PILLARS OF THE EMPIRE

Owing to the antiquity and rarity of this book, certain pages are regrettably absent, and readability is compromised due to the blurring of the original text. If you possess any insights regarding the availability of these missing sections, kindly inform us. Your assistance is crucial in ensuring the completion of this significant work for the benefit of future generations.

PILLARS OF THE EMPIRE

SKETCHES OF

LIVING INDIAN AND COLONIAL STATESMEN,

CELEBRITIES, AND OFFICIALS

BY

T. H. S. ESCOTT

GYAN

Published by

Gyan Publishing House
5, Ansari Road
Daryaganj, New Delhi-110002
Phone: 011-47034999, 9811692060
E-mail: books@gyanbooks.com

Distribution Network
gyanbooks.com
India, USA, Canada, UK, Australia

ISBN: 978-93-6208-286-2 (PB)
First Published, 1879

2nd Impression 2024

Printed at: Gyan Press, Delhi.

PILLARS OF THE EMPIRE
Author: T. H. S. ESCOTT

PILLARS OF THE EMPIRE

PILLARS OF THE EMPIRE

SKETCHES OF

LIVING INDIAN AND COLONIAL STATESMEN, CELEBRITIES, AND OFFICIALS

EDITED, WITH AN INTRODUCTION, BY

T. H. S. ESCOTT

LONDON
CHAPMAN AND HALL, 193, PICCADILLY
1879

TO

MESSRS. GRINDLAY & CO.,

THE PROPRIETORS OF THE *HOME NEWS*,

IN WHICH JOURNAL THESE PILLARS OF THE EMPIRE

ORIGINALLY APPEARED,

THIS VOLUME IS INSCRIBED.

PREFACE.

The Sketches of which this volume consists appeared originally in the *Home News*, where they were so well received that, at a time when India and the Colonies are of exceptional interest to Englishmen, it has been considered worth while to publish them in their present shape.

For Sketches IV., V., VI., VII., XII., XIX., XXII., XXXII., XXXVI., XXXVII., XXXVIII., XLVI., XLVII., I am indebted to Major Arthur Griffiths; for XIII., XXI., XXVIII., XXXV., XLI., to Mr. John Sherer, C.S.I.; for VIII., XI., XX., XXIII., XXIV., XXX., to Mr. John Macdonald; for X., XXV., to Mr. St. Leger Herbert; for XVI. to Mr. Cashel Hoey. For the rest I am myself responsible.

T. H. S. ESCOTT.

London, *November*, 1878.

CONTENTS.

INTRODUCTION.

THE RESPONSIBILITIES OF EMPIRE.

Characteristics of the British Empire and its policy.—Its cost and advantages.—Its services to humanity.—Loss and profit of India to England.—Social, economical, and industrial value of our colonies.—Influences of India upon Imperial policy.—Possible dangers of this influence.—Two kinds of Imperialism and Imperial policy.

THE story of the lives and achievements of the distinguished men whose careers are briefly sketched in the following pages, is the record of varied contributions to the British empire, of different illustrations of Imperial service, of many aspects of the Imperial idea. Sometimes that service has been performed on the battle-field, sometimes in the council chamber, now at home, now abroad, often in war, often in peace, and not always, necessarily, by individuals engaged in the official employment of the Government. While Oriental pageants have been in process of celebration, and dusky troops have been concentrating upon remote points; while the splendour and immobility of the Eastern world and the penetrating intelligence of Western civilisation have met as allies or enemies under an Indian sky; while there has been jubilee or consternation in the capitals of our Oriental dominions, the statesmanship which assisted to create, and which is essential to preserve, that empire, has been pursuing in England its unbroken way, calm, collected, resolute. While there have been wars and rumours of wars in our colonial dependencies, crises in colonial administrations, straining of colonial constitutions, the great central bureau at home has done its work steadily and well. The directing mind has not suffered itself to be agitated by alarms, but with admirable composure has addressed itself to the departmental business in hand, and has quietly drawn up the dispatches which, transmitted to the other end of the world, have carried with them usually a tranquillising and always a decisive influence. In these facts is one of the secrets of successful empire to be found. To whom, remembering this, will there not at once suggest itself an adaptation of the fine remark which Livy places in the lips of his orator, "It is not only of the aggregate of lands, but of the wisdom and devotion of living men, that this mighty empire consists"?—an empire won by heroes, and consolidated and preserved by statesmen.

It is an empire, moreover, which, if it is the greatest birth of time, is also the newest. The British Empire in anything like its present development, notwithstanding the Imperial titles which English monarchs in bygone times have assumed, is not yet one hundred and fifty years old. As it is an empire which has been bravely and gradually won, so also is it an empire which we may claim justly and generously to have administered. It has given us occupation, it has given us anxiety. It has only in a secondary degree given us wealth. Every other country in the world which at any age has owned foreign dependencies, has derived from them some immediate pecuniary advantage. The contributions which came yearly to Athens from her allies and dependants were an important element in the Athenian revenue. With the Romans it was, as Sir Alexander Grant has told us, the first principle of taxation that the provinces were to defray the expenses of the empire. When they conquered Sicily, as Sir John Lubbock has pointed out in an admirable article—to the researches embodied in which I am much indebted—contributed by him on the Imperial Policy of Great Britain to the first number (March, 1877) of the *Nineteenth Century*—"they exacted a tenth of the gross produce, and five per cent. of the value of all exports and imports." The same policy has been adopted in later times by Sicily, Portugal, Holland. As late as 1870 the military expenses of all the colonies were borne by the mother country. In 1875 our colonial empire cost us exactly a million and a half sterling, and a great deal more in arms, accoutrements, barracks, stores. Again, whereas France—the country which in this respect is, next to ourselves, saddled with the heaviest expenditure—pays some five millions a year for her navy, we pay twelve millions, the main, or rather the only cause of the difference being the risk which we take upon ourselves in guaranteeing our dependencies. Among other incidental charges that we have recently incurred in the interests of our colonies, may be mentioned the New Zealand war of

1865, of which the cost was £750,000, the colony paying subsequently £250,000 by a loan raised on bonds which we guaranteed; the Ashantee war of 1873-4, of which the cost was about a million; to say nothing of the Chinese and Kaffir wars. Between 1835 and 1875 we either advanced the colonies sums, or else guaranteed the payment of sums by the colonies on loan, on nineteen occasions, the largest total being a million and a half, the smallest, in the instance of Grenada, £7,000. Again, the colonies not only have the advantage of an Imperial Court of Appeal, but the cost of embassies, consular establishments, and of the Colonial Office is defrayed, not by the colonies, but by the mother country.

Considerable reciprocity of advantage doubtless accrues from this arrangement. Though our colonies are not yet converted to a belief in free trade, and decline to fix any differential duties in favour of the mother country—differential duties where they exist telling against us rather than for us—our trade with them is extensive and paying. When in 1874, in consequence of the earnest solicitation of the Australasian colonies, Lord Carnarvon accepted the cession of the Fiji Islands, these settlements declined to contribute £4,000 towards the government of the new possession, which cost us £40,000 in 1875, and £35,000 in 1876. The idea was not pressed, since it would have been, as Lord Carnarvon observed in his circular letter dispatched to the Governors of Victoria, New South Wales, Queensland, and New Zealand, "obviously undesirable, in a matter where the grace of the action depended upon its being voluntary, and where the amount involved was so small that it would be mainly valuable as proving the readiness of the great colonies to accept their membership in the common duties of the empire, to put the slightest pressure upon any one of them to make this joint contribution. It was, as I explained in my former dispatch, principally to give trial and effect to the principle of joint action among different members of the empire in such cases, that I invited co-operation in a matter in which the contributions proposed were so inconsiderable as to make it practically immaterial, except in connection with such a principle, whether the arrangement could be at once carried out." On the other hand, we have in the past few months witnessed a splendid illustration of something more than willing reciprocity on the part of our colonies. The anxiety which found expression both in Canada and at the antipodes to assist England with troops and with men and treasure, in the case of war, was the brightest testimony to a consciousness of the beneficence of British rule, and the most welcome guarantee of happy and profitable union.

In the case of India, as Sir John Lubbock puts it, "no English labourer, no English taxpayer derives a penny of direct advantage, or pays a penny less towards the revenues of the country, because we hold India." The only military expenditure for which India is chargeable is that involved by the presence of the troops actually doing duty there. The first Chinese war was caused by England's "determination to secure for India her revenue from the opium trade, which then amounted to £1,000,000, and is now worth £8,000,000, but it was not upon India that any of the expense fell. The second Chinese war arose out of a colonial and not a British grievance. But with the exception of two millions received in the way of indemnity from China, we bore the entire expense of the war, and actually paid £4,600,000." It is a fact which came out in the Parliamentary debates of last spring on the policy of the calling of Indian troops to Europe and which cannot be denied, that the pecuniary engagements into which the English entered by the Act of 1858 with the Indian Government, are really rather of the nature of an unilateral agreement. We pledge ourselves that Indian revenues shall be expended "for the purposes of the Government of India *only*." This qualifying word at once excludes Indian finance from a host of responsibilities to which it might otherwise be legitimately subject. It also furnishes a powerful argument against the policy of fusing, as there seems a tendency to fuse, the affairs of England and India. If the administration of the two countries is not to be, as it has been, carried on separately, and in a sense independently; if every Indian interest is a British interest; if what may seem to menace our ascendency in any quarter of Hindostan, menaces also our position as a people of world-wide Imperial sway—then it is clear that the little dissyllable "only" may make the burden of India intolerably heavy to the British taxpayer. "Even," to quote Sir John Lubbock, "the Crimean war was undertaken on the ground of Imperial policy, in which India was, to say the least, as much interested as Great Britain; but I need not say that all the expense fell upon us. I observe that the Mahommedans of India have memorialized us to help the Turks—so ingrained is the idea that all war expenses, whatever the object may be, ought to fall exclusively on the mother country."

Such are two—the chief—aspects of our British Empire. On the one hand, it has been, as a Quarterly Reviewer * asserts, an empire of conquest; on the other hand, it has been an empire of by no means inexpensive service to humanity at large, and of infinite advantage to the races subject to us. It is admitted by the severest critics of our Indian policy that we have wished and endeavoured to govern India for the good of the governed, and that our administration of that country, if far from perfect, has still been enlightened. That it is probably the most effectively beneficent which India has had; that under our sway the natives, though still taxed to the uttermost farthing, are taxed less heavily than they were under native rulers; that we do not derive any of our national income from India; and that if a plebiscite of the natives of India were taken to-morrow they would record their preference for our rule, rather than accept for it any other foreign substitute—these things we know. This may not be carrying humanity and the art of good government very far, but it is at least carrying it some way. As regards humanity, it

* *Quarterly Review*, No. 292, October, 1878. Art. "Rise of the Modern British Empire."

may be well to observe that had it not been for our colonial empire slavery would still flourish on the coast of West Africa, and the stricken negro would still tremble beneath the lash of the planter in the West Indies. The squadron which we kept off West Africa to stop the traffic in human lives, cost us for many years a sum varying between £1,000,000 and £300,000 annually. The expediency of continuing it was more than once questioned in the House of Commons, never on the ground of expense, but always on the ground of efficiency. As regards the West Indies, it must be remembered that when in 1833 the late Lord Derby brought in his Government resolution for the abolition of slavery, the Government had to consider the indemnification of a great vested interest. How were the West Indian proprietors to be compensated? A loan had been proposed, but the Government decided on a free gift of £20,000,000. Mr. Briscoe moved to substitute £15,000,000, but the Government proposal was voted by 304 to 56, amid the approval and the applause of the entire nation. Under these circumstances it is scarcely surprising that the Empire of England stands well, and has always stood well, in the eyes of the world—how well may be judged from an extract given by Sir John Lubbock, from Mr. Wood's work "On the Benefit to the Colonies of being Members of the British Empire." "In Hong-Kong," writes Mr. Wood, "we find a small barren island which, at the time of its cession to Britain, was inhabited only by a few handfuls of fishermen, now crowded with tens of thousands of Chinese, who have crossed from the mainland because they knew that under British rule they would be free from oppressive taxation, would be governed by just laws, and would be able to carry on a thriving and profitable trade. And so, in the once uninhabited island of Singapore, we see a motley population attracted from China, the Malay Peninsula, and India by a similar cause."

The controversy which took place not long ago between Mr. Lowe and Colonel Chesney on the subject of India's value to England points to precisely the same conclusion. Look, said Mr. Lowe, at the drain of men involved in the maintenance of an English garrison 70,000 strong. "The money which we spend can be repaid to us; but who shall give us back our men?" Surely the cry of "Vare, redde legiones!" was never uttered by the Roman Emperor in more mournful strain. Colonel Chesney's reply is that Mr. Lowe has overrated the number of men by at least 10,000, and that India herself does as a matter of fact give us back most of them. The only waste which would be really incurred would be found in the difference between the annual English and Indian death-rate. If the death-rate in India averages twenty per thousand, or twice that of England, it would appear that "600 more able-bodied Englishmen die yearly in consequence than would die otherwise." In addition, therefore, to the 60,000 permanently maintained in India, England loses only 600 men a year, or exactly as many as die in this country from railway accidents alone, and barely a third of the number which in the past year we have lost from casualties at sea. Of course Colonel Chesney should have added something for the number who yearly return home disabled prematurely by Indian diseases. Even thus it may be allowed that the drain on England, slight enough in itself, is "perfectly inappreciable compared with the effect of emigration." If in the last ten years 6,000 Englishmen have died before their time, more than a million have emigrated from this country never to return, of whom about one-half were adult males.

Again, Colonel Chesney argues that this additional mortality, such as it is, and the permanent withdrawal of 60,000 men from England, are an absolute benefit to all those who stay behind, inasmuch as they relieve the English labour market of men, whose presence at home would tend to keep wages below their existing level. Further, "if the Indian garrison were withdrawn to-morrow, the result would be not to give us an increased army at home, but that 60,000 soldiers would be discharged." There can be no doubt, that under the new system of short service and army reserves, England "will get the benefit of the reserves supplied from these 60,000 men, the cost of whose training has been paid by India"—an arrangement of which indeed India may have reason to complain, but certainly not England. As regards Mr. Lowe's contention, that the holding of India absorbs men without whom England could not carry on a European war, Colonel Chesney pertinently remarks, that England's greatest wars in India were waged "during the extremest crisis of her struggle with Napoleon;" that in our last war with France, the Government had usually more soldiers at its command than it knew what to do with—for instance, it could afford to detach troops which "might as well have been serving in India" on profitless expeditions to the Plate River and Walcheren; and that, if it be said that the conditions of war have entirely changed since then, the "Indian government has only to give the signal to draw recruits to its colours to any extent necessary from the perfectly inexhaustible supply available both with and without its borders, of many races possessing the qualities for making a splendid soldiery."

In the last chapter of his "Notes of an Indian Journey," Mr. Grant Duff sums up the pros and cons of our possession of India, deciding that on the whole the balance of advantages is against us, and that though it is *impossible* for us to think of giving up India, it is a source of weakness—of "glorious weakness,"—but still of weakness to England. The considerations which lead him to this conclusion are not so much the expenditure of men and money which India involves, as the alleged waste of energy which its administration entails, or which might have been more advantageously directed into other channels. This, too, is the view of other authorities of equal weight; amongst them, if I mistake not, a living Indian official, than whom no one has a better right to have his voice heard and respected on such a subject. But when it comes to calculating what the power which has been exhausted in governing India might have accomplished, if it had been devoted to the consolidation of our institutions at home and their development in our colonial possessions, we must be careful to guard against the logical fallacy known as begging the question. If the ability and energy consumed by India would, if India were not part of our possessions, have been spent in the service of England at home, or of our colonial dependencies abroad, then it may be admitted that India has made us *pro tanto* poorer. But is it so certain that we have given to India out of our necessities, and not out of our abundance? Is it not rather the case, that having at our disposal all the power and the industry which we wanted for Great Britain and her colonies, we had also a surplusage of these precious qualities, which, if India had not existed to utilise them, would have lain idle? Capacity for affairs, zeal and skill in dealing with affairs, are qualities which the very use of them generates; they are fortified by exercise and propagated by example. In proportion as the limits of the field of their display are widened, they themselves will be forthcoming; and it is a real danger lest, if we were to dwarf our dominions, we should, at the same time that we reduce the responsibilities of empire, impair our capacities for sustaining an Imperial burden.

Some of the most practical advantages which we derive from our Indian and Colonial Empire have yet to be mentioned. In the case of the colonies these advantages have been put before the public in a very striking manner by Sir Julius Vogel, and will be found recapitulated briefly in the sketch given of him in this volume. It is certainly not at the present time, with commercial and industrial distress of all sorts prevailing at home,—much of that distress being attributable to the fact that continental markets are closed against us, —that we can contemplate with composure the idea of renouncing those opportunities for British labour and capital which the colonies undoubtedly afford. To English enterprise and to English money, it may be said, the colonies would still be open, though the constitutional links binding them to the mother country were severed. But here sentimental considerations, and to a great extent also considerations of hard prosaic business, interpose themselves. While in the last five years there has been a steady increase in the number of emigrants from the mother country, there has been a rapid decrease in the number of English immigrants into the United States. Although the spirit of enterprise and of adventure is the birthright and tradition of the English race, our poorer classes are animated by a strange prejudice against setting their backs on certain misery and want at home, and discovering possible happiness and plenty in foreign climes. It needs all the argument in the world to induce a London pauper to avail himself of a free passage to the antipodes, though there be in addition the chance or certainty, when he has arrived at his destination, of a new start in a new country. Experience shows that this aversion to cross the seas is sensibly lessened by the gradual realisation of the truth, that when the seas have been crossed the exile will find himself on British soil and amongst British subjects. In the same way it is quite certain that if our colonies were severed from the mother country, a great and profitable outlet for English capital would be closed. What is from one point of view an Imperial question, is thus from another an industrial, an economical, and a social question. We are now witnessing in England on a very noticeable scale a gradual levelling-up of classes. To rise in life has taken its place as the chief legitimate ambition of each one. In almost every section of the population, sons are being educated above the level of their parents. It is quite certain that the ambitions which are thus implanted in their breasts cannot in all cases be gratified at home. And, indeed, if our colonial dependencies were to cease to be an integral part of Great Britain, it is not improbable that the consequences of what would practically prove a limitation of industrial area, would be fraught with political perils.

What is true of the colonies is equally true of India. Imagine the condition of the great middle class in this country, with their marriageable daughters and their fairly intelligent and educated sons, without the chances of the civil or the military career which India affords. The lad who succeeds in the competition for the Indian Civil Service is at once the architect of his own fortune and the possessor of the material for raising the fabric; the subaltern who secures an appointment to an Indian Staff Corps can at once do not only what he fails to do at home—live on his pay—but put money in his pocket as well. How far this natural gravitation of young Englishmen, who have their way to make in the world, towards India is the best thing for India itself, how far the exclusive officialism of Indian society is conducive to the good government of India, are subjects too large to be discussed here. The influences which India exercises upon England, and upon England's foreign relations, are the only other points on which it seems desirable to say a few words.

If we have an extensive Indian frontier to guard, and if that frontier is to be brought nearer year by year to that of Russia, it is scarcely reasonable to expect that we can have the same number of troops available for asserting our strength in Europe upon any sudden emergency. It is now perfectly clear that if our native Indian army is to be as trustworthy as it ought to be, it must have not only a larger proportion of English officers, but a larger admixture of English soldiers. It is, of course, exceedingly gratifying to know that when any emergency—such as an Afghan war—arises, we may probably receive offers of assistance from the native princes of Hindostan, but it is well to recollect first, that these native soldiers are quite as costly to move about and support, that they eat as much and expect as much as Prussian grenadiers, or any other perfect specimens of fighting men in Europe; secondly, that the experiences of the Indian mutiny should have taught us that such assistance from our great Indian feudatories, however gratifying, is not gratuitous. Holkar and Scindia may be ready to help us with men when we are confronted by the emergency of a border war, but, when the war is over, they will expect payment, they will demand, as they always have done, fresh grants of territory; and English prestige in India will not be strengthened by the boast which will always be possible for our allies to make, that England's victory could not have been secured without native arms.

There is another reason that makes many persons, who would not for a moment allow that we could think of renouncing our position in India, apprehensive of the consequences which India may exercise upon us at home. India, they say, at the present moment, is the chief source of that spirit of aggressive militarism which is fatal to the development of a free and peaceful country. There can, indeed, be no doubt that the impetus towards what is called Imperialism comes from India in a very great degree. The possession of India is regarded, not unjustly, as the symbol of our military power, and the visible embodiment of a standing military triumph. And when Imperialism is now spoken of, it is the military element which is one of its essential parts; it at once suggests the blare of trumpets, the nodding of plumes, the flashing of sabres, the clinking of spurs, the gallop of troops in the onset. To those who believe that militarism is the canker of England, the deadly enemy of those sound political and economical ideas, without which English greatness would be gone, India, as being the land of military pageants, a splendid testimony to the aggressive force of our national arms, a land in which a career is still open for the military adventurer, and the incentives to military adventure still exist as once they existed for Englishmen on the continent of Europe, is a name of evil omen, a premium on those martial passions whose indulgence is incompatible with the facts of national stability and prosperity. Nor is it on these grounds only that India has come to meet with small favour in the eyes of a certain school of English politicians. During the twenty years which have elapsed since the government of India was formally transferred by Act of Parliament to the Crown, some persons think they can discern a practically progressive tendency towards a fusion of the system of English and Indian administration. It is rightly contended that these two systems are radically different. The English Government is that of a democracy in all but name; the Indian Government is a military despotism—a beneficent despotism doubtless, or at least as beneficent as any despotism can be, but still a despotism. The English Government is not only a free, but an open government; acting by the full, searching light of Parliamentary institutions, dependent for its policy upon the will of a majority of English taxpayers, and traditionally bound not only to justify its conduct, but to produce the data upon which that conduct is founded. The Indian Government, on the other hand, is, by the necessities of the case, a secret government, compelled to conceal the shape which its policy will take before that policy is an accomplished fact, knowing nothing of free or representative institutions—which, indeed, cannot exist in the Indian air. In England it is public opinion which, in the last place, is the arbiter of parties and decides their destiny; in India no such thing as public opinion exists, and I have heard one of the ablest Anglo-Indian statesmen now living, bitterly complain of the absence of any salutary out-door criticisms, and lament that the only opinion which the intelligent Indian press reflected was that of a limited, a privileged, an exclusive official class.

Now no person can seriously suppose that any English statesman, or body of English statesmen, could be insane enough to engage in the attempt to assimilate the government of England to the government of India, but there are those who, rightly or wrongly, consider that there is a real danger lest India should become a predominating feature in our English Imperial system, and should so be used as an instrument for curtailing English constitutional liberties. Only a few months ago Sir Stafford Northcote spoke of India and our other foreign dependencies as occupying the same relation to England that England does to the Hebrides. Lord Salisbury has become of late as enthusiastic an admirer of a big England in preference to a little England as he was, a twelvemonth since, of the study of big maps. It is from such sentiments as these, proceeding from eminent official lips, that the inference is drawn, that somehow or other the centre of gravity of the English Empire is to be removed from London to Calcutta, and that, instead of India being an appanage of England, England may become an appanage of India. This was the change which these alarmists thought they could see foreshadowed when the title of Empress of India was added to that of Queen of England, and of whose consummation they consider that they can detect ever-growing signs.

When it is said that Imperialism is inconsistent with the free action of English representative institutions, what is meant is, not that we must choose between giving up our empire or giving up our constitutional privileges, but that our system of Imperial administration shall be carried on side by side with, and independently of, the United Kingdom, and that care shall be consistently taken not to bring England within the influence of that absolutism which exists for India. Hence the misgivings with which some excellent judges have observed, or fancy they have observed, a tendency to import India into the affairs of Europe; hence, in particular, the disapproval with which in these quarters the calling out of Indian troops to Europe was received. If, it is argued by these Mentors, our Indian military resources are to be at the disposal of any ambitious minister who chooses to flourish them as a menace in the face of the European powers, we shall have taken a fatal step towards that fusion of an Asiatic and British system of administration which must be fatal to English liberties, and which implies the establishment of the principle of personal rule. If—it is objected from this point of view—the resources of India and of England are to be employed indiscriminately and together in European affairs, it will involve the application to England of that Imperialism, in the sense of a central and more or less irresponsible autocracy, which governs India.

Such are the perils which anxious patriots discern in the relations of India to the English Crown, and such is a tolerably faithful account of the dangers which they detect as inherent in Imperialism. But there is, as Lord Carnarvon recently explained at Edinburgh, a true and false Imperialism—an Imperialism from which the sober sense of the English people instinctively revolts, and an Imperialism by whose principles they are determined to hold. In the sense in which Imperialism is a specious synonym for mere spread-eagleism, braggadocio, menace, restless activity, an ever-present passion of territorial aggressiveness, Imperialism does not and is not likely to commend itself to the deliberate judgment of the Anglo-Saxon race. But if Imperialism is to be defined as a resolute determination to retain and consolidate our foreign possessions, to allow of no encroachment upon them by aggressive powers, and to administer them, as far as may be, for the benefit and improvement of those who are already subject to us, then there is no nation in the world with whom Imperialism has taken such firm root as ourselves. If the voice of empire addresses to us those words which Pericles, more than two thousand years ago, enjoined his countrymen not to heed; if it endeavours to lure us on perpetually to fresh conquests and new annexations; if the arguments with which it appeals to us are those with which the Athenians, in the memorable dialogue of Thucydides, met the prayers of the terror-stricken Melians for mercy; if the feelings on which it trades are those of cynical and defiant self-assertion, then it is perfectly certain that Imperialism will obtain no permanent hold of the English mind.

The only idea of empire which can be a powerful instrument with the English people, must be something more than that of territorial sway and of military triumph. It must carry with it the conception and the performance of moral duties. Its watchwords must not be the rectification of frontiers, or even that more venerable word prestige; it must rely for its ultimate triumphs not upon the evanescent passions of a democracy, but upon the resolute and deliberate will of an educated and enlightened people. Here, at the present moment, we really seem to be in some danger. Politically we have bidden adieu to the old order of things, and for good or evil thrown in our lot with the new. We have in England, as the ultimate depositories of political power, a vast multitude of voters who have yet to be educated, yet to learn the lessons of Imperial sanity and political wisdom. As for their political education, that must depend very much upon the course adopted by the statesmen who preside over their destinies. It is not in schools alone, or even in lecture-rooms, and from the columns of the newspapers, that the masses imbibe those precepts which, sooner or later, they may be expected to convert into action. The statesman who, for the while, is in the possession of their confidence, moulds and educates them by the very means which he uses to secure their confidence. It is here that the real danger arises, here that the need of political sobriety is most apparent. Nothing can be easier than for the political leader who has the ear of a warm-hearted and enthusiastic race, such as the English are, by dexterous tactics and by the repetition of attractive phrases, to win their consent to a course which they will subsequently regard with remorse and dismay. But statesmen who were to adopt such expedients as these would be preparing for themselves a certain and a dangerous reaction; they would be sowing the wind in order that they might reap the whirlwind. If a national policy were to be exclusively or mainly dictated by considerations such as these, then there would be reason for alarm. The excitement would pass away, but the moral influences of the mood would remain, and when the temporary check or reverse came, as sooner or later it would come, it might be found that the natural sequel of a policy of sensation and impulse was the outburst of something very like revolutionary discontent.

T. H. S. E.

PILLARS OF THE EMPIRE.

I.

SIR GEORGE BOWEN, G.C.M.G.

HAPPY, it may be said—adapting for our purpose the Periclean aphorism on the status of women in the republic of classical Athens—is the colonial governor of whom least is said, whether in the way of praise or blame. Judged by this standard, which is, after all, that not only of Hellenic precedent but of common-sense, the present Governor of Victoria deserves, on the whole, to be considered a fortunate man. The turbulent period of loud-mouthed and irresponsible criticism through which he passed in the spring of 1878, was indeed a striking exception to the rule of tranquillity which has characterized the greater part of Sir George Bowen's career. Even then he suffered more from the censures poured upon him by imperfectly informed critics at home, than in the opinion of those who had the opportunity of judging of his conduct, and the antecedents of his conduct, on the spot. In England it is not sufficiently borne in mind that the collision between the two Houses, even though it may have resulted in "an unprecedented outburst of democratic frenzy," was to a considerable extent provoked by the Legislative Council. It was perfectly intelligible that the aristocratic representatives of the territorial interest should object to the Land Taxation Bill of which Mr. Berry approved, and which sought to exempt small properties from financial burdens. But the Council would have done well to have made a firm stand against this obnoxious measure, instead of deferring the expression of their wrath against the Government which passed it till the usual vote for payment of members in the Melbourne House of Commons came on for consideration. It was disastrous, that a great colony and a great capital should be thrown into confusion by a quarrel between the two Chambers of the Legislature. Sir George Bowen doubtless deplored the catastrophe as much as any one. But it should have been remembered when the policy of the Colonial Office in countenancing the steps taken by the Governor of Victoria was condemned, and when the Governor himself was accused of playing to the gallery—of cultivating popularity with the groundlings—that the free right to govern implies as its sinister correlative the risk of misgoverning. And such misgovernment, when it occurs, is no more to be charged upon the Governor or the Colonial Office than the credit for any conspicuous successes in government can be justly claimed either by the latter or the former. All that the Colonial Office, all that Sir George Bowen had to consider was, whether the Prime Minister was acting within the letter and spirit of his constitutional authority, whether imperial interests, as distinct from local interests, were menaced, whether the instructions which the Governor received from Downing Street were obeyed. If these questions could be answered satisfactorily—and a dispatch justifying his conduct, of a generally satisfactory character, was received at the Colonial Office, and has since been published—then, however much the facts of the situation might be regretted, Sir George Bowen could not rightly be held blameworthy.

This was not the first great crisis with which Sir George Bowen had to deal, and in dealing with which he exhibited a strength and determination, at the last resort, that abundantly justified the confidence reposed in him. Thirteen years ago—the year of the great financial panic in London, and, indeed, throughout England—when he was Governor of Queensland, Sir George Bowen was confronted by an emergency quite as grave in its way as that which overtook him last year. Among the consequences of the failure of the Agra Bank was the stoppage of money supplies in Brisbane. The Assembly, into whose hearts the disaster struck consternation, wished to issue irredeemable paper notes. It needed great firmness successfully to withstand a proposal in favour of which, as an immediate expedient, a great deal might have been said. Sir George Bowen was equal to the occasion, and strongly and triumphantly refused his consent to a step that would have brought a certain and perhaps an irretrievable financial Nemesis upon a considerable portion of Australia. The result was that an issue of ten per cents. was made, and thus the risk of a depreciation of the currency was—at great temporary inconvenience, it is true—averted. A few years later, when he was in New Zealand, he found himself in a situation scarcely less menacing. The Maori war was drawing to a close, and the British troops were to return. Sir George Bowen protested against their withdrawal. His protest was not entertained. With great promptitude and good humour he proceeded to make the best of the position. And he did make the best of it. The Maoris were organized into bodies for the improvement of roads, and other such works, and the experiment answered perfectly. The truth seems to be that while Sir George Bowen may be far from the ideal character one would wish to witness on the political stage when the cry is raised of breakers ahead, while he is perhaps deficient in resolution and in nerve when the danger is only drawing near, and while a little more decision in the initial stages of the difficulty would prevent its ever coming finally to a head, he is a really self-possessed pilot of the ship in the midst of the storm. In the case of Sir George Bowen we have not only the weaknesses of human nature to consider, but of Anglo-Irish nature—a very phenomenal kind of human development. Like the rest of his race, Sir George Bowen has a dominant desire to be all things to all men, and to be popular with all sorts of people. But of one thing there is no doubt, that unlike many of his race, Sir George Bowen's capacities are always increased and his nerves always strengthened when he feels that at last he is in the midst of the crisis. He may lack "the stiff upper lip" which sometimes prevents a crisis; he never yet has lacked the resource and presence of mind to deal with the crisis when it has actually arrived. Since the introduction of responsible government into the Australian colonies, occasions which, like that of 1878 in Melbourne, call forth all the strength of the Governor, are rare, and the principal field which his abilities have for their display is afforded by the friction that occasionally arises between the Home and the Colonial Government in cases where there is something of a conflict between different departments of State. Thus, as has happened more than once, a great shipowner is fined £100 by the Melbourne Administration because his captain has conveyed a lunatic from Calcutta, who had at once to be taken to an asylum, and who represents a tax on the Melbourne ratepayers of £60 or £80 a year. The shipowner protests. The Indian Secretary of State espouses his cause, and endorses his protest to the Colonial Office. The Governor of Victoria is remonstrated with, and the course which he finally adopts is decided by the counsel of his law advisers.

Sir George Bowen is something more than an able, a careful, an industrious administrator, as well as an administrator who, at a pinch, is capable of decisive action. He is one of the best-read constitutional authorities of whom the Colonial Office can boast. He is also a man of brilliant literary attainments and academic achievements, and of oratorical powers which have been, by dint of practice and discipline, brought to a high pitch of perfection. A scholar of Trinity

College, Oxford, he took a first-class, and became fellow and tutor of Brasenose. After three or four years he received the offer and accepted the post of principal of the college established in Corfu. Political advancement thrust itself upon him, and he was made the Chief Secretary of the island, under the Lord High Commissioner. At Corfu, too, it was that he made the acquaintance of the accomplished lady who subsequently became his wife. The present Lady Bowen was the daughter of a distinguished member of the Corfu Assembly—the Count Candiano di Roma, the representative of an ancient Veneto-Greek family—and it is permissible to observe that as a leader of society her ladyship has displayed such gifts and tact, that she must be regarded as a distinct element in the success of Sir George Bowen's administration. Sir George is not only the possessor of a tongue, ready beyond even the customary readiness of Irishmen, but of a singularly tenacious memory, splendidly stored with the accumulated results of a very wide reading. A fluent orator he has always been, and, as is the case with most fluent orators who have also effusive natures, the pearls of sincerity may not be the only things that fall from his lips. It is just four years ago that on the occasion of a vacation visit paid by him to England, Sir George Bowen was entertained at a magnificent banquet at Willis's Rooms. The Governor of Victoria then made a speech that will always dwell in the memory of those who heard it, and of which the tradition remains in England with many of those who heard it not. On the whole, Sir George Bowen is a man whom, for his rare culture, his great parts, his judgment, his knowledge of and skill in dealing with human nature, the mother country, and the dependency that he may, as the queen's representative, administer, have equal reason to regard with pride.

II.

SIR GEORGE CAMPBELL, K.C.S.I.

After an Indian career, extending over three decades, conspicuous throughout for strenuous devotion to duty as well as restless activity of service, Sir George Campbell has commenced public life *da capo* in England. He has held the highest judicial and administrative posts in our Asiatic Empire. He has been Judge of the Supreme Court at Calcutta, and Lieutenant-Governor of Bengal. He has lived continuously in the thick of controversy, and in the whirl of work. Hand and brain have never known what idleness was. He has initiated and executed policies, has held his own in face of the most persistent opposition, has perpetually been evolving new ideas on paper, while he was essaying the accomplishment of other ideas scarcely less new in fact. But the passion for work is as fierce and consuming with Sir George Campbell as with Mr. Gladstone; the necessity of doing something as continuous and as coercing. Not for him, as for so many Anglo-Indians who have returned, *jam rude donati*, to the land of their birth, are the soft delights of indolent days—the pleasant dawdling mornings at the pleasant club in St. James's Square, the afternoon whist, the regular attendance at the opera during the season, the frequent visit to the last new thing at the theatre, the not infrequent trip to Brighton—in a word, the constant endeavour to extract from what is left of existence all that is most pleasurable, sunny, and luxurious. Sir George Campbell is like the horse which, after having compassed a considerable journey, does not turn a hair, and is immediately led out of the stable to start off again. To all appearance he is as fresh and insatiate and insatiable of employment as during the discussions, in which he took so prominent a part, that accompanied the addition of the Punjaub to the English Crown, or in the investigation that succeeded the Orissa famine. He is not to be deterred by obstacles or difficulties; he is not to be intimidated by rebuffs. If he cannot induce the House of Commons to endorse his views on the Eastern Question, or on any particular branch of it which may have presented itself for discussion, he does not for one instant think of renouncing the attempt to convince it. If his speeches in Parliament fail to produce the effect that he intended, he writes an article in the *Fortnightly Review*. He has expressed his opinion on the subject of the Treaty of San Stefano at Westminster, and he has written quite the ablest, most lucid, suggestive, and just commentary upon it that has been published in the periodical which Mr. John Morley so admirably edits. He is, in fact, inexhaustible and irrepressible, and if boundless energy combined with infinite cleverness could insure the highest political success in England, that success must in the natural order of things fall to the lot of Sir George Campbell.

But it is not intellectual merit, it is not an immeasurable capacity for sheer hard work which wins the highest triumphs of the House of Commons, and it may be doubted whether Sir George Campbell's reputation as an English statesman will ever be equal to his fame as an Indian administrator. His Indian career is in a special sense part of Indian history: for the lines of its progress coincide with those of the march of Indian annexation. First in the North-West Provinces, then in the Punjaub and elsewhere, he has been a civilian in the van of the great army which has been constantly extending the British Sovereignty in Hindostan. The champion of the ryot against the zemindar, he would probably regard with no great enthusiasm the application of the principles of the new Imperial policy. It is desirable that the Queen's Government should cultivate friendly relations with the indigenous petty potentates of India. Sir George Campbell and others might be inclined to think that we are aiming too exclusively at the establishment of those relations, and that in doing so we lose sight of the facts that, after all, these native princes are little better than robber chiefs, and that it is to the masses of a "quick-witted and logical population" that our attention should chiefly be given. His devotion to these views will sufficiently explain the antagonism in which Sir George Campbell has found himself to more than one Governor-General, notably to Lord Canning; and may, perhaps, also furnish a reason why he was a Judge at Calcutta before he was Lieutenant-Governor of Bengal. Sir George Campbell's doctrines on other fundamental questions of Indian policy are tolerably well known. His administration of Bengal was signalised by great public services, and these services were of a character which caused him to arrive at conclusions of his own on the subject of "the principle of permanent settlement." In India, as indeed in other countries, the two chief engines of civilisation are education and facility of intercommunication—schools and roads. Sir George Campbell's efforts to promote both of these in Bengal were above praise. But neither roads nor schools are possible without money, and to raise the money Sir George imposed taxes—the local cesses—which were considered at home, and beyond doubt were in reality, an infringement upon the principle of the permanent settlement. The cesses themselves were a necessity, and the Lieutenant-Governor cast about for the means of their collection. In the old days the system which was then practically operative would have supplied the requisite machinery. But the machinery had now fallen into desuetude, and all that could be done was to provide for its revival. Believing that no advantage can be gained from the controversy "whether the money taken by Government from the land in India is revenue or rent," Sir George Campbell holds that "we now take as nearly as we can half the rent of lands not permanently settled," and says, "Either let us avow the principle of permanent settlement, adjust our whole system of revenue accordingly, and reap such advantages as result from permanency of assessment, or let us have the benefit of a new assessment proportioned to the increase of prices and values." One of the commissioners appointed to inquire into the Orissa famine, he naturally claimed considerable authority when the same calamity invaded Bengal. The attitude which he originally assumed was in opposition to that taken by Lord Northbrook, who, however, was eventually won over to the more drastic measures of Sir George Campbell. If, during the whole of this crisis, the Lieutenant-Governor of Bengal can be said to have committed any errors, they are errors on the right side. But Sir George Campbell's ideas could not long be made to square with the main principles of the Viceroy's policy; and, indeed, it may be doubted whether the individual lives with whom Sir George Campbell would find it possible to act for any considerable time in close concert. It is scarcely surprising that Lord Northbrook should have refused to consent to such a measure as the prohibition of the export of corn from Bengal, and indeed the one thing remarkable is that so crude a nostrum should have ever received the powerful advocacy of the *Times* in England. The arguments against such a measure, which is, of course, opposed to all the accepted laws of economic procedure, are conclusive. Nothing can be more certain than that if an embargo is placed upon a commodity, whether corn or anything else, when it has once been brought into a country, merchants will hesitate to bring such a commodity in, and to run the risk of having the goods, which are capital, hopelessly locked up. Again, if export is forbidden, there is no inducement offered to the natives to extract from the soil more than is required for their own consumption; and thus, of necessity, the standard of cultivation will decline. It was upon this issue that Lord Northbrook and Sir George Campbell found themselves hopelessly at odds —nor were the differences between them composed till Sir George was offered a seat on the Council of the Secretary of State for India at home.

An administrator of the highest energy, ability, and usefulness, some idea of the eventfulness of whose term of office may be gleamed from the admirable statements with which he has introduced the reports of the special departments of his province, and whose services in the famine period were even trivial, compared to the reforms which he instituted in the Native Civil Service municipal institutions throughout Bengal, and a general system of primary and secondary education, Sir George Campbell made an exceedingly useful member of the Indian Secretary's Council. Not only did he make several important speeches on the question of public works and irrigation—both of them topics on which he is now giving evidence before a Committee—but he was of great assistance generally to his colleagues. Sir George Campbell is eminently original, suggestive, ingenious. He is what may be best described as above all things a viewy man. He is sometimes, perhaps frequently, wrong, but then he is often right. He is so quick to arrive at a comprehensive conclusion of his own on any topic which the events of the hour may start, so original in the conclusion thus arrived at, and so tenacious of its main features, that he seldom succeeds in commanding the unqualified assent of any party or section. He has yet to show that he can subordinate his own ideas in minor matters to the general aims of others. He is essentially a politician of the eclectic order—his eclecticism being, however, the result of very remarkable originality. He is perpetually shaping new opinions, and propounding fresh doctrines, irrespectively of whether they accord with the general principles and practice of this party or that. He sits on the Liberal benches, yet he never hesitates for a moment to propound doctrines which are calculated to interpose another obstacle in the way of the collective action of the Liberal party. Thus he has Conservative ideas on some points, and uncompromisingly Radical ideas on many others. This is not the stuff out of which English party politicians—and in England no politicians who are not strong party men rise to eminence—are made. As has been said, Sir George Campbell has lately written an article of very uncommon power and knowledge on the Treaty of San Stefano. He advocates, like Mr. Gladstone, the expulsion of the Turks bag and baggage from Europe, but he declares himself strongly in favour of the real independence of Turkey in Asia. In other words, while practically denying the capacity of the Turks for sound and beneficial government in one continent, he appears to record his belief in the existence of that capacity when applied to another. A similar instance of the same tendency has just been afforded by Sir George Campbell in the House of Commons. Like the

Liberal leaders, he disapproves of the particular policy which the summons of the Sepoys to Malta at this time represents; but he does not object to the principle embodied in this policy, and, unlike the rest of the Liberals, he holds that we may legitimately employ black soldiers to fight the battles of England in the West. Sir George Campbell has already made very perceptibly his mark in the House of Commons. He is a vigorous and, as has been said, a strikingly original thinker. He is a persistent and a resolute speaker. It is exceedingly to be desired that he should continue to sit in Parliament, for he contributes materially to its wisdom. But he will never be a great Parliamentary leader. If Sir George Campbell had ever aspired to that position, he ought to have gone into the House of Commons at a much earlier age. As it is, he will go down to posterity as a very able and a very remarkable man, whose *forte* was Indian administration and whose foible was English politics.

III.

EARL OF CARNARVON.

SELDOM have those influences, advantages, and associations, to whose combined results may be attributed some of the best and most distinctive characteristics of English statesmanship, been so signally illustrated and so happily united as in the case of the late Secretary of State for the British Colonies. The inheritor of an illustrious title, he was born to great position, great wealth, great opportunities. But these possessions were not his sole birthright. There descended to him from a long line of ancestors, not a few of the qualities ascribed by the poet to that paragon of her sex who was "Sidney's sister, Pembroke's mother," and which have been common to the younger as well as the elder branch of the House of Herbert. Nothing that parental care and education could do towards bringing out these bright attributes into brighter relief was omitted. The Herberts have been for many generations a family of scholars as well as cavaliers, and, like Frank Leigh in "Westward Ho!"—the typical knight and student of a lettered and knightly period—have known how to turn a Latin stanza with ease, or draw their swords in the good cause with graceful intrepidity. A great department of State has seldom had for its two chief officers kinsmen at once so near in point of blood, and so distinguished in literary and academic attainments, as the Colonial Office when Lord Carnarvon was at its head. Lord Carnarvon, in addition to other laurels at school and college, gained a first-class at Oxford, when an Oxford first-class meant infinitely more of varied merit and polished accomplishment than it does now. His cousin, Mr. Robert Herbert, Permanent Under-Secretary of State, was *facile princeps* among all his contemporaries for elegant and accurate classical scholarship at Eton and at Balliol. Polite learning, a devotion to the scenes and countries which classical antiquity has hallowed, unsullied integrity and a consistent elevation of aim, may be described as the traditions of the House of Herbert. Lord Carnarvon's father was a scholar of wide knowledge, and poet of rare beauty. His uncle was admirable as a critic, and was also no mean orator, and, indeed, all the Herberts of that generation were men singularly accomplished and learned. Another cousin, Mr. Edward Herbert, perished by a horrible death in the massacre of Marathon—that historic spot which may be spoken of as the centre of the yearnings and the source of the inspirations of so many of his relatives—too soon, indeed, for his friends, but not before he had made his mark in scholarship, in literature, and in diplomacy. "Let us," were almost his last words in a letter written to a friend, "pray that we may die like Englishmen." The prayer was not unfulfilled, and when, from his place in Parliament,

Lord Carnarvon spoke of the tragic end of his kinsman, in a voice that trembled with emotion, he had the satisfaction of knowing that the halo of a heroic martyrdom rested upon Edward Herbert's premature grave.

It was thus a perfectly natural development that the descendant of such ancestors, and the son of such a father as the third Earl of Carnarvon, should have early showed signs of excellence in scholarship, in literature, and even in politics. Upon no young nobleman at the time of his entrance to Eton had more of attention been lavished, and that more immediately under the eye of his sire. Mr. Coleridge was the master who was more directly concerned in his education, and his private tutors were successively Mr. John Kent and Mr. Scott. While at Eton he gained the prize for the English essay. Even before his Eton days began he had shown signs of his aptitude for public speaking and for public affairs, and as a mere child delivered a speech before a considerable audience at a meeting of the Society for the Prevention of Cruelty to Animals. At Eton he took a keen interest in current politics, and was a constant speaker at the school debating society, better known as "Pop." His career at Oxford was the logical continuation of that which had been begun at Eton. After having graduated in the highest honours which the classical schools could bestow, and having derived no small benefit from the friendship and tuition of the late Dean Mansel, then resident at Oxford, Lord Carnarvon made the grand tour, extending it very far indeed beyond its conventional limits. His companion was Lord Sandon, now President of the Board of Trade, with whom he had much community of sentiment and sympathy. With him he travelled as far east as Erzeroum, and with him, too, he explored the Lebanon, and studied the Druses. Of this expedition he commemorated the results in a small volume, of which no higher praise is possible than that which is just—that it may be mentioned in the same breath as Mr. Kinglake's masterpiece "Eothen." On his permanent return to England, Lord Carnarvon led the life of a young nobleman who recognised the responsibilities as well as appreciated the pleasures of his station, and who kept his eyes steadily fixed on the opportunities of a political career. When in London he attended the House of Peers and went into society; when in the country he shot, hunted, yachted, and superintended his estates. But his mind was always open to the influences of the day, and the lesson of the stirring events which were then in progress was not lost. His active political career may be said to have begun in 1858—he had delivered his maiden speech in Parliament, a speech universally approved, and specially praised by the late Lord Derby, four years earlier—and, the late Lord Lytton then being Secretary, was offered, and accepted, the Parliamentary Under-Secretaryship of State at the Colonial Office.

Lord Carnarvon could not have commenced his official life under more favourable auspices. In Lord Lytton he had at least an inspiring chief. But the Colonial Secretary had himself so many and such absorbing occupations, that while he neglected nothing in Downing Street, he was very willing to leave not a few routine details to his colleague and subordinate. Lord Carnarvon thus acquired an intimate and practical knowledge of the machinery of the department, while there was ever present to him the animating spectacle of a bold and lofty policy—a policy, the results of which were successively the abolition of the old Australian mail service, the Incumbered Estates Act for West India, the dissipation of the misunderstanding between France and England in Africa by the happy and simple expedient of the exchange of Albuda and Portendic, and finally—the crowning achievement of all—the termination of the Hudson Bay monopoly, and the creation of British Columbia as an imperial dependency. Nor in estimating the influences which at this time were instructing Lord Carnarvon in his career as a statesman, should it be forgotten that the time was generally pregnant with great issues, that great principles were working themselves out on the continent of Europe in most dramatic shape, and that debates on the fundamental principle of foreign policy, to hear which was of itself a little education, were of daily occurrence in Parliament. Eight years later, in 1866, it again fell to the lot of Lord Derby, consequent on the death of Lord Palmerston and the defeat of Lord Russell's Administration, to form a Conservative Government. Lord Carnarvon was immediately offered the Secretaryship of State for the Colonies. He did not remain long at the post, resigning it in consequence of his disapproval of the

Conservative Reform Bill, and retiring together with Lord Salisbury, then Lord Cranborne, and General Peel, from the Cabinet. The next year came the dissolution and defeat of the Ministerial party in the appeal to the constituencies, and for six years Lord Carnarvon, with the rest of his party, was in opposition, and was the resolute but generous foe of the Liberal Legislation of Mr. Gladstone's Cabinet. In 1874 the Conservative reaction had reached a head, and Ministers, declining to meet Parliament with an unexpectedly large minority, resigned before Parliament assembled. Lord Carnarvon was at his old post and in the course of that very session gave signal proofs of the grasp and energy of his statesmanship. He had already—in 1867—completed what Mr. Cardwell had begun, by carrying through Parliament the Canada Dominion Act, and with much skill and patience entirely succeeded in reconciling the conflicting interests which the Act affected. Similarly, in 1874, it fell to him to complete the Ashantee war, which his predecessors had begun. Then followed the reorganization of the Government of the Gold Coast, the abolition of slavery in that region, and annexation of Fiji. Among the problems with which he successfully grappled at later dates may be mentioned the affair of Langalibalele, the treatment of Indians in the Mauritius, the civil war at the Malay peninsula, the solution of the long-standing difficulty with the Orange Free State and the final annexation of the Transvaal.

The salient qualities, as well as the chief performances of Lord Carnarvon's statesmanship, have already been indicated. It remains to say a few words, personal rather than political in their nature. As a speaker Lord Carnarvon has made a great advance in the course of the last two or three years. Though his voice is not one of great volume, he is more distinctly audible in any part of the House of Lords—probably the one Legislative Chamber in the world which is as remarkable for the gorgeousness of its decorations as its defiance of all acoustic laws—than the great majority of speakers who employ more stentorian tones. His speeches are perfect pieces of literary composition—admirable for their arrangement, lucidity, terseness, and point. As a debater he is exceedingly ready, quick, and courteous. He possesses, too, the power, which is in itself a great gift, of summing up the general results of a discussion with equal cogency and completeness—a gift that was shown more than once when the University Bill of 1877 was passing through the House of Lords. In addition to all this, and notwithstanding the predominance of the purely intellectual element in his speeches, he can fling, when occasion requires it, genuine passion into his words. No Cabinet Minister ever received deputations with more courtesy than Lord Carnarvon, and bestowed more attention to their arguments. Politeness has been defined as generosity in small matters, and how generous in small matters as in great, Lord Carnarvon is, colonists in all parts of the world know. His close and constant communication with the Colonial Agents in London did something towards securing a kind of indirect representation for the colonies in the Legislature. His hospitalities, both in London and at Highclere, to all colonists who have a claim to such attention, are pleasant memories with many of our fellow subjects beyond the far seas. His vigour and resolution were shown in the degree to which he increased the importance of the Colonial Office as a department of State during his administration, and his retirement from it was felt with a sense of personal loss throughout our Colonial Empire, and in not a few quarters at home as well. Had Lord Carnarvon accepted the offer which was made to him by the Prime Minister on Lord Northbrook's resignation, his name might have been not more closely associated with our Colonial than our Indian Empire. Pressing as it is understood were the terms on which he was then requested to undertake the Indian Vice-royalty, Lord Carnarvon, though not without due consideration, declined the honour, as, a few months later, he refused to take advantage of the opportunity which is said to have presented itself of replacing the late Mr. Ward Hunt at the Admiralty.

IV.

LIEUTENANT-GENERAL SIR NEVILLE CHAMBERLAIN, G.C.B., G.C.S.I.

The notion that great crises commonly produce great men and great minds to grapple with them is very generally prevalent, though it is not altogether or invariably borne out by fact. Nevertheless, periods of emergency, when tremendous issues are at stake, when the State is in jeopardy, or the throne in danger, are to some individuals what hot-houses and forcing-beds are to the various genera and species of the vegetable world. Rapid growth and abnormal development under such circumstances follow as a matter of course. The insignificant seedling or the unpretending plant shoots suddenly high above ground, and soon expands into the goodly proportions of a substantial forest tree. This has been frequently the case in the history of the world. The military tyros of Napoleon's earliest campaigns became ere long victorious marshals of France. Unpractised, nameless subalterns in the American Civil War were advanced in both North and South to great commands before that war was at an end. An early chance, turned to the best advantage at the right moment, and subsequently most tenaciously held, gave Osman Pacha European prestige; triumph over the seemingly insurmountable obstacles which had long hindered the Russian advance, placed Skobeloff and Gourko high upon the short list of Russian generals worthy the name. In this way, and at a juncture more perilous perhaps than any of those detailed, the great Indian Mutiny brought prominently to the front a band of gallant and intrepid soldiers, who, but for this crucial test, might have served on to the last—not without distinction cert inly, for some were well spoken of already, and to others another chance might also have offered later on—but yet comparatively unknown, except as deserving officers of the mediocre type. Foremost among those whom the trumpet call of danger found firm at their posts in the dread season of 1857 were the officers employed in Lord Dalhousie's pet province, the Punjaub, which they had admirably administered and governed since the submission of the Sikhs. It is hardly too much to say that their judicious attitude and courageous action saved the Punjaub at the time of the Mutiny, and therefore saved India. To the hands of the Lawrences, Lake, Lumsden, Macleod, Herbert Edwardes, James Abbott, Nicholson, and men such as they, were happily confided just then the fortunes of the North-West. Their enthusiasm was unparalleled. Equally remarkable were their consummate judgment and their cool heads. They were nerved to do and dare to the utmost of their power, but they were not less imbued with the necessity of cautious measures. What they accomplished the history of the revolt and its suppression is the best record, and among all who therein have established a claim upon the gratitude of Englishmen the name of Neville Chamberlain stands conspicuously forward amidst a galaxy of brilliant comrades and friends.

He was serving at the time in the command of the Punjaub Irregular Force, a body of troops composed of both horse and foot, which had been raised by the Lawrences for frontier service at a time when the peaceful administration of the Punjaub was a problem not too easy to solve. Chamberlain was eminently well fitted for the post. His Indian experience had been exceptionally brilliant; he had taken part in almost all the hard knocks which had been exchanged since he came to the country some twenty years before. With Christie's irregular cavalry he had made the campaign in Afghanistan, and was repeatedly wounded and cut about, and in this respect his luck has ever been hard, for it is said that from first to last Neville Chamberlain has suffered more from sword cuts and bullets than any officer of his standing and years. His gallant bearing in these sharply-contested affairs brought him under notice, and gained him an appointment upon the Governor-General's bodyguard, with which he was present at the battle of Maharajapore. His transfer later on to the personal staff of Lord Dalhousie was a natural transition, but when the war broke out against the Sikhs his uncontrollable military ardour carried him again into the thick of the fray. The reputation he had by this time achieved as a chivalrous, dashing young soldier, a splendid swordsman and rider, was very considerable, and on the formation of the irregular force already mentioned, no better selection could be made than he for its head. Aided and ably seconded by subalterns, as judiciously chosen as himself, he soon brought his command into a condition of such admirable efficiency that it was known and respected as a crack corps not only throughout India, but beyond it. He possessed in a marked degree many of the highest qualities of leadership. Resolute and determined if needs be, he was yet kind and conciliatory to all under his orders; there was little of the great *bahawder* in his demeanour —for one so gifted he was singularly modest and unassuming in his manner to all. This gained him readily the love of subordinates, the goodwill of those superior in rank to his own; their respect he also claimed from the prestige which he had clearly earned by his high courage in the field, courage which indeed has been called recklessness amounting to a fault. But this dashing leader of irregular horse was also more than a *beau sabreur*. He had studied and pondered deeply the lessons of war, was well read in military precedent, and could reason out with the best the logical consequences of any plan of campaign. No wonder, then, that when Delhi was beleaguered by the small force under Sir Henry Barnard, it was felt that Neville Chamberlain's arrival, although that of one man—no more—was considered an enormous accession of strength. His presence in the camp was spoken of as worth that of another thousand men. "All took courage," says a writer of the time, "from his stern, pale face." Especially were those who had eagerly pressed for vigorous offensive measures elated by his assuming the post of Adjutant-General, for they hoped he would throw his weight into the scale and counsel immediate attack. It was said that he had not hesitated to deprecate the timorous policy of those in chief command, and with eager impatience had ridiculed and protested against further delay. But, if these had been his views while remote from the scene of action, they were considerably modified on a closer inspection, and when he fully realised the desperate nature of the enterprise in hand. As might have been expected, his characteristic caution and deliberate common sense now got the upper hand. He would not willingly consent to anything like surrender or retrogression, but he was not less strongly opposed to the hazard of the "gambler's throw," as the project of a rash assault was not inaptly styled. But now, when his opinion carried weight, and at a time when he was fairly launched upon his deeply-important functions as chief of the staff, once more his proverbial ill-luck overtook him, and he became *hors de combat* with another serious wound. He was still incapacitated and confined to his tent when Delhi was actually stormed. There is perhaps no finer episode of its kind in warfare, and none which could bear more satisfactory testimony to the dauntless spirit that animated the man, than the eagerness with which he dragged himself, accompanied by a comrade in similar plight, still maimed and suffering, to the neighbourhood of the fight. He was determined at least to lend his presence, even if he could not personally take part in the struggle. And it so chanced that, while posted in seemingly inglorious inaction upon the ridge at Hindo Rao's, it fell to him to do essential service to the cause. Both by his advice when others wavered, by his authority and active interposition when the discontent of doubtful troops threatened to burst into real disaffection, he was able, as the fortunes of the day ebbed and flowed, to contribute in no slight degree to the ultimate success of our arms. The *rôle* he played was perhaps of an inferior character for one of his rank, but it was not without distinct influence upon the final result.

Since the Mutiny Sir Neville Chamberlain's only opportunity for distinction has been upon the North-West Frontier against the turbulent hill tribes. The disturbance among the frontier Afghans in 1863 took very serious proportions, and nothing less than a general invasion of the Punjaub was feared. Sir Neville's treatment of the insurgents was drastic and effectual, but his enemies fought well, and at the Umbeyla Pass the general himself, once again unfortunate, was so badly wounded that he could not remain on the field. A series of peaceful commands followed. Most recently Sir Neville Chamberlain has filled the important post of Commander-in-Chief at Madras, and this year he was selected to proceed on a special mission to Shere Ali, the ruler of Afghanistan. How that mission was peremptorily refused a passage across the Indian frontier, and the grave issues now occupying the public mind, are matters of which the historian of the future will have to treat. It is sufficient to say that Sir Neville Chamberlain would certainly have acquitted himself well had he been permitted to reach Caubul. He is one who has a large grasp of political questions, and has thought deeply on the great ones of the hour. Nor is it only as a diplomatist that he is likely to make a name in the future. Yet higher military advancement is doubtless in store for him. As a general officer he has a claim to further responsible employment. He is singularly free from prejudices, is not hampered by absurd notions of red tape or old-fashioned routine, and is therefore sure to enlist the willing co-operation of all who are under his command. Although a lieutenant-general already, he is still young in years, and younger yet in personal *physique.* His light, active figure, his indomitable energy, and the readiness with which he accepts the inevitable changes in modern warfare, all stamp him as a leader full of "go," and certain of a crowd of followers. No better man, if occasion should arise, could be found to command an Indian army corps than a general like Sir Neville Chamberlain, who has secured already the suffrages and hearty co-operation of our fellow-countrymen in the East.

V.

THE RIGHT HON. H. C. E. CHILDERS, M.P., F.R.S.

Cabinet Ministers are trained variously for their high calling. Some, to transpose the words of the great master, are born ministers, some achieve the rank by their own efforts, others have it thrust upon them. Some, like the infant Pitt, learn statecraft and elocution in their cradles; some got their first opening through good management or good luck, and gained advancement by sheer ability and weight of metal; not a few have climbed the ladder slowly and painfully, and graduating as under-secretaries or junior-lords, have arrived by right of survival, but by no special merit of their own, at the highest honours. The process through which Mr. Childers has come to the front has been none of these. His political education was acquired in the relatively unimportant arena of a new and remote country; the offices he filled worthily and well, were not in themselves of the highest dignity; his first experiences in debate were in colonial parliaments, at a time when these useful assemblies had hardly emerged from the embryonic stage. Having married early, he went out to Australia almost immediately after he had taken his degree, and was glad on his arrival at Victoria to accept the first appointment that came in his way. What was given him to do he did carefully and well, and as time passed he was advanced gradually to higher and yet higher functions, till at length, as Commissioner of Trade and Customs, he gained a place in the Colonial Cabinet, and sat as member for Portland in the Legislative Assembly. He had by this time identified himself so thoroughly with the country of his adoption, and had so obviously its best interests at heart, that on his return to England, after an absence of six years, he was at once entrusted with the duties of Agent-General, then a new appointment, for the colony of Victoria. But this was not sufficient for his energetic spirit, and he embraced the earliest opportunity of entering public life in England, and throwing himself with great energy into the election at Pontefract in 1859, succeeded, although returned second at the poll, in unseating his opponent on petition.

Now fairly launched, Mr. Childers soon made his mark in the House of Commons. He was not then, nor has he since become, an orator in the highest sense of the term; he never rises to eloquence, swaying his audience with a whirlwind of irresistible and passionate words; but he has been always a persuasive speaker, making his points well, and enforcing his arguments less by vehemence of effect than by their matter-of-fact conversational utterance. And upon certain subjects, with which he had long been intimately connected, he was at once admitted as an authority. Thus, as a member of the Parliamentary Commission which sat in 1863 to decide upon the whole question of our secondary punishments, he made his views known with so much distinctness and perspicuity, that, although he differed in certain vital points from his colleagues, his opinion was tacitly accepted by the public rather than that of the majority of the committee as set forth in their report. He was entirely opposed to the continuance of transportation beyond the seas in any shape or form, even protesting against the shipment of convicts, partially purified by a course of home discipline, to the youngest colonies, where their labour was most urgently required. The expedient, he maintained, could be but a makeshift at best, and must become, under the rapidly changing conditions of colonial existence, more and more inconvenient, till it finally altogether ceased. That his views were logical and sound, time as it passed has unquestionably proved. The fifteen years which have elapsed since they were made known have seen the absolute cessation of deportation, and we have long since decided to keep our criminals as best we can at home. The independent attitude of Mr. Childers in this discussion had gained for him the respect of political opponents, and no little favour from his own side of the House. He won yet more upon men by his genial manners and his handsome presence, while the conviction came the more strongly home to the rulers of his party that his brains and abilities were such that they should be secured for the purposes of administration. The first office he held was that of Junior Lord to the Admiralty, whence within a year he was translated to the Treasury as Financial Secretary. Three years later, when Mr. Gladstone came into power upon the top of the wave, Mr. Childers was selected to go to the Admiralty as its First Lord, and the tide of his fortune was at its flood. The measure of success which he achieved, if success it was, can scarcely be accurately estimated yet, but it may be fairly said in his favour that the task set him to perform was of colossal proportions, was surrounded by such tremendous difficulties that the stoutest heart might have feared to face them. The period was one of transition, when naval construction was still a moot point, and experiment could not be dispensed with. New ships must be put on the stocks, new armaments, new weapons, and new methods of naval warfare adopted and tried. On the one hand was the pressing necessity for outlay; on the other, the paralyzing policy of an administration of which he formed an integral part, pledged upon the hustings to economic retrenchment. Mr. Childers, placed thus somewhat on the horns of a dilemma, solved the difficulty by reducing expenditure where it could be done with the least harmful results. The reforms he introduced into the administrative machinery at Whitehall were trenchant, and their immediate effect was to rub up many prejudices and tread upon many corns; but they were much needed, and in the main judiciously undertaken and sensibly carried through.

It was less easy to deal satisfactorily with the burning questions which agitated the great department over which, at this important epoch, he was called upon to preside. He had to give a patient hearing to crowds of inventors wedded to their hobbies; to keep in good humour an army of subordinates who viewed his drastic treatment of the office with suspicion and alarm; above all, he had to keep in subjection a host of fractious admirals and punctilious post-captains, trained in traditions quite at variance with the new order of things, and not too willing to view his proceedings with unmixed satisfaction. There were Conservative officers in command of many of her Majesty's ships ready to cavil *sotto voce* at the spectacle of a civilian lord hoisting his flag—an unknown pendant hitherto—and sailing the seas at the head of a fleet of powerful ironclads; and there were many others practically trained who dissented from his theories in ship-building and his management of the dockyards. Led often into harassing and protracted controversies, made continually the butt of adverse criticisms, his troubles culminated when the ill-fated *Captain* went down—a favourite son of his own, be it said, among those who were lost—and an attempt was made to lay this great misfortune at his door. It was not strange that overwork and unceasing anxiety should by this time have seriously undermined his health, and that his friends and medical advisers, in alarm for his life, insisted upon his retirement from office, prescribing as the only panacea a period of absolute quietude, with complete abstention from public affairs.

Should it come to pass within this generation that the Liberal party recovers from its present rather disastrous eclipse, its return to power would certainly again bring Mr. Childers to the front, provided only that he retains his vigour unimpaired. In the interval since he last held office, and under the exigencies of that need for rest and change of scene which the state of his health so imperatively needed, Mr. Childers has been a diligent and indefatigable traveller, and he has again seen many cities and many men. A lengthened visit to the land of his first adoption has tightened still more closely the bonds which united him to Australia, and should his presence be required at the Colonial Office on some future day, he would find there a wide sphere of usefulness. But it is possible that he would be called neither there nor to his old post at the Admiralty, simply because the bent of his genius lies in other directions. Although the fact is not commonly known, Mr. Childers is a born financier. Figures are his *forte*. In the days before he held high office, City companies and commercial undertakings of every kind bid high for his countenance and personal support. He might have been a director a thousand times over; he may, in the way of business, control, if he pleases, unlimited sums. Although missing, perchance, that deftness of statement with which his leader, Mr. Gladstone, was wont to decorate his bald array of figures till they became the most glowing and interesting facts, he is nevertheless an apt pupil in the master's school, and might be counted upon to bring in and explain a Budget with more skill and judgment than any man of his standing in the House.

VI.

SIR ANDREW CLARKE, K.C.M.G., C.B.

SOME thirty years ago one of the fairest provinces of the Australian group of colonies was in a most deplorable condition. The system of transportation, which had but recently failed most conspicuously in the larger island, had been continued under other, and it was hoped improved, auspices in Tasmania, or Van Diemen's Land as it was then commonly called, but with consequences the most unlooked for and unsatisfactory. The colony had become crowded to excess with convicts in various stages between servitude and actual freedom; there was a glut in the labour market, little or no work to be done, and general distress prevailed. To grapple with this supremely difficult question Sir William Denison, an engineer officer of wide experience, accustomed to deal with large public works and large masses of men employed thereon, was especially selected and despatched to the colony, taking with him full instructions and large powers to set on foot measures of relief. Among the passengers on board the ship which conveyed the new Governor to his destination was a young subaltern, also of the Royal Engineers, whom the chances of his military service were also taking to the Antipodes. Between the skilled administrator charged with an important and delicate mission, enjoying already high place and a substantial measure of professional and statesmanlike prestige, and his youthful fellow-voyager, a great gulf intervened. They had only in common the honour of holding commissions in the same distinguished regiment—no trifling bond perhaps, for officers of Engineers are not the least strongly imbued, of all others in her Majesty's service, with the feeling of *esprit de corps.* Drawn thus together as comrades in arms, although in widely different grades, the first acquaintance between them developed during the long voyage into friendship, fostered not a little by the kindly encouragement of the elder, aided also by the ready tact and many amiable qualities of the younger man. The end of it was that on arrival at Hobart Town, when his Excellency landed, he was accompanied by an aide-de-camp, whom he had then and there appointed—Mr. Andrew Clarke. Thus entirely off his own bat, so to speak, unaided by interest or influential introductions, the young man gained for himself the first step upon the upward ladder, and this happy faculty of making and retaining friends has remained with him throughout his subsequent successful career. It stood by him in these early days of his colonial experience, days fraught with momentous colonial issues, when, as has been said, the last convict experiment had practically failed; when within a stone's-throw a vast island continent was convulsed by the discovery of a new El Dorado; when another colonial neighbour was plunged in war with a martial race; when, to crown all, the concession of constitutional government and representative institutions came to complicate the conditions of political life. In all of these young Clarke took an active share. He made the New Zealand campaign of '48 and '49, having been entrusted at its close with delicate diplomatic negotiations with a well-known Maori chief; he had been commissioned to proceed to the Victorian gold fields in the difficult and onerous post of Surveyor-General, charged with the settlement of claims and disputes connected with land. He was thus actively engaged when the proclamation of constitutional government threw into his way an opportunity of entering the political arena, and now, mainly in consequence of the popularity he had already deservedly earned, and of the friends he had made during the discharge of his functions as Surveyor-General, he was returned to the new House of Representatives as member for Melbourne. The position gained thus by a young soldier outside and beyond his own professional line was honourable in the extreme. But he soon proved that the choice had not fallen upon him without good reason, and in the years next following he came so prominently to the front, that he was called ere long to form one of the Colonial Government, and had a seat in Mr. Haines' Cabinet as Minister for Public Lands. So high was the opinion formed of his statesmanlike qualities, that a year or two later he was asked by Sir Henry Barkly to form an administration, but declined the honour, as he was upon the point of returning to England after an absence of nearly ten years.

To a man still in his first youth, energetic and full of vigour, the change from the stirring activity and constant excitement of political life in a large colony to the more humdrum duties of a district engineer officer in England, must have been sufficiently marked. But this change Colonel Clarke, like others of his cloth, accepted with the best grace in the world. His first patron, Sir William Denison, on relinquishing so high a post as the Governorship of an Indian Presidency, with the recollection that he had for a time acted also as Viceroy, could do the same; so could Chinese Gordon, as his friends love to style him, when from the command of the "Ever-victorious army," numbering many thousands of men, he settled quietly down as an engineer captain at Gravesend, remaining there, and in similar unpretending positions, until summoned by the Khedive of Egypt to be his Commander-in-chief in the expedition to the Soudan. Colonel Clarke similarly occupied himself usefully and uninterruptedly for several years, with the single exception of a special mission to the Gold Coast, to inquire into Ashanti squabbles, even then a fruitful source of trouble, a task in which he acquitted himself so well that it was remembered in his favour long afterwards, and he was actually offered the command of the expedition which Sir Garnet Wolseley manipulated with such wonderful success. The high qualifications of Colonel Clarke, and his undoubted fitness for more responsible duties were, however, destined to be recognised soon, and in 1863, not entirely without the good word of a former political colleague in Victoria,

Mr. Childers, he was appointed to be the Director of Naval Works to the Admiralty—in other words, he was entrusted with the control of those vast extensions of dockyards and naval arsenals which are among the great engineering feats of the present age. The gigantic labours which have converted a river estuary, as at Chatham, into a capacious land-locked harbour, capable of giving safe stowage to a whole navy at a time; the similar undertakings at Portsmouth, and the colossal scale in which surrounding and subsidiary buildings have been carried out, will testify always to the talents and breadth of mind of the man who superintended and controlled the works. Ten years or more of such congenial employment, during which he had the satisfaction of observing the works in hand steadily progressing towards completion, was properly rewarded by the honour of knighthood, and his translation to another, and a higher, although not a more distinctly useful, sphere. Sir Andrew Clarke found, on his arrival at Singapore, that he had no bed of roses in his new appointment as Governor of the Straits Settlements. Troubles were rife, especially in the neighbouring province of Perak. Faction fights of the most bloodthirsty character between clannish Chinamen, Malay piracy and turbulence, going the lengths sometimes of open affronts offered to the British flag, produced an unvarying condition of unrest. To deal with these difficulties was the first task of Sir Andrew Clarke's administration, and he grappled with them in his own way. Basing his line of treatment upon that principle of conciliation which he had hitherto so consistently and successfully observed in affairs of lesser moment, he set himself to work in good earnest to bring about a general pacification of the province. Unsparing always of himself, he started with all convenient dispatch for the troubled district, and with much patience, and still greater skill, brought the discontent to a close. Residents were established in the disturbed districts, a suitable scheme of revenue and finance introduced, and there was every reason to suppose that future peace and prosperity were assured to the province. Sir Andrew's treatment of the native races had been judicious and prudent. Frank always and outspoken, he was tolerant of their failings, considerate and kindly, yet firm and unyielding when an exhibition of determination and authority was needed to bring the wayward to their knees. He had already made substantial advance in their esteem when he was offered, and could hardly hesitate to accept, promotion to the Indian Council as member for Public Works. How, later on, the difficulties at Perak culminated in bloodshed, how the murder of Mr. Birch was promptly and vigorously avenged by Sir Andrew's successor, are matters beyond the scope of this memoir.

In India Sir Andrew Clarke has taken up the threads of a vast department, which, till he was nominated, had never known a supreme chief. The situation was one of extreme difficulty, therefore, and he has wisely proceeded so far with cautious steps. The new-broom theory has not been exemplified in his case, and he has been content to let matters go on for the present much in their old way. But with characteristic energy he has traversed great distances, and made himself personally acquainted with the condition of the greatest undertakings. He has in this way mastered the intricacies of the Indus Valley Railway, he has visited Madras and closely inspected its harbour works, as well as those of the port of Kurrachee, in Scinde. A man who thus devotes himself with persistent endeavour to see everything with his own eyes, and decide everything on his own judgment, cannot fail to succeed. At the termination of his tenure of office it will probably be found that if he has foregone the temptation of making hasty and showy reforms, he has, at least, accomplished a large amount of beneficial work in the consolidation of his department.

VII.

COLONEL COLLEY, C.B., C.M.G.

A MAN'S comrades and contemporaries, unless they be abnormally dull of apprehension, are by no means the worst judges of his character and the good that is in him. Jealousy may sometimes lead them into undue depreciation; exaggerated hero-worship may tempt them into undiscriminating praise; but their criticisms must generally be accepted as sound. Battling often with the same difficulties, having common aspirations, a common age, and perhaps a common profession, they are ready to make fuller allowances for failure, they will render a heartier acknowledgment for well-deserved success, than can be expected from others above or below the struggle. No officer of his rank and standing has received throughout the successive stages of his career, or receives now, from his fellows a more ungrudging recognition of superiority than Colonel George Pomeroy Colley. Coming of a good old stock, Colonel Pomeroy Colley can claim close kinship with one of the greatest of English generals. A Pomeroy, one of the Devonshire family, having gone to Ireland as chaplain to Lord Essex in the reign of Charles II., remained there, and later, one of his descendants intermarried with the Colleys, the same family identically as that which subsequently spelt itself Cowley, and adding the name Wellesley, was ennobled with the title of Mornington. The first Earl of Mornington was the father of Arthur Wellesley, Duke of Wellington.

At a very early age young Colley went to Sandhurst as a cadet, and, passing through the schools with flying colours, gained his first commission in 1853 in the Queen's, the well-known 2nd Regiment of the Line, which was stationed just then at the Cape of Good Hope. The Kaffir wars were at an end, and there seemed little prospect of active employment, but it was not long before the young ensign had an opportunity of showing the stuff that was in him. A skilful and facile draughtsman, he had taken honours, especially in military surveying, at Sandhurst; and his talents in this respect were soon turned to useful account at the Cape. Thus engaged for some years, he covered wide areas of land, and gradually acquired so much practical knowledge of the character and peculiarities of the African tribes that he was well fitted for the post of frontier magistrate, to which he was presently appointed. Colonel Gawler, of Cape renown, was his colleague and mentor, and no young administrator could have had one more experienced or more determined. There were times when both, stationed alone and almost at the mercy of the turbulent Kaffirs, seemed to carry their lives in their hands. A judicious blending of firmness and intrepidity brought Colonel Gawler through many trying situations, and the lesson was not lost upon his pupil. Colley's influence and ascendency over the chiefs were so undoubted that he was able on one occasion, by his advice and personal exertions, to stave off an imminent Kaffir war. For his services in this affair he was promoted, a year or two later, to a brevet-majority, and within the last few months he has also been made a C.M.G. Meanwhile, he had taken part in the expedition to Pekin, under Sir Hope Grant, and that ended, had competed for admission to the Staff College, which he entered in 1861. His progress through the college was one long triumph. It might have been supposed that in his busy and adventurous life, exiled often for months together in the bush, with a necessarily limited library, with no society but savage tribes, his book lore and scholastic attainments would have sensibly diminished. But, however active and laborious his employment, Major Colley never ceased to be a student—a voracious reader of everything on which he could lay hands. It was in these days that he came first to understand that if he would continue well-informed he must devote a certain time daily to his books. The difficulty, in the midst of his manifold and onerous occupations, was to find time, and it was then that he became what he has since unvaryingly continued, an early riser. The two or more hours before breakfast, when he lit his own fire and boiled his own coffee, multiplied by some fifteen times three hundred and sixty, have given him a deep insight into the literature of the day, and when books and authors are under discussion, he can hold his own always with the best. These studious habits served him in good stead at the Staff College, through which he passed in half the ordinary time with full honours, taking up many extra subjects, and doing so well in all that he came out, easily, first upon the list.

A succession of staff appointments in England followed the Staff College qualification, in which Major Colley gained routine experience in an office, with occasional practice in manœuvres on a large scale. When he could fling off the restraints of a garrison life, he sought to gratify his love of movement and adventure by continual travel and peregrination as far abroad as the limits of his leaves of absence would allow. In this way he visited Spain, Italy, Algeria, and the United States. He was actually in the Carpathians, studying the military geography of this frontier, and spending thus the vacation from the Staff College, to which he had returned as a professor of Military Administration, when the news reached him of Sir Garnet Wolseley's departure for Ashantee. Colley hurried home, resigned his professorship, and followed Sir Garnet to the Gold Coast with all speed. He arrived at a critical time. The whole hope of a final successful march upon Coomassie hinged upon the transport of supplies, and just at this juncture the entire arrangements for this service had broken down and collapsed. Time pressed; the season was advancing, and unless new plans could be matured, and that without delay, no movement could possibly be made against King Coffee's capital till the following year. In this emergency Sir Garnet cordially and thankfully availed himself of the services of the man who had appeared so opportunely upon the scene. Colley, by this time a Lieutenant-Colonel, was given *carte blanche*, and entrusted with full powers. No better selection could have been made. He was especially suited to grapple successfully with the difficult task entrusted to him. Having a singularly cool, clear head, and a brain which worked with mathematical precision, he was gifted also with great natural powers of organisation; he had, moreover, recently made the theory of administrative machinery in all its branches, including that of transport, his peculiar study, and this not only for the benefit of those who attended his lectures at the Staff College, but as the confidential adviser of Lord Northbrook, when Under Secretary of State for War. Above all, he knew certain portions of Africa, and the tribes which inhabited it, by heart; and there is in some respects a marked similarity between the varied members of the African family, notwithstanding the distances which divide them. No one could have manipulated more judiciously the petty potentates of town and village, upon whose goodwill and co-operation it depended whether human carriers to work the transport service would be forthcoming when required. By an admirable alternation between persuasion and peremptoriness he accomplished the object in view, and, having obtained his raw material, organised it so efficiently, with such admirable forethought, symmetry, and good sense, that never once in the series of extended operations which took place between the Prah and Coomassie was there a hitch in the arrangements for supply. Colonel Colley, who was the first to discharge in any English campaign the duties of an officer in charge of the communications, whom the Germans call the *etappen* commander, contributed in no slight degree to the glorious termination of the war. His personal exertions throughout this period were almost marvellous. He was ubiquitous; he seemed to take no rest. Carried now in a hammock, trudging next on foot, he managed day after day to cover forty or fifty miles' distance, and to supervise nearly the whole length of his long line of communications. This splendid physical energy, displayed continually under the adverse influences of an enervating, nearly murderous climate, is no less a proof of his spirit, pluck, and tenacity of purpose, than it is of his fitness to endure the real hardships of service in the field. No man could exhibit more strongly the *vis vitæ* in conjunction with great powers of mind.

An interval of comparative inactivity followed Ashantee, broken by further travel, by a special mission with Sir Garnet to Natal, and at length ending in his appointment as Quartermaster-General upon the Aldershot Staff. He had barely entered upon the duties of his new post when a tempting offer was made him to accompany Lord Lytton to India, which he was only too glad to accept. It had always been a theory with him that an English officer without Indian experience would be somewhat at a disadvantage if he came to chief command, and he felt that he could not gain that experience under better auspices than those which now offered. He went out accordingly as the Viceroy's Military Secretary, having thus, it must be confessed, no functions much above those of a purely social character. But the occasion of the Delhi Durbar and the difficulties connected with Quettah gave him opportunities which permitted him to prove his capacity, and he will have now far greater scope in his new appointment as Private Secretary. That he will discharge his new duties, onerous and responsible though they be, to the satisfaction of all, may be fairly assumed. He is a soldier *par excellence*—a deeply-read student in the great campaigns of all ages, thoroughly progressive, a close observer of all professional changes, ready to imbibe new lessons and make practical deductions therefrom—but that he will on occasion prove himself an undoubtedly able diplomatist too, is likely in the extreme. He has broad, sensible views upon all great questions of the day, and since his residence in India he has given much painstaking thought to those peculiarly affecting the great Empire in which he now holds so important a post. His manner to all who come in contact with him is such as to inspire confidence at once—quiet, self-possessed, and full, as it seems, of reserved power. He is, however, thoroughly genial in his social relations, sympathetic, friendly, and having a keen sense of humour, is always a pleasant companion. Last of all, he has much of the modesty and reticence which are among the evidences of true worth; and these many good points have gained him a widespread popularity which will win for him the devotion of a large band of disciples when he arrives, as, humanly speaking, he is certain to arrive, at the top of the professional tree.

VIII.

THE HONOURABLE KRISTO DAS PAL.

It would be difficult to name any Hindoo who has attained, among natives of his own race, a position exactly analogous to that which Syud Ahmed Khan holds among the Upper Indian Mahomedans. For one reason, the constitution of Hindoo society is less favourable than that of the Mussulman for the exercise of a social and political leadership on something like the European model. The religious and social distinctions, which we sum up in the generic word *caste*, interfere with the *solidarité* of the Hindoo population to an extent of which the Mahomedans, in spite of their many sectarian and class differences—imitated, in a great measure, from their former subjects—have themselves had no experience. Almost the only eminent Hindoo of whom the English public have lately heard is the religious reformer who many years ago threw off the trammels of caste altogether, and, as the chief of the Brahmists, came over to England to preach Theism. Baboo Keshub Chunder Sen, however, is a far less important personage among the natives of Calcutta and Bengal than his countryman, who is the subject of the present notice. The Honourable Kristo Das

Pal may be accepted as the leader of a large and influential section of Hindoos, whose political attitude towards the English Government corresponds in many respects to that of the Mahomedan Liberals, who are represented by Syud Ahmed Khan. There is this difference, however, that Syud Ahmed's followers are more uncompromisingly English in their tendencies than any other class of natives, Hindoo or Mahomedan, who are conscious of political opinions of any kind.

Like his Mahomedan countryman, the Honourable Kristo Das Pal owes his high rank among the foremost Bengalees of his generation solely to his character and ability. He first gained distinction as a journalist, and under his management the *Hindoo Patriot*—of which, we believe, he is also the proprietor—has long been recognised as one of the ablest newspapers in India. But it will be inferred from what we have already said, that the *Patriot*, which, like a small minority of its native contemporaries, is written in English, is much less advanced in its views than the Aligurh paper. It is what even old-fashioned Hindoos, if they were to borrow Western phraseology, might call a safe journal; and this partly accounts for its wide circulation among the educated classes. It has been Mr. Kristo Das Pal's ambition to act as the interpreter and representative of the more influential sections of his fellow-countrymen, rather than play the part of a reformer. Hence, in a great measure, his resolute opposition to some of the most cherished schemes of the greatest reformer, whether native or

English, whom Bengal has yet seen, viz., Sir George Campbell; or perhaps it would be more correct to say that his hostility was directed not so much against the end as the means. A discussion of this subject, however, would open out a series of questions with which English readers are unfamiliar, and in which they cannot be expected to feel any interest; but it may be observed that Mr. Kristo Das Pal, and those to whose views he gave expression, objected to Sir George Campbell's projects for taxation in support of local improvements, local self-government, as it is called, and a universal system of primary instruction, on the ground, partly, that the levy of the proposed cesses implied a violation of the arrangement by which, eighty years ago, the amount of the State's claim upon the soil was supposed to have been settled in perpetuity. There was a reminiscence of the old antagonism between the Lieutenant-Governor and the native editor when the former, during the debate on the Press Act, having declared that the Anglo-native papers were more seditious than all the vernacular journals put together, singled out the *Hindoo Patriot* as the most dangerous of them all. As a matter of fact, there is no more loyal journal in India than the *Patriot*. Mr. Kristo Das Pal, in short, is the literary champion of the zemindars, or landlords, and of the British Indian Association, which is perhaps the most powerful and intelligent of the many societies which the natives of India have formed after the English pattern. Whatever we may think of his views on the matter of ways and means, he must be acknowledged to be one of the most steadfast friends of progress, as well as one of the best writers and speakers that Bengal has produced. For a long time, too, Mr. Kristo Das Pal took an active interest in the control of local affairs; and he rendered valuable service during the prolonged discussions in the Legislative Council, and the public demonstrations in Calcutta, which, during the earlier portion of Sir Richard Temple's rule, ended in the establishment of a municipal constitution with an elective machinery similar to that which is in use in English towns.

It was an honour to which his services, his diverse qualifications, and his experience fully entitled him, when, at last, he was nominated to a seat in the Council of the Lieutenant-Governor of Bengal. He speedily established his reputation as one of the most skilful debaters in that body. His speeches show no trace of that looseness of thought and style which so often characterizes even the best efforts of natives who express themselves in English. On the contrary, they are just as compact and logical as any which we might expect from a practised orator addressing Mr. Speaker. An appointment such as that of the Honourable Kristo Das Pal was calculated to please the Bengalees, or, at least, the Calcutta population in particular; for it is in Bengal that the cry for elevation to the official level is sent forth more shrilly than in any other Indian province. The new member himself was, and still is—and very properly too, it may be added—one of the most persistent advocates of a more liberal system for the admission of natives to offices of dignity and responsibility. It is the substance rather than the shadow and mere symbols of power that natives of his stamp are anxious to conquer. Mr. Kristo Das Pal has also had his fair share of titles. That of Rai Bahadoor was conferred upon him in recognition of his public services. As member of the local Legislative Council, he ranks, of course, as an Honourable, and he is the only ornament of the Indian Fourth Estate, who rejoices in a Companionship of the newly-created "Order of the Indian Empire."

IX.

MR. GRANT DUFF, M.P.

THE name of the Parliamentary Under-Secretary of State for India in Mr. Gladstone's Government is immediately suggestive of Macaulay's famous dictum on the impossibility of promising success to any one in the British House of Commons. Mr. Grant Duff has long since made his mark at St. Stephen's. He has been in Parliament close on twenty-one years, and the position which will be assigned to him by political criticism must be pronounced definitely fixed. He is close upon fifty years of age; he has had six years' experience of official life; and if he is ever again promoted to place and power, it can scarcely be in the character of a subordinate. During the last decade the member for the Elgin Burghs has not made much Parliamentary progress, and has made a good many personal opponents and ill-wishers. There is indeed no man who has more of natural amiability, who is fonder of the society of his fellow-men, who enjoys the delights of conversation more thoroughly, who is more genial and generous in his hospitality, or whose house is a more agreeable one to visit, than Mr. Grant Duff. Similarly it is quite certain that if one was asked to select half-a-dozen, probably half that number, of Englishmen pre-eminent for thoroughness and variety of culture, width and depth of knowledge, political information, and worldly prudence, it would be impossible to exclude Mr. Grant Duff. If purely intellectual qualities, if an immense acquaintance with men and manners, if not merely to know more than others on the great questions of the day, but to possess an accuracy of knowledge proportionate to its superiority, could have commanded the highest success in Parliamentary life, that success would have long since been Mr. Grant Duff's. The truth is, we English have yet to emancipate ourselves from the traditions of Philistinism, and Mr. Grant Duff, as one in whom this emancipation is complete, is felt to be disagreeably in advance of his age.

That is the general explanation of the fact that the political success of the member for the Elgin Burghs has never seemed equal to his rare deserts. There are other more particular reasons at which it may be well to glance. Theoretically the sagacity and wisdom of no man is greater than that of Mr. Grant Duff. If a young man bent upon entering Parliamentary life were seeking for counsel, Mr. Grant Duff would give that counsel better and more wisely than any one else. He knows the House of Commons perfectly, he has felt every beat in its pulse; yet he has perhaps never turned this wisdom and knowledge to full practical account. He has never been able to keep his detestation of Philistinism and all its works within proper control; he has never been able to resist giving the

Philistines themselves a sharp rap whenever they have laid bare their knuckles in a tempting manner. He has been perfectly impartial in the administration of these stinging censures. He has attacked Lord Palmerston and Mr. Disraeli indiscriminately with the same keenness and candour that he did Sir Charles Wood, whose Indian financial statements he remarked, with a charming absence of disguise, were the dreariest, feeblest, and most confused to which mortal ears had ever been compelled to listen. As he has exposed the equivocations of the present Prime Minister, and inveighed against the temporising tactics of a Palmerston, so has he been unable to resist the temptation of falling upon Mr. Gladstone. The ecclesiastical crochets of the late Prime Minister are not unnaturally intolerable to a cultured Liberal like Mr. Grant Duff, and some six or seven years ago this detestation of them found utterance in an expression which Mr. Gladstone has, perhaps, not yet forgotten. The subject of discussion was education, and Mr. Gladstone consented to the principle of certain checks and safeguards in the interests of religion, or in other words, High Anglicanism. "What," asked Mr. Grant Duff, "are you to expect if, when the Liberal party is storming a forlorn hope, the leader of it turns round and fires a revolver in its face?" It is a very dangerous and inconvenient gift for a politician who has ambitions, the capacity for saying sharp things in an epigrammatic form. If invective be, as Mr. Disraeli has told us, the ornament of debate, sarcasm, when exercised upon one's friends, is apt to be the obstacle of a career. The pungent incisive taunt is too often refused forgiveness by magnanimity itself, and heaven-born statesmen who lead parties and form administrations are not always more magnanimous than the rest of the world. When Mr. Gladstone, upon Mr. Disraeli's resignation, after the general election in 1868, was called upon to construct a Government, it seemed as if Mr. Grant Duff were to be entirely left out in the cold. Lord Clarendon is understood to have signified the satisfaction with which he would have seen the member for the Elgin Burghs serving under him at the Foreign Office. During a long series of years, Mr. Grant Duff had left nothing undone, unseen, or unlearned which could qualify him for such a position. He had travelled over nearly the whole of Europe, had mastered the languages of different countries, had read most in them which was worth reading, had gained the acquaintance or the friendship of many of those persons in their capitals whom it was most desirable to know. His annual speeches to his constituents at Elgin had acquired a European reputation as the ablest and most exhaustive surveys of foreign affairs ever presented by an Englishman. He had spoken on the same class of subjects in the House of Commons, and had written the most clear and useful book on them in the English language. Moreover, Mr. Grant Duff had a sort of cosmopolitan fame. He was a true citizen of the world, and as, when on arriving at Berlin, or Vienna, or Munich, or at any other centre of statesmanship and diplomacy, the first thing which he did was to establish communications with those who were best able to introduce him to the political atmosphere of the place, so, after he had left it, he took care to continue the acquaintance, and often returned attention for attention, and kindness for kindness. Yet, conspicuous as Mr. Grant Duff's qualifications for the post were, he was passed over. It seemed as if no place in the administration at all were reserved for him. And, indeed, every other place except the Parliamentary Under-Secretaryship for India had been filled up. It was that which was allotted to the accomplished politician who, more than any of his contemporaries, had made the affairs of Europe his study.

After the Foreign Office, no department of State could have been more congenial to Mr. Grant Duff or more calculated to afford a field of display for his powers than the India Office. Indeed, as he soon found out, there were many converging points between the two, and the politics of Central Asia had long engaged his attention. He flung himself with rare energy into his work. Nor had the India Office ever an Under-Secretary who did more to extend the area of the duties of a subordinate position. His work was, of course, as must be the case with all Under-Secretaries, Parliamentary, but his Indian financial statements were really elaborate studies of the position and prospects of India, political as well as financial, and perhaps no higher compliment could be paid to their intrinsic merits than that they have stood the test of publication in a permanent shape, and that in this shape they are calculated to give the reader a clearer and a fuller idea of India than anything at all of the same bulk. His career at the India Office was associated rather with the development of the moderate policy of Lord Lawrence and Lord Northbrook than with any sensational *tours de force*. Twelve months after he left the India Office, on the occasion of the Liberal rout of four years ago, he visited India, and the memorials of his *impressions de voyage* are to be seen in the published "Notes of an Indian Journey." It has been objected to this little book that it is altogether of too light a texture to be really valuable, and there is no doubt something in the criticism. On the other hand, it should be remembered that the sense of responsibility with which Mr. Grant Duff wrote could not but operate as a certain restraint. He had already held an official position in connection with India; he might hold such a position again; and under these circumstances it would have been more than inexpedient if he had freely spoken his mind on all that he saw. Perhaps he has never appeared to more advantage as a critic, and in some sense an expositor, of our Oriental policy than in his latest speech on the Eastern Question in the House of Commons. At the same time no speech was ever more characteristic of the speaker, and the admirable impartiality with which he dealt his blows all round was a delightful spectacle for the friends and enemies of Ministerialists and the Opposition in turn. If Mr. Grant Duff did not hit so indiscriminately, did not, not only know so much, but also, unintentionally perhaps, aim the words of his knowledge over the heads of his hearers, we might have had a more successful politician, but we should not have had an abler statesman.

X.

EARL OF DUFFERIN, K.P., K.C.B.

In the autumn of 1873 there appeared in a Canadian illustrated paper a cartoon, in which was portrayed a stately matron presenting to Canada for service a page who, eyeglass in eye, with clearly cut and composed features, of which a broad and even forehead was no small part, seemed fitted for better than menial offices. Canada qualifies her acceptance of the new servant with an expression of fear that he may prove "too light for the place." The matron was England; the page offered for service was the Earl of Dufferin, then Governor-General of Canada, and the circumstances of the picture were those of the violent upheaval of Canadian politics, known as the Pacific Railway scandal. Trained at Eton and Oxford, Lord Dufferin, like many others who in after life have risen to illustrious positions, did not achieve academic distinction, and left the University without having given promise of future excellence, so far as such excellence can be predicted as the result of academic honours. These, however, by no means invariably afford a safe basis for prophecy, and it does not follow that Lord Dufferin profited less from his course at Eton and Oxford because he never attempted to win either the Newcastle or the Ireland. He is essentially one of those men who educate themselves—though not in the sense in which that expression is conventionally used. For much of that training for which he was not indebted to his own position by birth, his own bright and great power, he was indebted to his mother, one of the most gifted women of her age. The late Lady Dufferin, one of the three brilliant and beautiful daughters of Thomas Sheridan (the one, subsequently Duchess of Somerset, was renowned as Lady Seymour, the Queen of Beauty at the famous Eglinton Tournament, the other as Mrs. Norton, the poet and novelist), was grand-daughter of the wit, orator, and dramatist, Richard Brinsley Sheridan, and possessed in no ordinary degree the engaging qualities of her race. Her literary capacity generally, her style of writing, and especially of letter-writing, her faculty of sparkling conversation, were of the highest order. To those who knew her well she appeared as even a brighter star than her more distinguished sister, Mrs. Norton. Of the Sheridan brilliance the son of this attractive woman has inherited a visible portion.

Lord Dufferin had been Lord-in-Waiting to the Queen; had produced some literary work of the lighter description, and had been attached to Lord Russell's mission to Vienna in 1855, when he was selected by the Liberal Government in 1860 to fill the prominent and responsible position of British Commissioner to Syria, to inquire into the circumstances of the recent massacres in the Lebanon and in Damascus, and to suggest a scheme for the better government of the mixed and mismanaged populations of that troubled part of the Turkish Empire. The duties of this undertaking Lord Dufferin discharged with the marked ability which has characterized all the efforts to which he has seriously set himself, and the results of his labour were shown in dispatches of which the literary talent is conspicuous, and in the establishment of an administration in the Lebanon that has been followed by tranquillity. Of refined and literary tastes, with the bright and genial disposition and graceful versatility so well fitted for the gaiety and varied intercourse of society, Lord Dufferin appeared at one time, as though in philosophic indifference to the promising execution of the difficult Syrian mission, to be drifting away from the graver toils and greater rewards of political life to the dangerously seductive regions of cultured ease, surveying in pure Lucretian spirit the labourers on the troubled wave from the quiet vantage of a peaceful shore. In 1864 he was appointed Under-Secretary of State for India; subsequently Under-Secretary for War; and finally, in December, 1868, Chancellor of the Duchy of Lancaster. In none of these offices is there much opportunity of distinction, and it is not, perhaps, matter for surprise if Lord Dufferin as Governor-General of Canada appeared at first to the casual observer "a little too light for the place." His political ambition had never been obtrusive, and his tendency had been towards other tastes. Those, however, who beneath a sparkling and pleasant exterior had discerned the more solid and commanding qualities of temper and intellect read rightly. The keen observer would have seen in that presence the forceful and significant silence of one who awaits a trying issue with deliberate confidence. For it was but a little while before the "light man" had proved too weighty a combatant for the hardest hitter of the rough Canadian arena. Assailed for his admirable firmness in the Pacific Railway crisis with bitter and unsparing severity, threatened by the leading newspaper of the Dominion with perpetual execration, if not with the immediate violence of an indignant mob, Lord Dufferin could not be diverted from the constitutional course which he had assured himself was right, standing out in the event as no unequal match in questions of law for an Achilles among lawyers, as a patient and graphic constructor of admirably clear dispatches on the most involved subjects, and as an impartial and fearless interpreter of the maxims of constitutional rule.

The Canadian people then recognised what perhaps not even every English politician was thoroughly aware of, but what a few intimate observers had already realised—that in Lord Dufferin, to all the popular qualities of a *littérateur*, a man of society, a sprightly and charming talker, something of a poet, and something of a painter, a bold rider, a fair shot, and a good fisherman (for in all these characters he had been known), there were allied the robuster elements of a commanding will and a capacious intellect, the limit of which, after a variety of trials, has not yet been reached. So striking an impression was on this occasion formed of his fidelity to duty and his high abilities, that no voice has since been raised in Canada to censure any step he has taken in relation to any subsequent matter. He has forged for himself that happy and trenchant weapon of a constitutional ruler, the confidence of those with whom and for whom he acts, that what he does is probably right. Only those can fully understand the value of such a character who know how easily a Governor, on the one hand, may sink into obscurity beneath the shield of his ministers, and how effectively, on the other hand, he may exert upon the policy and feelings and tone of his advisers the great influence of a feared and respected name. There are Premiers who attempt to bully, and Premiers who attempt to cajole, but the worst of them go warily against a Governor whose word to the country is better than theirs. Lord Dufferin arrived in Canada in the summer of 1872, Sir John Macdonald being Premier with a large majority at his back, in times of political quiet which seemed still further assured indefinitely by the ensuing general election, at which the same party were confirmed in power. Then burst suddenly the storm of the Pacific Railway disclosures, and Sir John Macdonald was swept from office, and succeeded in November, 1873, by Mr. Mackenzie. The new Administration had to deal before long with the question whether an amnesty should be granted to the rebels of the Red River Rebellion of 1870. Unfortunately, of the offenders, whose crime varied in turpitude, some were French Roman Catholics, some Irish, while a victim of a murder for which they were responsible was an English Protestant, and over these divided claims arose the violent faction of conflicting nationalities and religious passion. Lord Dufferin severed the knot of the difficulty with characteristic chivalry. In awarding a commutation of sentence to the culprits, willingly exposing himself to censure, he took the burning question from the hands of his ministry, whose advice by the letter of his commission he was bound to take, though not necessarily to follow, and on his sole responsibility decided the issue. The step was constitutionally questionable, but it was the happy and bold settlement of a desperate dissension. The disappointed province of British Columbia, too, which had become part of Canada upon terms impossible of literal fulfilment, requiring the construction of a railway to the Pacific coast within a limited time, early created a serious trouble. Between the exorbitant appeals of the province and the deaf or indifferent honour of the Dominion, Lord Dufferin has succeeded in the no slight task of maintaining a just balance. His speech in British Columbia in the autumn of 1876 was a model of tact, firmness, and felicitous expression. The vehement resistance of the Roman Catholics of New Brunswick to the School Act of that Province; the Prince Edward Island Land Purchase Act of 1875; the soreness felt in Canada, the part of the Empire principally concerned, at the action of England towards the United States with regard to extradition; the difficult question of commercial Reciprocity with the United States; these are matters, amongst many others, in which the judgment and influence of the

Governor-General has been in no common degree exercised.

Nor is it alone in his capacity of dealing with the difficulties of political enterprise that Lord Dufferin has shown exceptional character; he has enjoyed in his appeal to popular affection as great felicity. His visits to the towns of the Dominion, his minute interest in every advancing undertaking, his exhaustive travels through all parts of the vast country, and his fervent and inspiriting record of his impressions in great public speeches which form memorable chapters of Canadian geography and history, his splendid hospitality, and his unostentatious kindliness, these have made him at once the most respected, the most valued, and the most affectionately esteemed Governor-General that Canada has ever known. The winter months are the time in Canada for the most signal festivities, and then, and especially during the session of Parliament, which, commencing generally about the middle of February, lasts from two to three months, the entertainments at Government House are as varied as they are sumptuous. Apart from the large balls and the State banquets, the afternoon parties, skating parties, curling parties, tabogganning parties, and private theatricals fill all the season; and the Governor-General, leaving a dispatch half written, or a painting unfinished, or a minister undecided in policy, will hasten to dance a quadrille upon skates or a valse in the ballroom with some pretty guest, or perhaps he will put three pretty guests together on a taboggan in front of him, and will steer them down the icy pathway that leads to overturning. These may seem small things when matched with the graver duties of government. But it is largely by showing the people of Canada how wide are the sympathies of the Governor-General, and how even in the least matters the happiness of all is his concern, that Lord Dufferin has succeeded in stimulating and confirming the regard of Canadians to himself as the representative of the Crown of England, and to the country from whence alone such a ruler can be supplied.

XI.

THE HON. SIR ASHLEY EDEN, K.C.S.I.

For years before he attained his present high position, the Hon. Sir Ashley Eden was generally recognised as one among the three or four ablest administrators in British India. His elevation from Rangoon to Belvedere was a distinction to which his exceptionally valuable services in Burmah, together with his earlier career in Bengal, fully entitled him. What Sir George Campbell was to Bengal, Sir Ashley was to British Burmah. The services which they rendered to their respective provinces were essentially alike, and even the characters of the two men seem to reveal many points of resemblance. Sir George Campbell's is no doubt the more speculative mind of the two, but both these rulers had much in common on the practical side, and they gave effect to their practical schemes in nearly the same manner. The development rather than the suppression of existing indigenous institutions was the keynote of their respective policies. The municipalities which Sir George Campbell established throughout Bengal were only an adaptation of the old *panchayets*, or rural communes. In the same way the indigenous *patshalas*, or village schools, became the primary schools—subject to Government inspection—of the administrations of Campbell and Temple. Even the Road Cess Act, which looks so exclusively modern, was based upon a series of researches that led to the discovery of many useful, though half-decayed, native institutions; and to it the cultivators are indebted for the first full record of their occupancy, rights, and obligations. As Sir George Campbell inaugurated an organized system of education in Bengal, so Sir Ashley initiated it in Burmah; the one began with the *guru;* the other with the *phoonghee,* or Buddhist monk, a stiff-necked Tory, compared to whom the Hindoo, or Mahomedan, pedagogue, was an advanced Radical. Unpromising tools, perhaps; but they were the best to be had, and the Lieutenant-Governor and the Chief Commissioner were not such indifferent workmen as to quarrel with them. The success which has attended both these great schemes has been remarkable.

The parallel holds good even as regards agrarian legislation. In Burmah the whole subject of occupancy rights was a chaos of contradiction and misconception, until Sir Ashley, three or four years ago, laid down a few easy and comprehensive rules for the information of the ryots. The land question, of course, is infinitely more simple in Bengal than in the sister province, and for the sufficient reason that in the former no zemindars intervene between the tenant and the State. Throughout his whole career at Rangoon, Sir Ashley exhibited an unerring perception of the real wants of his subjects, and of the simplest means for meeting them. He favoured the training of young

Burmans in veterinary surgery rather than in logic and metaphysics, just as Sir George Campbell preferred that his native officials should postpone the *literæ humaniores* to chemistry, the elements of law, and land surveying. Again, Sir Ashley was an indefatigable promoter of cattle shows, agricultural exhibitions, tobacco-growing experiments, and the like, precisely as Sir George Campbell was an enthusiast for "economic museums" at the headquarters of every district, as well as at the capital. Again, during the Famine crisis, Sir Ashley's services in Burmah were worthy of comparison with those of Sir George Campbell and Sir Richard Temple, and it was owing to his excellent management that the exportation to Bengal of such enormous quantities of grain was maintained during so many months without causing even the slightest derangements in the markets of Burmah. By his active interest in the Irrawaddy Valley Railway, and his admirable papers on the agricultural and other resources of Burmah, Sir Ashley has perhaps done more than any of his predecessors to demonstrate the capabilities of that magnificent province.

But, as has been already hinted, Sir Ashley's pre-Burmah career contained the promise of future distinction. The Secretariate is the golden key to advancement, and Sir Ashley entered the much-coveted department in about eight years after his arrival in India. His first appointment, 1852, was that of assistant to the magistrate and collector of Rajshaye. In 1856 he filled the post of magistrate at Moorshedabad, which he exchanged, after the lapse of three years, for the joint magistrateship and deputy collectorship of Baraset, whence, in two years more, he was transferred to the Revenue Board as junior secretary. During the long period 1865 to 1873 he discharged the duties of chief secretary to the Bengal Government with great skill and assiduity; and he was promoted in the last-named year to the chief commissionership of British Burmah. In 1874 he received the decoration of a C.S.I., and later that of a K.C.S.I.

Considering, therefore, the recent changes in the Provincial Department of Public Works—changes which throw the cost of construction and maintenance upon the respective provinces—it will be seen that in Burmah Sir Ashley has passed through an excellent apprenticeship for some of the most important duties of his new office. He may be depended upon for economical management of roads, light railways—if we are to hear anything more about them—and irrigation canals. In these respects there is more to be expected of him than of his predecessor, the present Governor of Bombay. To secure direct and speedy communication between Eastern Bengal and Assam would probably be a task much to the Lieutenant-Governor's taste, and it seems that indications of its early accomplishment are not wanting. But if in some directions he may prove himself a more useful administrator than Sir Richard Temple, there are signs that he may be considerably less popular. He is, perhaps, too downright in his modes of expression fully to please the sensitive Bengalees, while, next to Sir Bartle Frere,

Sir Richard Temple is perhaps the greatest Anglo-Indian master of the style that soothes and flatters. Here, again, he resembles the member for Kirkcaldy far more closely than he resembles Sir Richard Temple. One of the very first of his acts—viz., Act II., or the Public Works Cess Act of 1877—must have reminded the Bengal people somewhat unpleasantly of the terrible Sir George Campbell. The Act, however, which invests native honorary magistrates with police, in addition to their municipal jurisdiction, may perhaps have increased Sir Ashley's popularity among certain influential classes of the Calcutta public. On the other hand, he does not appear to be sufficiently enthusiastic on the subject of high schools and colleges, and the other more or less ornamental departments of Indian government, to satisfy the better educated people. But these are confined mainly to Calcutta and the large towns—which alone are not Bengal. Moreover, his support of the Press Bill rendered him, for a time, unpopular among all classes whatever. In reality, however, the grievance appears to have been, so far, more sentimental than real. Practically, the Press Law has remained almost completely a dead letter, and the Bengal vernacular papers are at this moment as unrestrained in their criticism of men and measures as they were before the notorious Press Bill became law.

It may be worth while to call attention to a mistake which Sir Ashley committed in his speech during the meeting at which the Bill was passed. He cited Sir George Campbell's own authority for the measure. What Sir George Campbell really proposed was summary trial for each case as it arose. We believe, however, that Bengal will be considerably the better for a course of Sir Ashley, after its experience of the sometimes too sympathetic manner of Sir Richard Temple. Sir Ashley's judicious efforts to introduce more pleasant relations between the ryots and landlords of Behar—a district in which the occupancy rights question has hitherto presented very formidable difficulties—are already beginning to bear fruit. The parallel case supplied by the measures of Sir Ashley's two predecessors was their successful intervention between the cultivators and zemindars of Eastern Bengal. In short, during his twenty months' tenure of office, Sir Ashley Eden has given sufficient proof of the highest qualifications for the office which, next to the Governor-Generalship itself, is the most important by far in British India.

XII.

SIR SANFORD FREELING, K.C.M.G.

The viceregal or pro-consular service of the British Crown is very variously recruited, and embraces all manner of men. Other public departments are, for the most part, governed by set rules, and he who elects to enter one of these is generally committed to it for better or worse, for the remainder of his days. The Treasury clerk, if he shows an especial aptitude for figures, may perhaps expand into the Finance Minister of some foreign but impecunious potentate, or he may be advanced to be the head of another branch of the national service. Often enough private secretaries are rewarded for years of self-sacrifice and labours that are nearly Sisyphean, by being translated to a lucrative but not undeserved sinecure. But, as a general rule, he who goes early to the Admiralty, Downing Street, Home Office, or Pall Mall, will continue to manipulate the fleet, prepare protocols, decide Poor Law questions, or control the various and complex operations of war until old age overtakes him, bringing with it a comfortable pension and assured ease. Not so the harvest gathered in by the wide-sweeping range of the Colonial

Office net. Everything is fish that comes to it—soldier, sailor, eminent barrister, experienced legislator, able if not entirely successful *littérateur*. The Colonial Office opens its gates gladly, and accords a cordial welcome to any and all, provided only that they have given earnest of capacity for administrative affairs. Yet more, it retains and advances them to more and more onerous posts when promise has expanded into performance, and they have practically proved that the confidence in their power to rule was not misplaced.

Mr. Freeling was serving as a young officer of artillery in the garrison of Malta when urgent entreaties for reinforcements came down from the Crimea in the dread winter of 1854. Placed in charge of a draft, which, by his own energy, he augmented still further by volunteers from the garrisons of the Ionian Islands, he arrived at Balaclava just in the nick of time. The men he handed over were in admirable trim, physically fresh and strong, in equipment efficient and complete. No small portion of the credit thereof was due to the officer in charge, and for this, and as a reward for his diligence in the soldierlike mission intrusted to him, Mr. Freeling, on his return to Malta, was appointed aide-de-camp to the Governor of the island, Sir William Reed. With the same chief he passed on a year or two later at Gibraltar, in the same capacity, and while there obtained his first footing upon the ladder of civil employment. The post of Colonial Secretary became vacant, and, through the good offices of the Governor, was secured for him, Captain Freeling accepting it gratefully, but only as a stepping-stone to better and more responsible work in the line of colonial administration. Although circumscribed in its physical limits, the diplomatic horizon of Gibraltar is by no means narrow. Questions of great variety and importance continually crop up; points of international law, vexed questions concerning the alien population, contentions with tetchy neighbours, who, not unnaturally, look upon the English as interlopers on the soil. The channel of communication in all such matters is the Colonial Secretary, and to any man of parts and adaptability, the training and experience gained therein could not fail to be useful in the extreme. It proved so to Mr. Freeling, who had now finally retired from the military service, when, within a few years of his advancement, first through his own merits and the kind advocacy of the then Governor, Sir Richard, now Lord Airey, he went to one of the West India islands as its Lieutenant-Governor. There was ample room even in this small governorship for the energies of an active administrator, and Mr. Freeling threw himself into the task with a will. It was his good fortune to contribute to the confederation of the Leeward Islands, so far as Dominica was concerned. Proceeding hence to Grenada, he was equally active here in carrying out constitutional reforms. Grenada owes it to him that it has a single Legislative Assembly instead of the old council and assembly, which never worked well. But even greater were the changes he initiated at Barbadoes when acting as Governor-in-Chief of the Windward Islands. This post he filled immediately before Mr. Pope Hennessy, and it is possible that had he remained longer, he might have carried the new constitution without the discontent and disruptions which gave Barbadoes soon afterwards a temporarily unenviable name. Yet more widely beneficial were improvements worked by his unsparing zeal and energy in the condition of the poor of the island. The various institutions, whether intended for their coercion or relief, were in a most unsatisfactory state. The gaols had been strangely neglected; they were seldom visited by the local authorities, and had never been properly governed. Not less mismanaged had been the hospitals and the leper asylums, in both of which deaths were more frequent than they ought to have been, and sanitary precautions were greatly overlooked. To all these matters Mr. Freeling addressed himself with vigour, fully realising that upon the due attention to such social and domestic affairs, no less than upon large questions of statesmanship, the success of an administration depends.

Returning from the West Indies, a period of retirement and inactivity followed, during which, very fortunately for himself, Mr. Freeling recruited his health and gained strength. He was soon to draw fully upon his resources in this respect. Lord Carnarvon, than whom no Colonial Minister has shown a juster appreciation of the value of the instruments available to carry out his policy, ere long, under circumstances very flattering to Mr. Freeling, offered him the Governorship of the Gold Coast. The situation called at the moment for an especially good man. The political aspect was threatening in the extreme. Weakness and want of judgment in dealing with the neighbouring tribes might have brought on another Ashantee war. The Ashantees still consider that they allowed themselves to be beaten too easily in the campaign under Sir Garnet Wolseley, and they were longing for another chance of measuring their strength with us. More than this, the kings and chiefs of the British Protectorate had never been thoroughly enamoured of British rule; the abolition of slavery they had accepted only with reluctance, and having become much impoverished thereby, they were proportionately discontented. These and similar difficulties surrounded the administration of the Gold Coast, and it was clear that nothing short of the utmost tact and discretion, combined with promptitude and resolution in him who was at the head of affairs, would suffice to keep the peace. That these qualities were to be found in Mr. Freeling, Lord Carnarvon plainly indicated when he begged him with some insistance to accept the vacant post, and the ready and unhesitating affirmative which Mr. Freeling gave was a fair earnest that he was worthy of the trust reposed in him. Almost immediately after his arrival on the Coast he was called upon to act with vigour. A turbulent tribe, the Juabins, who had been allowed to settle within the Protectorate on the condition that they kept quiet, had secretly collected arms and ammunition, and was on the point of invading the Ashantee Kingdom. An attack thus made from a British base, so to speak, and presumably with British sanction and support, could not fail to embroil us also with the

Ashantees, and it was of importance, therefore, to coerce the Juabins and inflict summary punishment upon them without loss of time. The handful of Houssa constabulary at Accra was sent off post haste by Mr. Freeling to disarm the Juabins, while he brought up further reinforcements from Cape Coast. The Houssas behaved admirably. Marching day and night nearly incredible distances, regardless of fatigue, they fell upon a large force of Juabins most unexpectedly, and in the surprise captured nearly all their ammunition and guns. Moving thence with equal rapidity from place to place, they completely crushed the movement, and after three weeks upon the frontier, returned in triumph, justifying fully the vigorous policy which had made such good use of them just at the right time. Nor was this the only occasion upon which the Governor acted with commendable pomptitude. Other detachments were repeatedly dispatched long distances to quell disturbances, and unwearied attention was paid to the force, in order to maintain it always in the state of the highest efficiency, ready to march anywhere at a moment's notice and do anything.

The immediate result of these judicious measures in dealing with turbulence and discontent has been a hitherto unknown sense of tranquillity in the colony. This, with the unceasing efforts of the administration to develop internal communications, opening up roads into the interior, securing them, repairing the old castles, and arming them with good ordnance, have given a tremendous impetus to trade. As the country becomes more and more settled, commerce has naturally increased, but no previous progress can compare with that of last year. The credit of this is due in a great measure to the present Governor. His constant watchfulness for the symptoms of approaching disturbance, his treatment, prompt and unsparing, where an exhibition of force is really necessary, his anxiety to promote all schemes for the development of internal resources, whether by his own intelligent initiative or by according a cordial support to the proposals of others, all these mark him down as a man eminently well fitted to rule. It is also greatly in his favour that he has been everywhere uniformly successful. Success may in truth be a matter of chance, but to have the credit of commanding it is a distinct advantage to an administrator, as are also other natural accidents, such as a fine person, the gift of ready eloquence, intuitive tact, or conciliatory ways. But it is in Downing Street that the character of having been always successful is the strongest recommendation. It is now so much the practice with the Colonial Office to leave its representatives abroad unfettered and with full power to act, that it throws practically all responsibility upon them, and judges them by the measure of success or failure which attends their endeavours. Mr. Freeling's official good fortune has gained him already the confidence and approval of his chiefs. He owes to it—coupled, of course, with his undoubtedly useful public services—his recent advancement to knighthood; and if it continues unabated, as there is every reason to hope it will while his sound judgment and indefatigable energy remain unimpaired, there is every reason to hope that he will find his reward by translation to some larger province, with wider capabilities and in a better climate than any of those he has hitherto ruled.

XIII.

THE FIRST BISHOP OF LAHORE.

CRUEL and unjustifiable as were many of the Spanish conquests, both in North and South America, it is still probable that they were undertaken with a clear conscience, and even with a righteous spirit. Devoted to the glory of Spain, the heroes of these adventures, who were little better than bandits, cherished the inspiring conviction that they were destined to bring, by persuasion if possible, or in the last resort by force, pagans of strange and sometimes sanguinary rites into the bosom of the great Mother Church. No such religious zeal was ever felt by the brave seamen who carried the English flag through unknown seas, or by the hardy merchants who pressed their way to strange cities where the most friendly reception they could expect was one marked with inactive suspicion. Least of all was a spirit of proselytism abroad amongst our early adventurers in India. Far from desiring to draw others to their faith, they took pains to conceal what little personal religion they possessed. There was a root of sincerity in much of this. It is not true that the Latin Church ever taught that bad men could be faithful children of her community; but it is true that Catholic freebooters sometimes chose to believe that unjustifiable actions might be sanctified in the end by the devotion of power to the interests of faith. The tide of English national adventures beyond sea set in pretty well at the same time that the Puritan spirit was coming prominently into notice, and a leading idea of Puritanism was that the elect and the non-elect were perfectly different classes, that those who had a call and those who had not, were entirely divided in their objects and their hopes, their pursuits and habits. Many of our early captains and stalwart traders, finding within themselves small traces of the spirit of God, led lives which might have aroused the suspicion that they were altogether unbelievers, though nothing could have been further from their thoughts than active scepticism.

Signs of this despairing indifference are apparent in the late dates of the churches in India: that of St. Thomas, at Bombay, one of the earliest—1720; St. Mary's, at Madras, about a century old; whilst the edifice of the Expectation of Our Lady, near the same place, was built by the Portuguese in 1547. In this state of feeling it was not likely that much anxiety should be experienced about the conversion of the heathen, and accordingly we find that though the Danes established a Protestant mission in Tranquebar so early as 1706, which was in the latter part of the century supported by the Society for the Propagation of Christian Knowledge, yet it was not till after the arrival in Bengal of the Baptist emissaries in 1793, that the cause of preaching the gospel to the heathen really took root amongst the British population. It progressed very slowly, meeting with much opposition and discouragement, though in the end triumphing over the obstacles thrown in its way by the Government. The mutiny at Vellore in 1806 was made the pretext for denouncing direct attempts at proselytism, on the score that the religious prejudices of the natives were so easily awakened. It was merely the method of operation, and the want of culture evinced by some of the missionaries, which raised alarm. The Church Missionary Society was founded early in the century, and soon enlisted the sympathies of a body of the chaplains of the Company: the names of Brown, Martyn, Corrie, and others became watchwords with those who were interested in the progress of Protestantism amongst the Indian masses. It cannot be denied that this active and open propagandism by clergymen in Government employ was to a certain extent a breach of neutrality on religious questions, and it is creditable to the forbearance of the old Company that the directors did not come to a misunderstanding with these excellent men. The establishment of a bishopric in Calcutta marked the era in which it began to be seen that the functions of the missionary and those of the chaplain were scarcely interchangeable, and that the task of building up a Protestant Church in India in connection with the State establishment at home, and of inviting and inducing the natives to join it, were separate. As time wore on, the chaplains entirely withdrew from missionary work, and the enterprise has gone on by itself till results have been reached which are numerically expressed by 120 missionaries, 95 native clergy, and 80,000 native Christians. The last figure does not seem high amongst such millions—there are as many Jews in half-a-dozen German towns taken collectively. Nor, it must be added in candour, are the converts as a body at all of a moral stamp sufficiently high to influence favourably the surrounding populations. The work of individual conviction is of course slow; and then, again, abandonment of caste, and change, in some respects, of national habits have been insisted upon, and therefore native Christians have grown to be a separate class, by the side of, but not amongst, the people. The surprising success of Christianity in the days of Xavier, was a kind of sudden enthusiasm, produced, in a measure, by the character of the man, and terminating with his life; and one is almost tempted to believe that if the country is ever to be evangelized, it will be by some similar *tour de force*, only on a prodigious and astonishing scale.

The appointment of a missionary to the See of Lahore indicated on the part of Government a belief in two points: first, that the subordination of missionaries to the general discipline of the Church tends to strengthen the position of that establishment as a whole; and next, that the spread of Christianity is calculated, in the long run, to increase the stability of our political dominion in the East. With regard to the first point, occurrences which took place a short time ago in the Island of Ceylon show that it is not a matter of such little moment as it might seem; and as to the second, the influence of religion will aid in the consolidation of the Imperial power, if the more the natives learn of Christianity the more the conviction shall grow upon them, that the British supremacy does not look for its permanence to force, nor to the material advantages it affords, nor even the intellectual expansion it encourages, but to the success attending a duty fulfilled, and founded on hope that looks beyond the gates of time.

Thomas Valpy French was a Rugby boy, commencing his school career in Arnold's time, and ending it under Tait. He then went to Oxford, and took his degree in 1846—a first class in classics—and was soon after elected a Fellow of University College. In September, 1850, he sailed for India, having as his companion the Rev. E. C. Stewart, who has just been elected Bishop of Wiapu, in New Zealand, so that the two friends have both succeeded in reaching the colonial bench—or, to speak with closer correctness, the outland bench. French was for eight years at Agra, where he established a high-class educational institution, called St. John's College, one of the objects of which is to afford culture to Hindoos of the better-born classes, including instruction in the principles of Christianity. He devoted himself with great industry to the study of the languages connected with Eastern lore, as well as the mere vernaculars, and is known as the "man of seven tongues"—Urdu, Hindi, Punjabi, Pushtu, Persian, Arabic, and Sanscrit. With regard, indeed, to the two latter, they scarcely consent to yield all their secrets to the leisure of a busy life, and, therefore, we must suppose rather that Dr. French takes the clever interest in them of a scholarly mind, than that he has vanquished their difficulties. The Mutiny came upon him, still working in what was then the capital of the North-West Provinces, in all its fury, shaking, as it did, the foundations of the British power to their very centre. He managed to take his native Christians with him when the retreat to the Fort was decided upon, and his firmness in insisting upon their admittance greatly endeared him to them when the danger was past. The excitement, if it tended at the time to keep people going, in most cases was followed by a painful reaction, and Dr. French was obliged to return to England when things grew a little brighter.

In October, 1836, Daniel Wilson, Bishop of Calcutta, a man not unmarked by eccentricities, but of a character in which there was much grandeur of a rugged sort, was in a boat on the river Sutlej, when he suddenly arose, and, stretching his right hand in the direction of the Plain of the Five Rivers, exclaimed in a loud voice, "I take possession of this land in the name of my Master, Jesus Christ." Runjeet Singh was then on the throne; the prophecy or intimation, seemed an idle cry flung on the passing breeze. But the great lion died, and was burnt on a pyre of sandal-wood, with four living queens and five slave girls, to whom existence was no longer an object when their lord was gone. The smoke of that funeral fire was succeeded by the smoke of civil war, and in the end by that of battles of surprising slaughter, and when the dreadful canopy was cleared away and peace returned, the land was British. In 1852, a meeting was held at Lahore, presided over by Archdeacon Pratt, when a missionary society was founded under the presidency of Sir Henry Lawrence. And in 1861 the Home Committee decided on starting a mission in the Deraját, partly induced thereto by the munificent promise of £1,000 towards its inauguration from General Reynell Taylor, the Commissioner of that rugged frontier territory lying between the Indus and the mountains of Afghanistan. To superintend this work French was fixed upon as the man whose zeal and knowledge best fitted him for it, and thither he proceeded; but the climate is wretched, and he threw himself so completely into his duties that health again broke down, and he had to return to England. But, nothing daunted, 1869 saw him again in Lahore, to establish a school of divinity in that capital, and once more—scarcely a subject of wonder—bodily strength gave way before mental exertion and an anxiety attendant on heavy duties under trying conditions of atmosphere. And so in 1874 he was again in the old country, and on this occasion, obtaining the parish of St. Ebbe, Oxford, it seemed probable that his Eastern career was at an end. But as those who have once tasted the freedom of the prairie and the forest languish in the confinement of the streets and squares, and envy the birds of passage passing over their heads, who leave us to our mists and fly far, far away in search of alien sunshine and brighter skies, so Dr. French faltered in the platitudes of parochial routine, and turned his thoughts to that ancient land of his adoption and his love.

To appoint a missionary as the first bishop of the Punjaub was at once complimentary and conciliatory to that society of which the Government was once too suspicious, and promises a possible fulfilment to that strange announcement of the gaunt old bishop in his boat on the Sutlej. Without strongly marked or salient features, Dr. French has sustained from the first a reputation for earnestness, worth, and high-mindedness; and these qualifications are quickly discovered and appreciated by the native population. Thoreau said that he could not despair of the earth so long as it possessed the power of bringing forth from unpromising mould, or even the *débris* of its own ruins, the pure beauty and fragrance of a lily; and an age marred by cupidity of gold, by feeble faith, and by depreciation of ideal ends, has still a future before it when it can produce the simple integrity of a good man's life, and can pause in its frivolous career to admire what it is scarcely able to understand.

XIV.

SIR BARTLE FRERE, BART., G.C.B., G.C.S.I.

The qualities displayed by the erewhile Governor of Bombay in dealing with the Kaffir rebellion have sensibly raised him in the official and the general estimation. An able administrator he had already proved himself; tenacity of purpose, once his resolution was fairly taken, he was known to possess; but his most favourable critics had scarcely credited him with the promptitude and vigour, the capacity of meeting a great and sudden crisis in an attitude of perfect calmness and undisturbed strength, the masterly combination of those attributes which lie at the root of success, whether in the councils of war or peace, that he has consistently exhibited since the outbreak of the Cape troubles. In a manner that has been much commented on at home, and has received the impartial praise of all whose praise he holds valuable, he has risen to the successive responsibilities imposed on him by the imperious hand of events; and when he returns to England he will bring with him a reputation which, not inconsiderable at the time of his departure to South Africa nearly two years ago, has been elevated and amplified to a degree that he may himself scarcely have foreseen.

This is the second, and it is incomparably the more real and substantial success achieved by Sir Bartle Frere on that continent, of which Tacitus wrote, that it was always producing something new, and which has for centuries abundantly maintained the character given it by the Roman historian—now affording the field of the most marvellous feats of exploration and research, crowning the labours of a Livingstone with the exploits of a Stanley; yielding its secrets of forest and flood, lake and mountain range, to the man who has the courage and skill requisite to pluck them from its bosom; at one moment revealing a hidden wealth of precious stones, at another, fresh opportunities of imperial annexation; now compelling us to send forth an expeditionary force against a barbarous potentate; and now suggesting to greatly daring minds the grand experiment which, under the name of "flooding the Sahara," is probably yet destined to be made. It is true that the negotiations which six years ago closely associated the name of Sir Bartle Frere with South Africa cannot be said to have ended in failure; indeed their outcome was generally considered a triumph. But it was not a triumph arrived at by the means or in the spirit originally contemplated. No better envoy to the Sultan of Zanzibar could have been selected in 1872 than Sir Bartle. He had first met that dusky potentate at Bombay, and Seyyid Burghash retained a vivid recollection of Sir Bartle's Oriental majesty and power, as well as his Oriental fame. Burghash was probably less impressed than he ought to have been by the auspicious omens which attended Sir Bartle Frere on his outward journey. Before he left England he had received a benedictory address from the Evangelical Protestants; *en route* to Zanzibar, while spending a few days at Rome, he received the special blessing of the Pope. Unfortunately the approval of Christendom was of insufficient weight with Seyyid Burghash, who splendidly entertained his distinguished visitor, but when politely informed by him that he must forego the slave trade, expressed himself unable to see why a treaty which he had concluded with Lord Palmerston should be rescinded by a process so summary. Moral and diplomatic pressure failed, and it was only when a British man-of-war, for which Sir Bartle Frere had telegraphed to his Government, lay at anchor in the offing, that Seyyid Burghash was brought to see that the arguments of the envoy were unanswerable.

But the desired result was gained, and that was enough. Sir Bartle Frere returned to England with his prestige immensely increased, and was greeted as the Christian diplomatist, who had put down the slave-trade at Zanzibar by the force of Christian persuasion. This view of the matter was due not only to Sir Bartle Frere's great capacities, but to the good influence which may be said to have watched over him from the first moment of his birth. He has shown how thoroughly he deserves all the good gifts which Fate and Fortune have showered upon him, and, seeing that these were perhaps unique in their value, it is impossible to pay him a higher compliment. His uncle, Hookham Frere, the friend and literary associate of Canning in the *Anti-jacobin*, wrote the best translation of some of the plays of Aristophanes in existence, made a brilliant marriage, and very seriously mismanaged our affairs in Spain during the Peninsular war. He was recalled from his embassy, and went down to his grave as one of the most distinguished men of the time. His nephew, Bartle Frere, has inherited a good deal of his uncle's intellectual force, though not precisely the same intellectual and literary tastes which were pre-eminent in his gifted and scholarly relative. Sir Bartle Frere has a ready and powerful pen, but he has also a taste for scientific investigation with which Hookham Frere would have had no sympathy. On the other hand, he resembles his accomplished uncle in having a lively fancy, a delicate and prolific imagination; and it is not impossible that if his administrative duties had been less absorbing, he might have won the laurels of poetic fame.

His powerful family connections—powerful both in India and England—would never have secured for him the successes of his career unless he had possessed rare gifts of his own. His life in India was that of a conscientious, courageous, indefatigable official, who rose rapidly through all the grades of his profession and who never deviated into a blunder. Arriving in Bombay in 1834—having gone out, characteristically enough, by the new overland route, then new, unknown, and dangerous—he served in subordinate grades till 1842, when he became private secretary to Sir George Arthur, the Governor, whose daughter he married in 1844. A few years later he became Resident, and afterwards Commissioner, at Satara, and in 1852 Chief Commissioner of Scinde, and during his incumbency twice received the thanks of the two Houses of Parliament. From 1859 to 1862 he was a distinguished member of the Supreme Council of India, and in the latter year was appointed Governor of Bombay. It may be that on some occasions during his period of office—1862-67—as Governor of Bombay, he did not exhibit all the sagacity which might have been expected of him. As for the failure of the Bombay Bank, Sir Bartle Frere was apprised too late of the menacing aspect of affairs to interpose with advantage. Moreover, he possessed a firm belief in the buoyancy of Indian finance in general, and the brilliant future which awaited Bombay in particular, as a new centre of the cotton trade, after its temporary paralysis in America, consequent on the Civil War. His chief success as an Indian administrator came from the presence in him of those qualifications which have proved eminently useful in building up the fabric of our Indian Empire — his birth, breeding, character, chivalry, patience, resolution, tact, and courtesy.

These, also, it may be presumed, were the qualities which caused him to be selected to accompany the Prince of Wales when he visited India, and certainly the Heir Apparent could have had, as the event proved, no more valuable mentor than Sir Bartle Frere. It has seldom been given to one man to carve his name in more enduring characters in the history of two continents. When his term of office at the Cape has expired, Sir Bartle will return as one who is still a member of the Council of the Secretary of State for India. Nor is it an official secret that several times in the course of last year his opinion on difficult questions of Indian policy was asked and delivered. But it is not only in his capacities of Asiatic and African statesman that he is known to the English public. No Indian official of his time has ever been identified with so many philanthropic or beneficent movements at home. He has given energy, labour, and money to every enterprise of every party in Church and State for the promotion of good to India, Africa, and their inhabitants. At one moment the good object has been the assistance of Indian missionaries, at another the emancipation of East African slaves. He was elected President of the Geographical Society, and here, too, he did good work. Though he is now sixty-three years of age, he shows, one is glad to hear, no signs of exhaustion, and when he comes back to England there will yet be work for him to do. It is possible that he may still find his place in the august assembly of the hereditary Legislature, and possibly as Viscount Roydon or Firmingham—taking his title from one of the estates held by his family—he may be added to the number of matured Indian and Colonial statesmen who are already in the House of Lords, and whose knowledge and advice are of growing good to the destinies of the Empire.

XV.

LORD GEORGE HAMILTON.

Among the younger members of the Conservative party in the House of Commons there is no one who has made anything like the same mark within so short a period as the Under-Secretary of State for India. "Rising young men," according to popular parlance, are comparatively abundant in their ranks, promising young men are yet more plentiful; but it is exceedingly rare to find one of the number who has actually commenced the process of rising, or has gone any way to fulfil the promise of his political infancy. While some there are who remain rising young men to the end of the chapter, and who are as near to and remote from public eminence or influence at the age of sixty as at six-and-twenty, there are others who, after a spasmodic flash, dedicate a career to extinguishing themselves in the gloom of dulness. Four years ago the borough of Oxford sent to Parliament a gentleman of whom it was confidently predicted that he would do great things—Mr. A. W. Hall. In his first and second session he made a couple of excellent speeches, one of which drew forth a cordial compliment from Mr. Gladstone. Since then Mr. Hall has been a silent member, only once violating his vow of taciturnity, and that a few weeks ago, when he ambitiously essayed to instruct the House of Commons on the policy of England in the East, and signally failed. The present Sir Mathew White Ridley is an instance of the rising member, who was expected to carry everything before him, who has done nothing, who it is still believed must do something, and a belief in whose Parliamentary future can only be dictated by the charity which "hopeth all things." In each of these cases there was some reason to anticipate at least a modest modicum of achievement. Mr. Hall has had considerable experience in county business before he entered the House of Commons; had been in the habit of essaying his oratorical powers in the character of champion of Church and State at provincial meetings, and moreover, had been trained in that school which Sir Stafford Northcote has pronounced the best possible for a future Parliamentary leader—the hunting-field; he had, in fact, been not only a sort of diocesan fire-brand, but master of the Heythrop Pack. Again, Sir M. W. Ridley had won distinguished successes at Oxford, was a scholar of Balliol, and a favourite pupil of Mr. Jowett. But in the House of Commons this gentleman has only signalised himself by making four years ago the worst speech that had been heard for a decade when it fell to his lot to move the Address. It is, indeed, not improbable that he will some day or other attain office. Nothing can be more certain than that if he does so it will be because he is an influential county member, sprung of ancient lineage, and in the possession of immense wealth.

Lord George Hamilton belongs to a category quite different from either Mr. Hall or Sir M. W. Ridley. When he entered the House of Commons, ten years ago, there was no consensus of prophetic voices that he might, if he would only take the trouble, prove a second Pitt or Canning. Certain points in his favour there were. He belonged to a gifted and a famous house. He was more or less closely allied with illustrious families. He had the purest Whig blood in his veins, that of the Russells and the Gordons. His mother was the daughter of the sixth Duke of Bedford, and half-sister of the veteran Earl Russell. His father was the model of a Marquis in appearance and in accomplishment, had also proved himself the model of an Irish Viceroy, and for these reasons had been created a Duke by Mr. Disraeli. Mr. Disraeli himself had celebrated the physical and the social distinctions of the race of Hamilton in "Lothair." Beyond this there is little to be said. Lord George Hamilton had been "educated" at Harrow, in the same way that many scions of noble families are educated at our great public schools. In other words, he had learned nothing. He had shown, of course, that he possessed the high and intrepid spirit which was his birthright; and, in addition to that, he had won large popularity among his school-fellows by his genial and pleasant ways. After he left Harrow he went into the Foot Guards, and had he remained in the army and seen service he might very probably have risen to a great position. Suddenly the dissolution was announced, and by the force of family circumstances he found himself pitch-forked into politics. He fought the Conservative battle in Middlesex, and fought it pluckily and well. He made slashing speeches, denounced Liberalism and all its works in a style which the party-managers approved, and took his seat in the House of Commons as a member of that brigade of handsome, well-dressed young men whose idea of statesmanship consisted in badgering Mr. Bright, imitating the melody of cocks when Mr. Mill rose to speak, and declaring upon every occasion that Mr. Gladstone was a hybrid growth between Robespierre and Antichrist. Shrew judges of political aptitude did not hesitate to say that Lord George Hamilton was cast in superior clay to that out of which the ordinary *beaux sabreurs* of Conservatism were moulded. On several occasions he gave substantial evidence of the fact that he was disposed to regard a seat in Parliament as the legitimate opportunity of honest industry and strenuous exertion. When therefore, in 1874, Mr. Disraeli was called upon to form an administration, and offered Lord George Hamilton the Indian Parliamentary Under-Secretaryship, there were several persons who believed and said that events would speedily justify his choice, and that Lord George Hamilton would make his mark. It was, however, scarcely surprising that at the India Office itself his promotion should have created something of misgiving. His predecessor had been Mr. Grant Duff, the ablest Parliamentary Under-Secretary that the India Office had seen for a long time, and the doubt was certainly excusable on the part of those who entertained it, whether Lord George Hamilton would prove himself at all capable of standing the formidable test of comparison.

The best comment upon such misgivings as these is the simple fact that he has stood it. It is no exaggeration to say that among the many difficult things which Lord George Hamilton has done well, it would be scarcely possible to mention one which Mr. Grant Duff himself would have done better. He has now been four years in his present position, and the time has arrived when we need no longer adhere to the maxim of Cicero, *apropos* of the possibility of young men exhibiting capacity for statesmanship—*De pueris difficile est laudare quia nondum res, sed spes, est*—and can speak not only of Lord George Hamilton's promise but of his performance. He has proved himself a clear, cool-headed official, capable of very hard work, grudging the expenditure of no amount of care or industry in the getting up of subjects. In the House of Commons he has won a high reputation as a speaker. He has attempted no flights of pyrotechnical eloquence, but has contented himself with admirably clear expositions of very often exceedingly complicated subjects. Thus the speech which he made two years ago on the depreciation of silver was recognised on all hands as a statement not less exhaustive than lucid, and secured for him the generous praise of so severe a critic as Mr. Goshen. His speech on the Indian Budget last year was both a masterly account of Indian finances, and contained, moreover, something which may be described as a contribution of permanent value to Indian administration. In it, as will be recollected, he introduced an improved scheme for recording the facts and figures of Indian expenditure, the credit of elaborating which must be admitted to belong entirely or in great measure to himself—of which the cardinal principle was a distinction between the money spent on Indian works, ordinary and extraordinary. The result of this is not merely an economy of labour and a simplification of figures, but also a large increase in the intelligibility of the accounts themselves on the part of the English Parliament. A better understanding of Indian finance by the House of Commons may reasonably be expected to go no little way towards the better government of our Indian Empire. What he could do in the way of popularising Indian affairs, that Lord George Hamilton has done, and our Indian fellow-subjects on this account, if on no other, owe him a considerable debt of gratitude. Again, one of the chief functions of a Parliamentary Under-Secretary, in the case of our foreign dependencies, is not only to explain to the House of Commons, and through the House of Commons to the nation, principles and facts which are too often wrapped in mystery, but to conciliate opponents, and to disarm hostile critics. Here, again, Lord George has done capitally. His manner is perfect, and his answers to puzzling or awkward questions are as good as his manner. Since he has had a seat on the Treasury Bench Mr. Smollet has grumbled less than usual: while even Mr. Fawcett has minimised his habits of virtuous molestation of the representatives of the Government. It is further to be accounted as a strong point in his favour that at a time when criticism was never more irrepressible or outspoken, Lord George Hamilton has the discrimination in virtue of which he can accept and appreciate sound advice, and the courage which prompts him lightly to put aside merely vexatious censure, however denunciatory it may be. Destined, as he probably is, if only his physical strength is sufficiently enduring, to hold a high place in future administrations, he could have no better apprenticeship to official life than at his present post. His work at the India Office is, of course, mainly financial, but he is necessarily obliged to see much of work that is not financial—military and political. At the Foreign Office he would have had none of these advantages; at the War Office his experience would have been almost exclusively military.

Nor, it may be, is the only financial training which Lord G. Hamilton has received the result of his duties at the India Office. His sister-in-law is the wife of Sir Charles Mills, of the eminent banking firm. A frequent guest at Sir Charles Mills' house at Sevenoaks, Lord G. Hamilton is naturally thrown into contact with gentlemen of sound as well as varied commercial knowledge whom he might perhaps not otherwise meet, and he has in a rare degree that gift, than which few others are more valuable, of assimilating and profiting by the information which chance may throw in his way. The combination of gifts and qualities possessed by the Parliamentary Under-Secretary of State for India is such as to assure to him the highest career.

XVI.

GOVERNOR POPE HENNESSY, C.M.G.

In the autumn of 1766 Mr. Edmund Burke paid a visit to his aunt, Mrs. French, of Loughrea, in the County of Galway; and his mother, who was there at the time, after a brief reference to the "quick and speedy" birth of the "foxy daughter," through whom it was destined that the name and race of the great statesman should be continued to our time, wrote a letter of tender and pleasant gossip to her "dear Nelly," her niece, Mrs. Hennessy, of Ballymacmoy, in the County of Cork. Mr. Burke was in those days, though his fame was yet young, regarded as quite the man for Galway. While they were at Loughrea he and his brother visited the City of the Tribes, and "as soon as they got into Galway the bells rang for them. The Monday following the Corporation met, and voted the freedom of the city to be sent to Ned in a silver box." So writes the proud, fond mother, and, sweetly garrulous, flows on—"My dear Nelly, I believe you will think me very vain; but, as you are a mother, I hope you will excuse it. I assure you that it is no honour that is done him that makes me vain of him, but the goodness of his heart, which, I believe, no man living has a better; and sure there can't be a better son, nor can there be a better daughter-in-law than his wife." He was then in the dawn of his genius and power, and she in the bloom of her grave and tender beauty. Mr. Pope Hennessy stands, we believe, in the relation of great grandnephew to the lady to whom this charmingly characteristic letter was addressed, and who was, it is easy to see, the favourite niece of the mother of Mr. Burke.

Lord Dufferin, in one of the last of those Canadian speeches in which the wit and wisdom, "the fancy, the manhood, the fire of his race" are so delightfully blended, claimed for the Irish a peculiar possession of the imperial Roman gift of ruling colonies and dependencies with skill and with sympathy. This at all events ought to be true of those Irishmen who feel proud of being imbued with the political spirit of Mr. Burke. It no little contributed to the large and easy energy with which his namesake, Lord Mayo, administered India. It has animated and sustained Mr. Pope Hennessy in the difficult, sometimes invidious, tasks which the Colonial Office has found for him within both western and eastern tropics. That respect for subject races which inspired the prosecutor of Warren Hastings, a constant regard for those noble principles of policy which pervade the speech on "Conciliation of the American Colonies," have not been wanting throughout the career of the Governor of Hong Kong. No man among colonial viceroys has represented the majesty of the Crown with a more serious sense that, as Lord Carnarvon well expressed it lately at Edinburgh, "as to all these different races the obligation is laid upon us, which we have accepted, of giving them protection, and of gradually raising them in the scale of humanity."

Mr. Pope Hennessy was born at Cork in 1834, was educated at the Queen's College of that city, and was for a short time a clerk in the Privy Council Office, at the same time keeping his terms for the Bar at the Inner Temple. He had already written a striking pamphlet against mixed education, and was known by his friends to have admirable political talents, nor to want ambition to propel them, when the general election of 1859 offered him an opportunity of entering Parliament. His position in politics was original, indeed unique. He was at heart a Tory of ancient days, as Jacobite as her most gracious Majesty is said in her secret soul to be. But this did not prevent him, any more than it did Sarsfield, from sharing the strongest popular sympathies with his own race. He won the cordial support of the King's County priests and tenant-right party. But in his election address there was one curious sentence which is worth recalling to memory nowadays: he professed himself "a supporter of the foreign policy of Mr. Disraeli." The King's County Conservatives were glad of the chance of sustaining a candidate who would support Mr. Disraeli on any subject. Mr. Pope Hennessy was in consequence returned at the head of the poll. Such a strange expression of personal loyalty probably stirred Mr.

Disraeli's curiosity; and Mr. Pope Hennessy was one of the forty gentlemen invited to dine with the Leader of the House of Commons to hear the Queen's speech read the evening before Parliament met. This is not the proper place, nor would it afford space enough, to sketch his parliamentary career, which opened well and was a sustained success. His relations with the Tory party were close knit in the cold shade of opposition, and especially on questions of foreign policy, upon which he again and again attacked Lord Palmerston with vigour, and not without effect. He first brought Mr. Stansfeld's connection with Mazzini to the notice of the House of Commons, a circumstance which caused that rising statesman to resign. His advocacy of the cause of Poland gained him a European reputation. The Emperor Napoleon received him with great distinction when he visited Paris soon after a memorable debate, and, it was believed at the time, charged him with a secret message on the subject to the Emperor Francis Joseph, by whom he was also received on his way to Cracow. There he was welcomed so enthusiastically that the *Times* predicted that the Diet, if restored, would probably elect "Pope the First" King of Poland. Mr. Bernal Osborne was credited with the joke that he would perhaps be content with the title of Count, and that Count Corkwhisky would make a perfect Polish title. Had he remained in Parliament he would have attained a high position as a debater, and would not improbably have held office. But Irish constituencies are fickle, and in 1865 Mr. Pope Hennessy found himself *out*, and not at all likely in the then state of Irish politics to get *in* again for some time.

In the following year Lord Palmerston died, and soon afterwards the wheel of office turned round. The Duke of Buckingham, aware that Mr. Hennessy wished for employment under the Colonial Office, appointed him Governor of Labuan, an inconsiderable situation so far as rank and salary are concerned, but an interesting field for a young administrator. He found that the revenue of the colony had never been able to meet the charges upon it without assistance from the Imperial Treasury. Within a year he so stimulated its finances that the colony became self-supporting. His Excellency at the same time organized an excellent native police to replace the garrison, which was withdrawn in 1871. He had early formed a high estimate of the Chinese population as an element of commerce and civilisation in those latitudes. He somewhat scandalized the local European society by appointing a Chinese merchant to be a judge of his court and justice of peace. When a great noble of Borneo slew, as he might slay a snake, a poor Chinaman who was a naturalised British subject, Mr. Hennessy, who, besides being Governor of Labuan, was accredited as Consul-General to the Court of the Sultan, proceeded to Brunei with a gun-boat, which had arrived conveniently for the occasion, and insisted that the offender should be tried by his peers, and executed in their presence. Great was the sounding of gongs that night round the consulate—multitudinous the display of coloured lanterns. Soon after the Chinese settlers paid the most solemn testimony of their loyalty to Labuan as a country of adoption: they carried to it, from the Flowery Land, the ashes of their ancestors. A migration of the dead came to found and hallow the homes of the living.

Mr. Hennessy spent four years at Labuan. There, in a field where he had complete command, his character as a colonial administrator was formed. There his constitution, aided by the early hours and abstemious tastes which had always been his habit, became so perfectly inured to the tropical climate, that neither in the East or West Indies nor in Africa has he ever felt fever. There he married his charming and devoted wife, the daughter of a principal member of his Legislative Council. There was born the fair, bright-eyed boy, who afterwards died of the venomous air of the Gold Coast.

In 1871 Mr. Pope Hennessy was promoted to be Governor of the Bahamas; but on his way through London, occasion arose to dispatch an officer of rank and tact to arrange with the Dutch Government, first at the Hague and afterwards in Africa, for the transfer of their settlements on the Gold Coast. Lord Kimberley directed Mr. Hennessy to undertake this duty, in which the friendship of the late greatly gifted Queen of Holland much helped him. The ratifications of the treaty were exchanged at the Hague in February, 1872, and on the 6th of April, with all due state and ceremony, the Dutch tricolor was replaced by the union jack at Elmina, and the Governor of his Majesty the King of the Netherlands handed the great symbol of his authority, the ancient gold and ivory baton of Admiral de Ruyter, to her Britannic Majesty's "Acting Governor-in-Chief," who in honour of this occasion received the Companion's Cross of Saints Michael and George.

After a stay of a little more than a year in the Bahamas, Mr. Pope Hennessy was promoted to Barbadoes, with instructions to promote the confederation of the Windward Islands. Similar instructions had been given to his immediate predecessors, but they had shrunk from an obnoxious and troublesome task. Lord Carnarvon, in addressing Mr. Pope Hennessy on the subject, expressed his great regret that Sir R. Rawson had made no progress in this direction, and desired him to publish both Lord Kimberley's and his own dispatches, so that there should be no possible mistake as to the policy of the Imperial Government. The question being thus absolutely launched, the Governor applied himself to his task with energy, yet with every disposition to conciliate opposed interests. But when that happens in a British dependency to which Lord Carnarvon referred at Edinburgh, when "the reins of power are in the hands of a very small white minority," it is not easy to persuade them to modify a constitution under which they enjoy absolute supremacy. The animosity which pursued Mr. Hennessy was due not so much to his having proposed confederation, as to his openly-expressed sympathy with the condition of the negro race. Through the outrageous attacks made upon him, he bore himself with perfect calm and dignity. "What a cool, hard head he carries!" said a great official to a friend of his when the storm was at its fiercest. "Yes," was the reply, "we do not often produce heads of that calibre in Ireland; but when we do they are as chilled shot." Already there have been occasional signs of somewhat similar troubles in his administration of Hong Kong, otherwise highly prosperous and successful; and wherever wrong is wrought within his view by class to class, on the ground of race, caste, creed, or colour, then those who do wrong will be sure to have an ill time of it until justice is done. "More power to his elbow!" as the old Irish proverb says.

There was a portrait of Sir Arthur Wellesley when he was a Sepoy general, published by Home of Calcutta. The head and figure are curiously like Governor Pope Hennessy as he looked when he was last in London. Ten years of difficult labours in unwholesome climates had yet spared to him the abounding energy of youth, the active step, the gay, bright spirit, the well-stored memory, the rapid, easy flow of variously informed and richly coloured conversation. He had found leisure to pursue under larger stars the studies of science which had had such a charm for his youth. He had followed with instant interest from far away the march of history, the play of parties, the fortunes of his friends. He was still a believer in "the foreign policy of Mr. Disraeli," and looked forward now and then, like a dream, to a time when, his career of colonial service fairly completed, he might again sit in the House of Commons. Meantime it is to be hoped he may not always be consigned to tropical colonies. After eleven years spent between Cancer and Capricorn, is there not room for a change to fresher verdure and cooler airs?

XVII.

MR. R. G. W. HERBERT.

It has been more than once suggested that a change which would amount to a practical revolution of the whole system of Imperial administration should be introduced into more than one of the great public offices of England, and that certain departments of State should be exempted from the operation of the law that gives each a new chief when a new Ministry comes into power. The Colonial Office is one of those that have been included in this hypothetical category. Colonial affairs, it is urged, require close and continuous study. The average life of a political administration is three or four years, and the consequence is that just at the moment when a Secretary of State for the Colonies has acquired a mastery of official detail, he receives his *congé*, and his successor has to go through the process of initiation from the beginning. Theoretically there is something to be said in favour of this view; practically, the argument for revolutionising our present system of Government has no weight whatever. It would, indeed, be impossible to select any single department of State which had any special claim for this exceptional treatment. Experience of some sort or another is equally valuable, equally necessary in the case of all. As a matter of fact it is invariably forthcoming. The Permanent Under-Secretary of State supplies in each instance whatever is wanted of fixity of tenure and professional training. It is the business of the permanent official to know—to have the facts and data on which decisions are based at his fingers' ends; it is the business of the temporary chief to decide—to bring the judicial and administrative ability with which a place in the Cabinet pre-supposes he is endowed to the evidence contained in documents. Unless the Under-Secretary of State, who is superior to the vicissitudes of Parliamentary majorities, had stored away in his literal and metaphorical pigeon-holes a very considerable amount of departmental information, and knew not merely the tendency, but the antecedents of affairs, the great man who is the creature of that majority would find his position impracticable. The natural result of party government is, therefore, to increase the powers of the permanent officials of Government. As an illustration of this may be mentioned the case of Mr., now Lord, Hammond, who, for twenty years as Permanent Under-Secretary of State for Foreign Affairs, had scarcely less to do with the foreign policy of England than Lord Palmerston himself. Hence the necessity that these posts should be filled by the very best men that money can secure—a necessity, on the whole, duly recognised and acted on throughout the public service.

Of the Permanent Under-Secretaries of State there is none more distinguished, none more capable, none more completely a master of the duties of his office than the gentleman who fills that position at the Colonial Office, Mr. R. G. W. Herbert. It was Lord Carnarvon's last act before quitting the office which he filled for four brilliant and eventful years, to induct his successor into the work that awaited him. But the Colonial Secretary had to be acquainted with other things than the character of the business to be transacted and the best mode of transacting it. There is much pomotion at the Colonial Office—many berths to be given, a fair proportion of knightly and minor dignities to be distributed. The candidates for these offices and honours are proportionately numerous. It requires an intimate acquaintance with the claims of each, and a very correct insight into Colonial feeling, if justice is to be done and sensitive susceptibilities are not to be wounded. Here Mr. Herbert's counsel has always proved invaluable, for the Permanent Under-Secretary is not only gifted with great administrative powers, but has studied human nature all the world over, and has a surprisingly minute acquaintance with the business and the chief members of every one of our Colonial dependencies. As Prime Minister of Queensland for nearly six years, Mr. Herbert is naturally no stranger to the past and present history of that prosperous settlement. But the comprehensiveness of his mental grip, the extraordinary faculty that he has of gathering into a focus whatever bears upon, or is associated with, any Colonial capital of which casual mention is made, is apt to produce an exaggerated impression of his rare knowledge. It is not merely the routine and superficial acquaintance which office training and access to State archives gives. He is, if the expression may be used, on speaking terms with our Colonial fellow-subjects in every quarter of the globe. The citizen of Melbourne, Sidney, Hobart Town, Quebec, Singapore, from the easy familiarity which he finds Mr. Herbert display with the affairs, and even with the principal personages, of his own town, might fancy that the Permanent Under-Secretary had made them and it the exclusive subjects of his study. The tact of the man of the world and the application of the painstaking official are not enough to explain this aptitude. Mr. Herbert is a gentleman of the highest intellectual powers, and these powers have been most perfectly developed and brought to an admirable pitch of efficiency by the combined influences of academic culture and large experience of life in many climes. Academic attainments in themselves go but a very little way, but when there is a fitting temperament they constitute the very best foundation on which the teachings of experience can rest. Knowledge of life, observation of affairs, are the necessary supplements, but when these are forthcoming, the statesman or administrator who has received the best that Eton and Oxford can give is sure to be one of the best representatives of the educated Englishman. All that Eton and Oxford can give have been received by Mr. Herbert. The most brilliant distinctions of school and college life came to him as by a natural succession. At Eton he gained the Newcastle Scholarship, he then won a Balliol Scholarship; and in the course of his

Oxford career, during which his contemporaries were Calverley — the C. S. C. whose initials are well known as that of the author of some of the best and brightest modern *vers de société*—George Brodrick, Chitty, and Hornby, the present head-master of Eton, he won successively the Hertford, Ireland, and Eldon Scholarships, the Latin verse prizes, a first class at moderations, a second at degree, a fellowship at All Souls.

The bent and character of more than one brilliant career have been originally decided by accident, and it is in a great degree the result of an accident that the name of Mr. Herbert has become so closely identified with the Colonial Empire of England. On leaving Oxford, when he had commenced his studies for the Bar, he received the offer from Mr. Gladstone—then Chancellor of the Exchequer—of the position of private secretary. The resignation of Lord Aberdeen's Ministry before long deprived him of this employment, and he returned to the Inner Temple. But lawyers' chambers and their occupations he found exceedingly uncongenial work, and before he took the irrevocable step he determined that he would see something of European civilisation outside England. When Sir George Bowen was appointed the first governor of the new colony of Queensland, Mr. Herbert received from the Duke of Newcastle the offer of the Colonial Secretaryship. He accepted it, and, almost before he was aware, he found himself closely identified with the politics of the dependency. The first Parliament that Queensland ever had met in 1860, and it opened with the Colonial Secretary as Prime Minister. That office he continued to hold till 1866—the longest term of power ever enjoyed by a Tory Government. Even then he was not in a minority. He resigned, not through any miscarriage of his policy, or defection of his supporters, but because private affairs compelled his presence at home. Mr. Herbert's Colonial reputation had long since preceded him to England. He had to pay the penalty for his success, and he was given to understand that he was too good a man to be lost to the public service. The celebrity of Colonial statesmen too often consists of the degree of publicity with which they get into difficulties, and the degree of success with which they make good their escape. Mr. Herbert's distinction was of a more felicitous character. The period of his administration had been marked by the completion of great measures, the organization of the whole system of civil government, the settlement of the educational question and the land laws, and by the opening of the first railway which Queensland ever saw. Within two years of his return he was appointed one of the assistant-secretaries to the Board of Trade, and just eight years ago he was removed to the same position at the Colonial Office, becoming in the following year, 1871, Permanent Under-Secretary of State. Such is Mr. Herbert's career, and never was substantial success the reward of more solid qualifications. Popular in the Colonial Office, Mr. Herbert is popular also in the world of London society, a bright talker, and what is less common, perhaps, a fairly tolerant listener. There is a good deal of humour in his composition. He is not an optimist, and he scarcely conceals his disbelief in the doctrine of human perfectibility. Nevertheless, if he does not think that everything is for the best in this best of all possible worlds, he perhaps considers that the world is as good as could reasonably be expected, and that matters are on the whole rather better than might have been feared. Finally, he possesses a quality which is invaluable to the gentleman who fills an anxious and responsible post: officially he does not know the meaning of the words hurry or discomposure. Tidings of Colonial revolution might arrive without causing him visible excitement, and would simply suggest themselves as incidents—all coming in the day's work—each to be dealt with in its proper turn.

XVIII.

SIR MICHAEL HICKS-BEACH, BART., M.P.

Never was that quality, which may be described as the touchstone of administrative capacity, and of the possession of which Lord Beaconsfield has, in the course of his career, given such conclusive and abundant proofs—the power of making the best selection that circumstances permit for the most responsible offices of Imperial administration—more signally displayed than when, on Lord Carnarvon's resignation, he appointed Sir Michael Hicks-Beach to the Secretaryship of State for the Colonies. In the course of a spirited, and judicious, speech which he made at the banquet given last summer to Sir William Jervois, the Colonial Minister modestly spoke of his conscious inferiority to his distinguished predecessors in his high office, but, he added, with a touch of justifiable pride, that at least none of them could have gone to the Colonial Office more profoundly impressed with the responsibilities of the position, or animated by a stronger desire to discharge its duties to the best of his abilities. That is a feeling which, in the case of Sir Michael Beach, has not been destined long to remain in the optative mood. He not merely dedicates all his powers to his new post, but he has shown that the powers which he thus dedicates are of an exceedingly high order. A great Colonial Minister it would be premature to pronounce him, seeing that he has only been at the Colonial Office a little less than the third of a year. But there is every reason to believe that he will, in the fulness of time, prove himself well worthy to follow any of the distinguished men who have held sway before him in Downing Street.

Sir Michael Beach is only now in his forty-second year. There is no member of his party, of at all the same age, who is of anything like the same calibre. Colonel Stanley, Mr. Sclater-Booth, Lord Sandon, are each of them able and painstaking politicians. Colonel Stanley makes a respectable War Minister, and thoroughly deserved his promotion to the Cabinet. Mr. Sclater-Booth and Lord Sandon are entitled to an equally favourable estimate; beyond this there is little to say about them. The Colonial Secretary is made of altogether different stuff, and cast in a very different mould. He is from association and conviction a Tory of a somewhat stern and unbending type. But with his uncompromising Toryism he unites a vigour of intellect, a hardness of head, a strength and independence of judgment, which were regarded as pre-eminently the attributes of Liberalism, in the days when Liberals prided themselves more on their strength of mind and respect for reason than on emotional sympathies, impulsive almost to fanaticism. Strong Tory as Sir Michael Beach is, he is no bigot, and on ecclesiastical matters especially is without passion or prejudice. Short though his tenure of the Colonial Office has as yet been, he has completely mastered, by dint of sheer hard work and resolute will, some of the knottiest problems with which a Colonial administrator can be called upon to deal. He was scarcely installed there before the Constitutional difficulty in Victoria engaged his attention, and in his treatment of it he exhibited a degree of quiet strength that took not a few persons by surprise. Nor has he been less personally successful in the mode in which he has grappled with the Cape troubles. Firm and cool, he takes his resolutions carefully, and executes them without compromise. Equally removed from obstinacy and vacillation, he possesses, and he makes all with whom he is brought into contact feel that he possesses, the very gifts which the Minister of the complex and varied Colonial Empire of Great Britain should have.

Sir Michael Hicks-Beach has been in the House of Commons just fourteen years; a decade since he made his first acquaintance with the routine of office at the Poor-Law Board and the Home Office. His work was done with a thoroughness and ability which testified to the soundness of the view that the occupations of a country gentleman who does not disdain to attend to county business, are no bad training-school for Imperial statesmanship. In the course of the Irish Church debates of 1869 he proved that he had readiness of speech and considerable power of argument. The Prime Minister, when he offered him, in 1874, the Chief Secretaryship for Ireland, was influenced by considerations of which, both in his writings and his practical policy, he has always recognised the weight. Lord Beaconsfield has never failed to exhibit the same distrust of political specialists as of the statesmanship which ostentatiously boasts that it rests upon a basis of scientific data. He has placed before all other attributes that common sense and knowledge of men and things which are gathered in the great school of the world. These conditions were exactly forthcoming in Sir Michael Hicks-Beach, while as for other conditions, not less necessary, though infinitely easier of subsequent attainment by dint of industry and practice, Mr. Disraeli trusted for their development to time. When it was announced in 1874 that the Chief Secretaryship of Ireland had been given to Sir Michael Hicks-Beach, there were some who predicted the member for East Gloucestershire would scarcely display that combination of caution and promptitude which is a necessity in dealing with critics so keen and interrogators so indefatigable as the Irish members of the House of Commons. Sir Michael Hicks-Beach had no sooner been nominated to his post than he applied himself with assiduous energy to mastering the details of his official work. He delegated to his subordinates nothing that it was possible for him to do himself. When letters arrived on the subject of the narrowest local business of some obscure Irish town, he examined personally the questions raised. The long vacation of 1874 he devoted exclusively to the investigation of Irish fishing, on the spot, and since then not a year has passed without his spending a much larger portion of time than Irish Secretaries are officially compelled to do, or usually have done, in gathering, at first hand, the materials on which his policy was based. To Parliamentary capacities of a high order Sir Michael Hicks-Beach added general courtesy and good humour, which was sorely tried, but which seldom failed. All this brought with it its reward, and the general expectation which found expression in the autumn of 1876 that Sir Michael Hicks-Beach would be raised to the Cabinet as soon as practicable, was not destined to remain unfulfilled.

In one of the many poems in which W. M. Praed recalls the memory of the old Eton days, "School and Schoolfellows," this quatrain occurs :—

"I wish that I could run away,
From House, and Court, and *Levée*,
Where bearded men appear to-day
Just Eton boys grown heavy."

"Heavy," in the metaphorical sense, in which it is here employed, the Secretary of State for the Colonies has certainly not become. But there is, nevertheless, much of the "Eton boy" which is still preserved in his manner and his presence. So far as it is consistent with the breeding of the man of the world, there is about him a decided smack of the *brusquerie* of the fifth-form Etonian. Just as it was impossible to be in the society of Mr. James Lowther, who has replaced Sir Michael at the Irish Office, without being reminded of the typical Yorkshireman, as he may be seen on Doncaster race-course, so it is difficult to look at Sir Michael Beach himself without the idea of the Eton boy coming to one's mind. And, perhaps, the Colonial Secretary would not be sorry to know that he carries thus about with him the *cachet* of his old school. There can be little doubt, at least, that he believes the kind of education which he has himself received to be about the best that the world can give. Probably he is not far wrong, and, as the experience of several centuries has shown, the best political leaders and the most popular statesmen are those who have been at Eton and Oxford. The older generation of Conservative politicians now alive must soon pass away, and when the time comes for the selection of a Prime Minister from the younger ranks, the chances of the present Colonial Secretary, who has many of the qualities which Englishmen admire and respect, will have to be taken into consideration.

XIX.

GENERAL SIR EDWARD ALAN HOLDICH, K.C.B.

THROUGHOUT the second quarter of the present century the military profession seemed to offer few attractions to the young soldier. There was little or no promotion. Long years of profound peace, years which tended more and more to class the soldier's trade with what was obsolete and useless, had produced an utter stagnation in the army. Subalterns were grey-haired, captains corpulent, with grown-up families, majors half imbecile, colonels had one leg in the grave. As for a general officer, he was seldom seen out of a glass case in some military museum or club. The prospect of active service, of any professional employment beyond the pursuit of Irish rebels or the suppression of rowdy riots, grew more and more remote. Officers spent their lives in exile beyond the seas or in country quarters at home, with no occupation, as it was said, but to expectorate over a bridge into the stream below. Under such circumstances, therefore, the newly-joined ensign or recruit faced an interminable vista of blank idleness, permeated by not one single ray of encouragement. To have prophesied, therefore, that any young gentleman who received his first commission in 1841 would be a lieutenant-colonel twelve years later would have borne the stamp of improbability upon the face of it. Such rapid advancement was out of the question for any but Princes of the Blood Royal, or possibly for a peer like Lord Cardigan, determined to lavish fabulous sums to purchase himself a regimental command. Yet this good fortune, rare, and, to a certain extent, unexpected, fell to the lot of the subject of the present sketch, and if his quick promotion made him an object of envy to less fortunate comrades, it could not be denied that he had won his honours by sheer hard work and good service in the field.

Edward Holdich was serving as a lieutenant in the 80th Regiment at the outbreak of the first Sikh war. Of the army assembled under the orders of Sir Hugh Gough, and in which the Governor-General of India, Sir Henry Hardinge, with the true spirit of the soldier, cheerfully and loyally served as second in command, the first infantry division had a distinguished general officer, Sir Harry Smith, at its head. Sir Harry was young Holdich's relative, and on taking the field he offered the young man a post upon his personal staff. While still but a lad, therefore, the latter was called upon to play a by no means unimportant part in serious operations and to bear the brunt of battle. The young aide-de-camp stuck to his chief through everything. He was present at Moodkee and at Ferozeshah, the critical battle in which defeat would have led to overwhelming disaster. The high courage of our leaders on this occasion—the Generals Gough and Hardinge, resolving to conquer or die, the fine spectacle of the Governor-General himself sleeping among the soldiers at the outposts in order to share their trials, and placing his son in the forefront of the battle next day so as to inspire confidence in his troops—these are great memories in the past, and likely to set a splendid example to soldiers of every rank. They were not lost upon Holdich, or upon his chief, who in the first action fought on his own account at Aliwal, won it against tremendous odds, and achieved success not inferior to that in the principal operations of the campaign. The duties of an aide-de-camp to the general in chief command at any hard-fought day are in the highest sense onerous and responsible, but young Holdich did his work right well, as he did again later on at the decisive action of Sobraon, in which he was so severely wounded that he could take no part in the closing scenes of the war. After that, and still as aide-de-camp, he accompanied Sir Harry Smith to the Cape of Good Hope when that general assumed the governorship of the colony. Here fresh opportunities offered of gaining experience and distinction. The Kaffir war which presently broke out was no unmixed success, it is true. Perhaps no English general was ever called upon to play a more difficult part than Sir Harry Smith; no public servant was ever more ungenerously and unfairly used. The policy of cheeseparing, niggardly economy had been pushed to its extreme limits; the Cape was nearly denuded of troops, adequate reinforcements were denied, and yet the sins of failure, the crime of suffering victory to elude fingers too weak really to clutch it, were visited upon the chief who was by no means personally to blame. Sir Harry's dauntless behaviour when hemmed in and imprisoned by hordes of Kaffirs at Fort Cox; the bold and intrepid courage with which, at the head of a small but gallant band of mounted riflemen and attended by his personal staff, he broke through the beleaguering savages, and galloped a dozen miles at top speed till he gained the shelter of King William's Town, are matters of history, feats to which we can do ample justice in these later days. But, in spite of his own gallantry, and of the manifest injustice of condemning a general unheard, the Administration at home was determined to recall Sir Harry Smith. The greatest living soldier, the Iron Duke himself, in his place in the House of Lords, declared that he was proud to say that he had not observed any serious error in the whole of the operations of Sir Harry Smith—"I distinctly approve of all—of all the orders he has given his troops, and of the arrangements he has made for their success." Nevertheless, the general was sacrificed to popular clamour, and surrendering the command to General Cathcart, who superseded him, he came home.

Returning once more to regimental duty, Major Holdich was soon fortunate enough to see more active service in the field. His regiment was in Burmah, and took part in the Burmese War; it was engaged also against the great robber chieftain in the fastnesses of the Donabew district, and after a period of inaction, chafing bitterly at the chances afforded to others in the Crimea, it presently passed over to India, and did its share in suppressing the great Sepoy revolt. By this time Edward Holdich was a C.B. and a full colonel in the army, although still a regimental captain low down on the list, a striking but somewhat rare instance of the anomalies of brevet rank. Had his regiment gone to the Crimea he would probably have commanded a brigade, of which his own regiment under his own colonel, might have formed part. As it was he soon rose to an independent command upon the Nepaul frontier, and at the close of the operations was appointed to the Staff in Bengal. Here he remained for the years immediately following, till presently the slow process of time brought him, while still quite a young man, to the top of the tree, and without having served as a regimental lieutenant-colonel he passed up to the rank of a general officer. The whirligig of time had, in fact, brought its revenges, and it seemed not unlikely that it would prove a positive disadvantage to General Holdich that he had got on so early and so well. The rank of a major-general is a highly-prized and, in many cases, long-looked-for distinction; but it is sometimes a misfortune to attain to it. Commands are not plentiful, and the long list of eligible candidates makes choice sufficiently embarrassing to the powers that be. Some must inevitably be left out in the cold, and thus it is that many an active and energetic man in the prime of life finds himself relegated hopelessly to the shelf. It was not so exactly in the case of General Holdich, who received two divisional commands, one at Cork and the other in Dublin; but before he had exhausted his period of service in the latter, his excessive and somewhat unsatisfactory good luck overtook him, and, rising now willy-nilly to the rank of full general, he was compelled to relinquish his command. There is now unfortunately little left for him to accept. The posts which a "full" general can accept may be counted on one's fingers. The two great Mediterranean fortresses; Cyprus, perhaps, when regularly organized and annexed; the chief command in India; Ireland—when these are mentioned the tale is told. That one or other of these should fall to a man still in the full vigour of all his faculties, and almost in the heyday of youth and strength, seems probable enough. One has only to look at Sir Edward Holdich as he walks with springy step, his slight, spare frame erect and active, his eye still bright and keen, and his whole appearance indicating that he still possesses the priceless boon of health and youth, to see that he is still full of untold units of work. Those who have served under his orders know him as an excellent soldier, prompt to decide, of sound practical views, having behind him years of experience, a clear, intelligent mind, backed up by a plentiful fund of sterling common sense. Of quiet and unassuming demeanour, he can upon occasion assume the eye to threaten and command; but his habitual courtesy and kindliness of heart win for him willing service and cordial co-operation from all. It would be a thousand pities if the country were to be prevented from drawing still further upon the energies and brains of a man so thoroughly capable in every sense of the word.

XX.

THE INDIAN FOURTH ESTATE.

THE Press of India—*embarras de richesses!* It was by no means an easy task to make a suitable selection of men whose functions in the State fabric might be symbolized by pillars of every description, from the mighty pier, or buttress, which is more useful than ornamental, to the column which, though more ornamental than useful, is an essential component of every properly regulated structure. He would be a bold man who should specialise for a like object any of the two hundred and odd editors of British India. Each being a *primus inter pares*, we have considered it desirable to treat the present subject, not as a Pillar, but as a Colonnade—or, more properly, as the vast abstraction known in Western countries by the name of the Fourth Estate.

The growth of the Press is in many ways the most striking phenomenon in the history of British India. It may even be said that the institution itself is unique in its kind. But in many respects, too, it inevitably suffers by comparison with the Press of England. The leading contrast is almost too obvious even for an allusion. Here the Press is the mouthpiece of the people, with whom political responsibility ultimately rests; there—and we refer to the Anglo-Indian section in particular—it is chiefly the pastime of an extremely limited public without any political responsibility whatever. The English Press is the voice of the nation; the Anglo-Indian Press is the voice of a small portion of the three or four score thousand Englishmen, few of whom would remain in India an hour longer than they could possibly help. The contrast, as regards responsibility and representative character, may be illustrated by the fact that, in the event of a great political crisis, the Viceroy of India could, at a moment's notice, suspend every newspaper between the Himalayas and Cape Comorin. Say you what you like, and we shall do what we like, are the words in which the administrators of British India might summarise their theory of the relation between themselves and the journalists, both Native and English. Politically, there are only two estates in India—a beneficently despotic bureaucracy of sixteen gentlemen, and their two hundred million subjects.

These circumstances, no doubt, justify to some extent the frequent assertion that the tone and matter of the Anglo-Indian journals are rather more parochial than Imperial. In India, however, as elsewhere, journalists must consult the tastes of their readers. Is there one Anglo-Indian in a hundred who would not prefer a paragraph of station gossip, or an announcement about a *burra mem's* garden-party, to the most eloquent dissertation on a great public question of land tenure, revenue, finance, and the like? For the ordinary English bird of passage these topics possess no interest whatever; it cannot be expected that they should. So much may fairly be admitted. But there is another side to the picture. In the first place, the English journals are themselves by no means free from the taint of parochialism. Do not even the London papers devote whole columns to topics which are essentially as trivial as the silliest gossip published in any *mofussil* print? But secondly, though the Anglo-Indian papers wisely accommodate themselves to the ordinary taste, they not only supply the heavier material for the few who may demand it, but they often handle it with a skill and vigour unsurpassed, as regards kindred subjects, by the Press at home. It would be easy to name some Anglo-Indian journalists who, from their assiduity, ability, and life-long experience in the country, are just as competent as the ablest members of the Government to criticize the most intricate questions of administration.

Again, it would be ridiculous to assert that any of these members can speak on the great questions of finance and commerce with anything like the authority which the Anglo-Indian public, including the Fourth Estate itself, willingly concedes to certain well-known journalists in Calcutta and Bombay. So long as men of this stamp are to be found at its head, it will be impossible to deny that the Indian Press must exercise an influence—none the less real because indirect—upon the local and supreme autocracies, and the current of public affairs. The Press, in short, is the sole available antidote against the enervation of Bureaucracy. We might name one writer in particular whose vigorous onslaughts on official senility have richly deserved a C.S.I. at least. In the next place, the Indian writers enjoy one great compensation for the lack of the representative power wielded by their English brethren—and that is their independence. The English journalist is often perhaps too representative, and his head-quarters too like a factory where goods are reeled off to suit the tastes—wise or foolish, refined or vulgar—of consumers, just as longcloth, bottled beer, and shady dramas are produced in other kinds of workshops. In England the individuality of the writer is too often merged in the abstraction of the firm. But in India the journals which have been more or less familiarly known here for the last twenty, thirty, or forty—and, in the case of the oldest of them all, nearly eighty—years, have always borne the stamp of their individual editors. Their names always suggest the names of the men who made them what they were, and who wrote with the authority of knowledge and ability, though not of official position.

In a word, the less favourable view of the significance of the Indian Press becomes less and less applicable as time goes on. Its power will increase as the Government of India passes from the bureaucratic stage to the sphere of general politics. (Imperial would have been the more appropriate adjective, but for its unlucky association with a kind of shoddy statesmanship.) The frequent regret and complaint of Anglo-Indian writers that they are removed from the central current of the world's affairs, becomes less justifiable every year—we might almost say every day. For instance, are they not at this hour as vitally interested in the Balkan Mountains as in the Hindoo Khoosh and the Suleiman? An Anglo-Indian journalist might have considered himself a politically detached atom so long as India, in so far as the public of England and Europe cared for it, might have lain somewhere on the invisible side of the moon. But now that the subject is one in which every European Cabinet entertains the liveliest concern, there is no reason why he should not regard the exercise of his calling to be at least as important in India as elsewhere. It is often said that the Civil Service offers the only career worthy of an able and ambitious Anglo-Indian; but the Press is gradually affording more opportunities for labour no less useful and honourable, though less dignified and remunerative, than even that of the higher stages of office.

But all this while we have said nothing of that portion of the Press for which its conductors claim the honour and title of *the* Indian Press by pre-eminence. The twenty or so Anglo-Indian papers represent, as they contend, only the views of the few thousand White Brahmins who have come to sojourn in the country; but the one hundred and eighty Hindoo and Mahomedan editors are the spokesmen of the two hundred million, and more, natives of the land. This claim we may, and must, to a great extent, concede at once. The Native papers may be wise or foolish, loyal or the reverse; but, such as they are, they constitute the true Press of India. The Press Law was an acknowledgment of the fact. Measured by the European standard, the Press circulation, or, more properly speaking, its subscription list, is ridiculously small; but the length of its list is no index to the amount of its influence. An immense number of natives are affected one way or the other by newspapers in which they may never have invested an anna of their own. And it is an undoubted fact that in nineteen cases out of twenty the Native editors express themselves, as regards at least the essentials of administration, in a manner most loyal to the paramount Power. The spectacle of a free Press in an Asiatic despotism sorely puzzled the soul of Sir William Muir's Russian friend; but in India at least—we cannot answer for Turkestan—the singular contradiction is an affair of ordinary experience. The natives of India, journalists and all, are alive to the fact; and, what is more, they fully appreciate it. Though many Governors-General have warmly supported the freedom of the Press, it cannot be said that its liberty is the work of any of them in particular. Lord Wellesley banished the first Anglo-Indian journal to the Danish settlement of Serampore, and succeeding rulers expelled editors, and harassed the papers with licensing and censorial regulations. Still, it cannot be said that our Native fellow-subjects and our countrymen in India conquered the liberty of the Press for themselves. It is not so much the result of Metcalfe's legislation as the fruit and the characteristic of the genius of the race to which Fate has appointed the greatest task of the kind ever imposed upon a nation of conquerors.*

* I have received the following communication on the subject of the foregoing article from a friend of great experience, who is well qualified to speak on such a matter: "What Sir Henry Maine has said about the general culture of Indians is true as regards the Press. The English public judge from the seaboard towns. Except in Lucknow, Lahore, and Poona, where I believe the local papers are in the hands of certain associations, the Mofussil native Press is almost entirely without influence. And even in the seaboard towns the Bengali element is strong and deceiving, because it must be remembered that the Baboos, though decidedly first in intellectual advancement, are *politically* of no moment whatever. Had the rise of the Press been treated as a narrative, its story would have allowed of some very curious illustrations. Take, for instance, these two brief statements,—what an astonishing growth in public opinion and its influence they betray. In 1823 the secretaries of the Government wore a green uniform, and were in the habit of walking before Government House in the evening on a path still called the 'Secretaries' Walk.' Silk Buckingham was then editor of the *Calcutta Journal*. It is true he had previously censured some of the acts of the Government, but his last offence was saying that at sunset a very sinister description of grasshopper was to be observed on the plain. For this, Mr. Adams, then acting as Governor-General, had Buckingham put on board ship and *deported* then and there out of the country. Years after, by continual complaint, Buckingham obtained a pension, but never more did he set foot on the Plain of Calcutta. That, as I say, was in 1823. In 1878, Mr. R. Knight travelled through the famine districts in Agra. He censured Sir George Couper's arrangements in the *Statesman*. No *deporting* in 1878! Sir George wrote an elaborate defence of his conduct in immediate reply to Knight, which he submitted to the Government of India. And the Government of India, sitting in judgment in the case of Knight *v*. Couper, passed an order of acquittal in sympathizing, but not enthusiastic, terms."

XXI.

THE INDIAN NON-OFFICIAL.

THE old East India Company had many grand qualities: it desired to be just; thrifty, and prudent in its financial arrangements, it was often splendid in its designs, and always magnificent in its rewards. It was defended on its dying bed by John Stuart Mill, and does not need the eulogy of feebler pens. But it had one singular prejudice, amounting at times almost to monomania, which was jealousy of the immigration of settlers. Of merchants on a large or small scale, who took scant interest in politics, and came into collision only with such natives in the ports as were agents for land produce; of tradesmen who peaceably pursued their avocations in the sea-board towns, the Company took little notice. In the three presidency cities the chief jealousy of the non-official was shown in the persecution of newspapers; we say persecution advisedly, for it was more than prosecution. By a most singular weapon of tyranny called "deportation," the Government in 1823 put the proprietor of the *Calcutta Journal* on board ship, and turned him, for ever, out of the country. And up to Lord Metcalfe's time as acting Governor-General, the Press was always more or less subject to annoyance.

But the prejudice against English planters, landowners, and settlers generally, in the rural districts, lasted with the life of the Company; and, indeed, the singular outbreak of ill-feeling between the local government of Bengal and the indigo interests, in 1859 and 1860, may be said, in some measure, to have been a posthumous result of the Company's old infirmity. Of what is known as the *Nil Durpan* disturbance, more need not here be said than that everybody seemed under a spell to act as reflection would have shown them they should not have acted. It was like a scene in one of Mr. W. S. Gilbert's fairy caprices. The Bengalee drama, which should have been left to perish of literary insignificance, was attacked or defended until it gained celebrity. The Government secretary circulated it, as if he had been promised a commission on its success. It formed the subject of a useless trial; the wrong person was made answerable for its malignity; the judge spoke in terms befitting the counsel for the prosecution; the bishop publicly rebuked the judge;—indeed, every one was clearly under an incantation to forget himself. But this outburst was what the doctors call a *sequela* of the disease; the malady was really over, for it was the Mutiny that taught Englishmen that their interests in the country were common, and that in the day of danger the non-official found his natural place by the side of the official. The old Government jealousy of the interloper, of course, in its day, did a good deal of mischief. It tended to encourage a priggish and interfering behaviour on the part of Government officers on the one hand; on the other, it fomented a very unreasonable opposition to public measures on the part of the planters and settlers. These latter were not, it is true, an immaculate body, but they were made worse by being denounced and misjudged. That they were (with one or two illustrious examples, indeed, of philanthropic worth) occasionally harsh and unjust to those with whom their farming requirements brought them into contact, was doubtless true; that they sometimes went so far, in Bengal, as to encourage agrarian riots, and themselves to give employment to bands of clubmen, is also known. In different parts of the country, circumstances tended to modify the relations between officials and non-officials in district life. The coffee planters of the Wynaad, and other parts of the Madras presidency, were more independent of the Government. In Tirhoot, again, a common love of sport, and especially the English passion for riding, formed a bond which often drew into close intimacy the indigo farmer and the Government servant.

A fruitful source of misunderstanding between the planter and the authorities had always been the necessity for litigation which his position as temporary lessee of lands enforced upon him. There was no court available for his frequent needs, except the native civil courts spread throughout the districts; and for these the planter had a contempt which, unfortunately, often led him into conduct accountable indeed, but not to be excused. These rural judges were, in former days, very badly paid, some of them not getting more than £10 a month; and it was a notorious fact that a decision was not beyond the reach of money. To expose and get removed such a venal officer was a long, tiresome, and precarious business; to bribe him, a very easy one. He was sometimes bribed. The descent once made to these bad practices, worse followed: struggles in chicanery with native opponents; the processes of law set in motion out of malice or revenge; annoyances of every sort carefully thought out. The Englishman, perhaps, would be for the time worsted; he would shut himself up in his factory, and defy the myrmidons of the disreputable court. These again would besiege his door, infest his outhouses, and insult his servants, not indeed without apprehension of small shot in the calves of their legs from an upper chamber. This was all subject-matter for exaggeration, for accusations and reprisals. The immorality, too, which had only slowly disappeared from amongst the official classes themselves, in consequence of the improved facilities of communication, the greater publicity of social life, and the increasing number of spectators and critics in the shape of outsiders, lingered of course in the solitary houses of the settlers far removed from the ken of their fellow-men and the influences of society. The institution of the Curtain and the other appliances of Zenanah life were not wanting; the hookah and the bottle occupied hours which afforded splendid leisure for reading or reasonable amusement;

and the exquisite nights of Eastern latitudes were disturbed with the jingle of native music, and the chink from the anklets of the bayadere. In some of these secluded places the Mutiny came like a shock of fate, and Sense was dragged trembling into the presence of its natural enemy, who is Death.

But this great social upheaving brought with it, too, the remedy for the unnatural state of things which had too long prevailed. The starched demeanour and assumed superiority of officials would have always prevented any understanding between parties apparently bent upon misjudging each other. But common danger, common reliance, and common valour effected, as if by the wand of a magician, a reconciliation which cannot but be lasting. History has claimed for her own department the courage, tact, and administrative abilities of men who, like Venables in Goruckpore and Azimgurh, upheld the credit of the British name; but many gallant deeds have escaped notice which were carried out by non-officials, for the love and honour of the old country, quite as much as for personal defence. Without manner of doubt the Empire was supported—in that dread hour—by many a pillar whose Doric simplicity has robbed it of celebrity or prominent notice; indeed, whose very existence has scarcely reached the ears of posterity. Before the Mutiny came on, the gradual introduction of railways had begun to work a great and useful revolution. Society commenced to recruit its ranks from a body who had been brought up beyond earshot of the traditions of the Services. The old members of the army and the civilians were esteemed and liked —if they possessed qualities to call forth such sentiments—but not merely on account of their position. And the railway officials, forming often an important item in the society of large stations, created a link between official and non-official circles, which has been of the greatest benefit. It seems impossible to believe that misunderstandings which once existed should ever arise again. But forbearance will be necessary on the part of both sections; if, on the one side, officials put away an arrogance of manner calculated to irritate and engender opposition, non-officials should be cautious, whilst maintaining personal independence, to concede the due respect for the function which is no longer claimed for the individual. On this understanding alone can official life be carried out with dignity and efficiency.

The great vice of public opinion in India is the undue vehemence with which propositions, often by no means distinctly apprehended, are held and enunciated. The government of a vast multitude of peoples, virtually living in a century long anterior to our own, must, if conducted with any view to their happiness, be a task of immense difficulty, and one requiring the patient consideration of the best intellect available. An individual mind can scarcely hope to strike upon a panacea which has any chance of permanent success. We sincerely trust and believe that there is a great future for the injured interloper of former years; that as justice of the peace, municipal authority, member of council, local magistrate, philanthropist, *amicus curiæ*, he will have every opportunity given him for exercising legitimate influence. But we confess we do not look forward with any comfort to an increase of statesmen, to any accession to the ranks of those who have got entirely new plans of administering our Eastern Empire. It is in the last degree improbable that any person who would, under other circumstances, have risen to great political influence, should have hidden his light under a bushel so long, as to have attained middle life—surrounded by the full opportunities of Indian life—without any one finding out he was a genius. Local knowledge is of the greatest possible service to a mind otherwise capable of turning facts to good account; but not of itself. And if people would only understand that the sole method of utilising their experiences very often lies in the sacrifice of supplying them for the use of others, we should often be spared a great many crude schemes, which are so far harmful that they distract the attention which wiser ones demand.

One painful point remains. The frightful convulsion of 1857—1858 created a chasm between natives and Europeans which has not yet been bridged over. With all his faults the old planter was often a very friendly neighbour with the zemindar; with all his impracticable egotism, the old civilian had many a cherished and valued companion among the native community. This state of things has temporarily passed away; outsider and official agree in the sinister article of faith, that " the niggers are not to be trusted." But a remark of Lord Napier of Magdala is eminently true:

"Every man who, by haughty or inconsiderate conduct, alienates the regard of his native fellow-subjects, throws a stone at the British power in India." And the reverse is, of course, true also—that it is not necessary to be an official of the Government to greatly aid in the support of the empire, by conciliatory behaviour to the conquered race. In the prospect of a great increase of settlers in connection with the cultivation of tea, the spread of manufactures,—ultimately, perhaps, the development of mineral resources,—how satisfactory it would be to think that north and south, east and west, sturdy Englishmen were not only laying the foundations of their own fortunes, but by gaining the regard of the natives were consolidating the power of their nation over the vast and interesting continent which wonderful events have placed under its charge.

XXII.

SIR WILLIAM JERVOIS, C.B., K.C.M.G.

It was the mischance of his military service, hitherto sufficiently stirring, which stranded Captain Jervois, then an officer of some fifteen years' standing, upon the Island of Alderney just when Europe was aflame and his comrades and contemporaries were winning honours in the Crimean War. He was engaged, it was true, upon engineering works of great scope and importance, still his employment was at best inactive and dull compared with the great game afoot elsewhere. While other soldiers were growing famous, as true soldiers best love to grow famous—in the actual clash of conflict—while colleagues and school friends were fast distancing him, as it seemed, in the race for preferment, while brother officers of his own corps were gaining sound practical experience in their own scientific walk of the military profession, it was hard fate to be engrossed with contractors' specifications, with the details of draughtsmen and the shortcomings of clerks of works. The enforced inaction must have been the more irksome to a young man who had already, like Horace, "fought not without glory." In the first years of his career, when still quite a lad, he found no outlet for his energies at the Cape of Good Hope beyond purely civil duties, but the time came when he was called upon to do more than construct roads, build bridges, and establish frontier posts. The Kaffir War of 1841 arrived opportunely to give him many openings, of which he availed himself to the full, not only in the execution of valuable surveys of vast tracts of land in close proximity to the enemy, but in the active operations of war. Not strangely, then, he looked askance at his more fortunate fellows, envying them their luck, and wondering whether his turn would come again. It came—in truth, it was already close at hand, but the direction was not perhaps that which he would have chosen for himself. A royal visit to Alderney brought him under the immediate approval of august personages, and the Queen's recognition of the good work he had done in the insular defences was followed by promotion and removal to the London District as Commanding Royal Engineer. This, as it turned out, meant continued exclusion from active service in the East, but the move had other important consequences. "There is a divinity which shapes our end, rough hew them as we may." Something more than chance took Major Jervois to the great centre of life, where, standing in the gangway, as it were, he found himself unexpectedly called upon to play a conspicuous part in great changes then pending.

The period was now approaching when a fresh revolution was to take place in war. The new and startling discoveries of mechanicians, chemists, and engineers, were to be turned to account in the development of the processes of destruction. The inventions of our Armstrongs, our Whitworths, and our Pallisers, began to invest modern artillery with the most terrible and deadly power. In length of range, in weight and calibre, modern guns daily became more and more formidable, and the apprehension grew, not without cause, that no fortifications on land, and no ships afloat, as then constructed, would have any chance in future struggles. A total revision of our navy and of the whole of our land defences was imperative. The latter were, moreover, proved to be as ludicrously inadequate in extent as in their character; the former, it was soon shown, would be sunk at the first encounter with ships armour-plated and carrying the new guns. From this moment dawned a new era in defensive as well as in offensive warfare, and with the former Colonel Jervois was associated from the first. His official position had already secured for him a place upon that Barrack Accommodation Committee, which had brought about such great and salutary changes in the sanitary condition and general comfort of the troops, and the services which he had then rendered, his shrewd, sagacious intellect, and his sound professional skill marked him out clearly as the man of all others to assist in the development of the new ideas of attack and defence. Colonel Jervois was first nominated Assistant-Inspector-General of Fortifications, his chief being the renowned Sir John Burgoyne; he became Secretary next to the Defence Committee of the United Kingdom; later he was appointed to serve as member of the special committee which was to report upon the application of iron to the defences of ships and of land fortifications. The labours in these several and very onerous capacities, through which he passed triumphant, were herculean in their character, but the success which attended his efforts paved the way to his further and rapid advancement. Almost naturally, Colonel Jervois slipped into the post of general adviser and responsible authority on all matters of fortifications.

The vast works which were growing into being at the most vital points, at Portsmouth, Plymouth, and Portland, on the Medway, at Harwich, or on the Thames, were under his immediate control; he might be buried near to one or other of our great arsenals, and remembered like a new Sir Christopher Wren, by the epitaph that his monument lay around. More than this, such value by this time attached to his opinion that his counsel was eagerly sought on every side. He went to Canada on the special invitation of the Colonial Government to confer and report upon the frontier defences; he did the same for the harbours of Nova Scotia and New Brunswick; he visited and examined the seaboard fortifications of the forts of the United States. The great Mediterranean fortresses next claimed his attention; Bermuda also; Quebec was fortified according to his recommendation; he advised concerning the harbours at the mouth of the Red Sea; and he accompanied Lord Mayo to British Burmah to do the same for Rangoon and Moulmein. By this time, indeed, he had earned a world-wide reputation. Foreign States, Switzerland notably, submitted to him the whole scheme of their national defences, and were glad to follow his advice. So highly was he esteemed upon the Continent, that when a special mission of scientific officers was dispatched to inspect the fortifications of Antwerp, General Brialmont said, surprised, "Why do you come to us, when you have in Colonel Jervois an engineer almost without equal in his time?"

To this high reputation as a military engineer South Australia owes its good fortune in securing Sir William Jervois as its present Governor. Summoned hastily from the Straits Settlements, to which his able management of the Perak troubles had at length given peace and quiet, he joined Colonel Scratchley at Melbourne to co-operate with him and discuss the question of Australian defences. While thus engaged the Government of South Australia suddenly fell vacant through the deplorable illness of Sir William Cairns, and Sir William Jervois, to the delight of the people, was forthwith inducted into the place. He has held office little more than six months, and yet the announcement of his departure for England was hailed with unfeigned regret, not unmixed with apprehension that he did not mean to return. Such rumours were groundless. Sir William's temporary leave of absence had been rendered imperative by the pressure of private affairs; but the general expression of regret at his departure and the fear that accompanied it were the best proofs of the estimation in which he is held. Already Sir William Jervois has given abundant evidence of that untiring energy which is one of his strongest characteristics. To matters of deep Colonial importance he has given the fullest and most concentrated attention. In such works as the engineering operations for improving the mouths of the Murray, and reducing the difficulties of its navigation, he is naturally quite at home; but his eager spirit throws itself also into all questions which affect the general welfare of the province. He has a plain, straightforward method of dealing with men which soon wins them over to his views. His manner is short and sharp, after the way of his cloth, and his speech rapid; he goes straight to his point without circumlocution or delay. This plain-speaking, all who serve with or under him have already learnt to appreciate. He may tell colonists just as he has told colleagues or subordinates, many home truths in somewhat brusque, decisive language, but the evident honesty of purpose which underlies them removes almost before it is formed any unpleasant impression they might occasion. When the scarcity of domestic servants in South Australia has grown into a positive nuisance he will not hesitate probably to recommend the importation of Chinese, just as he would have told the Canadians they must substitute new for old methods of defence. This conviction that all his public utterances have but one object—the advancement of the public good—has secured for him, and will probably preserve, his popularity. He will have the opportunity of largely increasing it on his return by his hospitalities at Government House. It is not too much to say that the success of each *régime* is not a little dependent upon social conditions. Adelaide has so long been widowed in this respect that it welcomes with additional pleasure the return of a Governor who comes back as a family man.

If it be Sir William Jervois's intention to pursue further the career of the pro-consul which he has now fairly entered, and in which he has already achieved an undoubted measure of success, he is very happily placed at his present post. South Australia is still junior in point of years to many of its neighbours, but it is not far behind any of them in enterprise, breadth of policy, or intelligence. The education of governorship will be well carried on in such a province, and he who graduates here with honour may reasonably expect translation to higher spheres. There are many concurrent signs that at no great distance of time larger, if not more interesting, changes close by may fall to Sir William Jervois should he elect to remain at the Antipodes. Having so decided, it may be counted as nearly certain that he will continue to gain the goodwill of those over whom he is called to preside.

XXIII.

HENRY GEORGE KEENE.

THERE are many well-informed persons who, on reading Mr. Grant Duff's recent allusion to the Anglo-Indian poet, by pre-eminence, may have confessed their ignorance of the fact that Anglo-India possessed a poet of any sort. British India, it has been said, has produced men who have written profitably and pleasantly upon most topics, from Buddhist topes to black-beetles; in philology, especially, her claims are almost second to none; she boasts of at least one author who, if Fate had not relegated him to the department of gazetteers and statistics, might have won high distinction as the historian of India no less than of "Rural Bengal" and "Orissa;" yet her literature has not flowered into poetry. Mr. Grant Duff's anonymous allusion really had reference to Mr. A. C. Lyall, but it might have been not altogether unjustly applied to the gifted civilian who fills the post of District Judge at Agra. Mr. H. G. Keene is not merely a dexterous, melodious versifier, but a poet of genius, whose miscellaneous essays, with their unmistakable characteristics of humour and wit, run like a thread of gold through the drab of Anglo-Indian journalism. They constitute a highly suggestive indication of the loss which the Anglo-Indian public would sustain from a hard-and-fast rule prohibiting officials—so long as they conformed, as, in fact, they always have honourably conformed, to certain obvious restrictions—from writing to the papers. At the same time that it confers a benefit upon a public steeped in *ennui*, and upon editors in distress, the indulgence affords a congenial pastime to the few choicest spirits of the most hardly-worked Civil Service in the world, and a welcome set-off to an official drudgery the most complete and monotonous.

"In the long pedestrian performances for which the natives of India are so remarkable, they often provide themselves with a supply of parched grain, which is carried in the girdle, and munched from time to time as the traveller proceeds. He is thus enabled to obtain a little nourishment without the delay and trouble of stopping to collect, prepare, and cook more substantial kinds. This slender *viaticum* is called Chabeena, and in the long and dreary path of exile the Anglo-Indian is, in like manner, often glad of any kind of read-and-run literature which may give him mental support without calling upon him to bring together and study more nutritious matter."

These words are quoted from the preface to a collection of short essays which Mr. Keene published at Meerut more than twenty years ago, and to which, following his own analogy, he applied the title "Chabeena." Mr. Keene, like many ornaments of the Civil Service, has accomplished substantial and valuable work in the laborious fields of historical and archæological research; but the foregoing comparison holds good of perhaps the greater bulk of his literary labour—with this qualification, however, that, though sustaining and easy of digestion, the *viaticum* is neither dry nor parched. The first, it seems, of his published series of compositions, the "Chabeena" is a good specimen of the author's style and the catholicity of his tastes. The first paper in the collection is an excellent description of the routine of Anglo-Indian life—especially of its narrowness, its dulness, its immense boredom—though we must add that these qualities are detailed with the warm sympathy of an observer who sees even in that apparently uninviting life endless possibilities of enjoyment as well as of prosaic utility. The next paper in the collection—that, viz., on "Limitations of Indian Liberty,"—is a brief commentary, from the point of view of Indian conditions and experience, on John Stuart Mill's essay on "Liberty," and opens out a vista of speculation upon which many writers have expended their ingenuity, and which in these critical times is likely to prove more attractive than ever. The essay is also noteworthy as containing many useful and extremely practical suggestions in regard to the decentralisation policy which is now an accepted and happy fact, though when Mr. Keene wrote, it was still "in the air." The "Chabeena," together with much of Mr. Keene's subsequent work, are among the first indications of a species of Indian descriptive literature which is steadily growing, and which, now that the public are manifesting a new and even keen interest in Indian affairs, ought to become popular in England. An author who should unite power of expression with versatility of insight and sympathy, might soon, one would think, establish his claim to a hearing; and as a writer on such Indian subjects as the English public would care for, Mr. Keene's combination of endowments is second to none. In verse, at least, he is not one of those who can only harp on one string. In his poems, if we may change the simile, we hear, not only the singing of the brook, but likewise the murmur of the sea.

This variety of quality distinguishes his last volume of verses, "The Death of Akbar, and Other Poems," published two or three years ago. The eponymous poem, together with the fine verses called "The Tents of Shem," "Anti-Locksley, or, the Pervert's Apology," and "The Other Side," are very popular in India, and deserve to be known in England. "The Death of Akbar" is only a dramatic fragment, the readers of which, we think, will regret that the author has devoted so little of his talent to the noblest form of poetic composition. "Anti-Locksley," as our Anglo-Indian readers will remember, was written on the occasion of the conversion of an English member of the Civil Service to Mahomedanism. Some deemed it a piece of irreverence towards Heaven, no less than towards the gods at Simla; but we need hardly say that it is nothing else than a legitimate reproduction of what might be supposed to be the reasoning by which a pervert would justify his resolution, alike to his conscience and before society. We have only space for a portion of the poem:—

"Yes, the step is taken, and I for my part have done
With wine and the flesh of swine, and the faith of the Carpenter's Son;
I have done with the creed of the Cross, and left off going to pray
Where a eunuch-minded prater preaches for praise and pay.

I am sick of civilisation, with all its cant and sham,
Its wars that are waged in the cause of trade, with the flag of the Lamb.

* * * * * *

"Yes, I am sick of it all, and your world will call me back
When it teaches the weary camel to pick up a fallen pack.
There is no God but Allah! he needs no help from man.
Whom He will save, He saves without theological plan.
Was Bethlehem's manger meant to end in Oxford schools,
And your prating preacher haranguing a crowd of frivolous fools—
Defining a God who dwells in a temple not made with hands,
Intoning through his nose what nobody understands?

* * * * * *

"What has your civilisation done for the people here?
Has it made them prosper?—or poorer, think you, year by year?
Skulking in rotten cabins, like foul and famished ghosts,
While you live at Simla, concocting statistics and well-paid posts,
Standing like trees between the soil and the beams of God,
Furnishing each clodhopper with one supporting clod?

"This is not your ideal? Well, and what is it, then?
Flatulent Bengal students aping the manners of men!
People that hate you like poison, praising you up to the skies,
Greeks of the Lower Empire, building a throne on lies.
No, no, I've done with it all—it's cruelty, cant, and pride,
And I turn to the life of the desert, the tent, and the untaught bride."

The next poem may be regarded as "The Other Side" to the despairing picture drawn by the Pervert. It describes a time of famine, and—

"The cry of the reapers whose labour was sped
On the drought-smitten plain,
The cry of the children that wanted for bread,
Of a people in pain:
Who saw that they suffered and toiled and were
Patient in vain.

"And who said of a truth our desert and reward
Are at terrible odds,
And far in the hills sleeps our temporal lord
With our negligent gods:
While we starve here, begrimed in the dust
Of our waterless clods."

They, too, were of the same mind with the Pervert; but at last—

> ". . . The sound of their sorrow went forth
> On the wings of the breeze,
> Being borne by the lightning to hills of the North,
> And under the seas,
> To the Queen at the Isles, sitting throned in her
> Splendour and ease."

The next verse celebrates the charity and munificence of the English nation:—

> "Till the terrible odds of the strife passed away,
> And there came, once again,
> In the season appointed, the genial ray
> And the affluent rain,
> And boon Bhagirutti once more in her valley of grain."

And then the appeal:—

> "Shall not these things, I pray you, be mentioned while men
> Keep our memory alive,
> And the writer of chronicles uses the pen
> That upbraids us with Clive,
> And with taking the honey, and leaving the bees but the hive?"

We may quote the following comparison from "The Tents of Shem":—

> "The corpses of dead cities, the dry bones
> Of a lost world in indistinct decay."

The next quotation is also noteworthy, from its suggestion of the significance of Semitic ornamentation:—

> "Looking on lordly arch and tall minar,
> The glowing sandstone shaft upon the green,
> We feel how void of grace our own lives are,
> And what the race that left them must have been,
> No forms of bird or beast, no shape of man,
> Intrude distraction:

But with a comely geometric plan,
The arabesque allays the thought of action.
The leaning lotos, with inverted urn,
Over the carven lintel seems to turn;
And over all, like fairy links and fetters,
The solemn Scripture-letters."

As adaptability for quotation is a test of authorship, we may cite the following from the same poem:—

"Knaves, when you dupe them, bluster; fools complain;
The wise man smiles, but trusts you not again."

"Discretion," "Last Love Song," and "The Sulky Man's Farewell," are written in the humorous vein—the last-named being a very droll, rollicking, and amusing narrative of the worries of an Anglo-Indian official in the hot weather, when his wife is about to start for England. Here are three of its stanzas:—

"Once for all receive my warning,
Lay aside your doubt and scorning,
Think, on waking every morning,
'Faithful Charlie thinks of me;'
Though his mind be aught but plastic,
Thinks in earnest, if fantastic,
Till, at night, his judgment's last tick
Stops, in slumber, true to me.

* * * * *

"Then all day the Moonshee's droning,
Tales of forging, lying, 'boning,'
Sham complainants, falsely groaning,
Show their wounds produced by paint,
Clearing of encamping stations,
Roads and schools, and sanitations,
Tabulated operations
Make a coil would rouse a saint!

"Measure up that stack of kunkur,
Flog me yonder larcenous younker,
Splash the tatty, swing the punkah,
Close the office, hear the band!

> Then, though neither saint nor sinner,
> Home to fast in place of dinner,
> Clear away, and then begin her
>   Greeting by the Overland!"

Perhaps the best in the collection is the introductory piece, "Weeds of the Woodland," a poem graceful in form and expression, and distinguished by a rare delicacy and tenderness of feeling.

Much of Mr. Keene's literary work has been inspired by the historic locality with which he has been intimately associated. His guide-books to Agra and Delhi are learned, accurate, and detailed, and as delightful as they are learned. Their art criticisms, notes on local industries, architectural styles, legends, history, and the like are of very great value. An intending tourist desirous of acquiring the utmost amount of knowledge about the architectural glories of Upper India, and in the shortest possible space of time, can do no better than wander over these famous localities with Mr. Keene's books for his guidance. The Archæological Society and Museum of Agra also owe their existence to Mr. Keene. On all matters relating to Mahomedan —or "Saracenic"—art and antiquities he is acknowledged to be one of the two or three most competent authorities in India, and certainly the most competent in his own quarter of the country. Mr. Keene's last work has been an enlarged reprint of his "Fall of the Mogul Empire," which covers the obscure interval between the Mogul revolutionary period up to the battle of Paniput, and the time of Generals Lake and Wellesley. Mr. Keene is now said to be engaged on fresh historical work, including some sketches of the careers of the "Adventurers" who were carving out their fortunes in India at the dawn of the English era. The subject is full of romantic interest; the field is almost unexplored, part of it being known only to Mr. Keene himself, and the labourer, we need hardly repeat, is well equipped for his task.

XXIV.

THE HON. SYUD AHMED KHAN, C.S.I.

Of the measures which Lord Lytton has adopted for the advancement of natives to offices of dignity and responsibility, none has been more deservedly popular than his appointment of the venerable leader of the Mahomedan Liberals to a seat in the Legislative Council. The honour has been recognised by Hindoos and Mahomedans alike as a tribute to Syud Ahmed Khan's abilities, and the honesty, disinterestedness, and nobility of his character. It would be easier, perhaps, to estimate the value of his services to his country by reference to the visible fruits of his energy than to the force or contagion, so to speak, of his personal influence and example. Yet it is in this last respect that he chiefly interests one. The Syud belongs to the Socratic order of men—the men who inspire their fellows with their own enthusiasm, and are the well-springs of ideas to which others will impart a practical form and direction. In this sense, Syud Ahmed Khan has occupied, for a great many years past, an almost unique position among the Upper Indian Mahomedans. In fact, the lateness of the acknowledgment of his great claims has been the result of an accident. But for his imperfect command of English, Syud Ahmed Khan would long ago have been promoted from the Subordinate Judgeship—whose duties he discharged so admirably at Benares—to a seat on the Bench of the High Court. He was, and is, devoid of ambition in the vulgar sense of the word; and his late advancement was not merely unsought, but, on Syud Ahmed Khan's own part, no doubt wholly unexpected.

The wisdom of Lord Lytton's selection will be apparent from a more detailed account of the Mahomedan Liberals—or "Naturalists," as their less advanced co-religionists call them—and the kind of work to which their present leader has specially devoted himself. The name "Naturalists" was invented by way of allusion to the preference of Syud Ahmed's party for Western science and knowledge generally, in contradistinction to the old-fashioned, and often worse than useless, learning of the orthodox Mahomedan schools. The English reader will suspect that the term may sometimes be no less suggestive of dissent and reproach than of approbation. No doubt it is. But this is only another way of saying that reformers are usually in a minority. The views of the Mahomedan Liberals have frequently provoked the most violent opposition from the uncompromisingly orthodox parties. Even many of the warmest admirers of Syud Ahmed Khan personally, still maintain his political and social doctrines to be utterly antagonistic to the spirit, and inconsistent with the vitality and progress, of Islam. But though the Naturalists are in a minority, they comprise among their adherents the best educated and the most intelligent of the Mahomedan population, and in reality their influence is far greater than their numbers, and is steadily increasing.

Their most ambitious and also most promising effort in the direction of an educational policy is the recent foundation of the Anglo-Mahomedan college at Aligurh. It is to Syud Ahmed Khan that the chief credit of the project belongs. It may be doubted whether a beginning would have been made with the institution even now, but for the patience and resolution exhibited by him under great difficulties and discouragement. His idea was to found a college, on the model, as regards residence, course of studies, scholarships, fellowships, and other endowments, of an English college at Oxford or Cambridge. In course of time, subsidiary institutions were to be established at the leading towns. The project met with the approval of many chiefs and gentlemen of distinction, Sir Salar Jung himself contributing a very large proportion of the sum required for an endowment fund.

The same spirit pervades their political doctrines. They are English in everything—the essential elements of their religion excepted. The vague aspirations towards a revival of native rule, to which so many Mahomedan and Hindoo writers give expression, find but little favour among the Naturalists. On the contrary, the Naturalists often speak as if they believed that an English conquest or occupation of all Mahomedan territory between the Punjaub frontier and the Balkans would be the very best thing that could happen. Next to Lord Beaconsfield and Lord Salisbury the Mahomedan Progressists seem to be the most emphatic in their approval of the Asian Protectorate, and the annexation of Cyprus. Many of them regret that the English Ministry did not proceed to even greater extremities, by insisting upon definite and detailed pledges for the just government of Asiatic Turkey, and even upon the nomination of English or Anglo-Indian officials who should superintend the execution of the promised reforms. They entertain, of course, a loyal respect for the head of their faith, but they assert, as unreservedly as any foreign critics, that the ruin of the Porte is simply the unavoidable end of official incompetence and corruption. A selection of articles from the last two years' issue of their chief organ, the *Aligurh Institute Gazette*, would form a curious and instructive record of the views of an energetic and influential, though numerically small, section of the Indian Mahomedans, as regards Russo-Turkish, Russo-Afghan, and Indo-Afghan politics. It need hardly be said that the Mahomedan Progressists would heartily approve of any punishment which Lord Lytton might inflict upon Shere Ali. In this respect, however, they only resemble the great majority of the Indian Mahomedans, that is to say, if we accept the drift of the comments in the Mahomedan vernacular papers as an index of native opinion.

Of the *Aligurh Gazette*, named above, Syud Ahmed Khan was, and still appears to be, the editor. It is one of the best native journals in Upper India; but the English reader must not be led by English analogies into a misconception as to the influence of a native

Indian newspaper. The *Gazette* boasts of a steady circulation of three hundred, or at the very outside, three hundred and fifty copies a fortnight; but, as is shown in an article published in a recent number of the *New Quarterly Magazine,* the circulation, or, in other words, the subscription list, may be a very inadequate measure of the real number of readers, and the many others who are indirectly affected by the paper, though they may never have bought or read a copy. The important fact is this, that journals of this description express the opinions of the classes who influence the multitudes. It is not every Mahomedan paper, however, which would denounce the misrule of Mahomedan countries in the terms made use of in Syud Ahmed Khan's organ. As stated in the articles already referred to, the *Gazette* declares that the woes of Turkey are attributable in great part to the religious teachers, or Moulvies, who read only one book, and who are not unlike the Mollahs one sees idling about the mosques in Hindostan. The Turkish Ulema, continues the *Gazette,* deserves to be drowned in the Black Sea. A good example of its style and matter may be found in the number for the 31st of August, containing a reply to certain depreciatory observations of Lord Northbrook's on the loyalty of the Indian Mahomedans. "Every Mahomedan, whether a 'Naturalist' or not, knows," says the *Gazette,* "that no native Government has ever been so successful in making life and property secure, or ruled more 'peacefully and impartially,' than that of the English." As to Shere Ali, it reproaches him with folly and ingratitude, in a strain which distinguishes the utterances of nineteen native journals out of twenty on this great question of the hour. Syud Ahmed Khan also enjoys a high literary distinction among Mahomedans generally. His "Essays on the Life of Mahomet" is a work which possesses a wide reputation. Much interest and value attaches to a little book which he published some years ago in the course of the controversy which Dr. Hunter raised on the question—Whether Mahomedans were bound by their religion to rebel against the Queen?

XXV.

THE EARL OF KIMBERLEY.

THERE is no older family in Norfolk than that of Wodehouse. But titular ennoblement is by no means the necessary accompaniment or the guarantee of antiquity, and though since there have been Angles in England there have been Wodehouses in Norfolk, a peerage was not among the possessions of the house until it was conferred on the great-grandfather of the present Earl of Kimberley. Born fifty-two years ago, the ex—or rather the penultimate—Secretary of State for the Colonies succeeded his grandfather as Baron Wodehouse while still at Oxford. In 1847, he won a first-class and a wife. Equipped with these encouragements to serious occupation, he addressed himself at once with the steady and workmanlike energy which forms a characteristic part of his nature to the struggle of political life. His talents received early recognition, and Lord Palmerston, on his return to power, in December, 1852, after the three hundred days' dexterous reign of Lord Derby and Mr. Disraeli, selected him for the post of Under-Secretary at the Foreign Office. Here he remained until, as Envoy Extraordinary and Minister Plenipotentiary to Russia, he was occupied with the delicate negotiations consequent upon our successful termination of the Crimean War. Again, for two years, from 1859 to 1861, he was Under-Secretary for Foreign Affairs, and having filled the same position at the India Office in 1864, he was in October of that year appointed Lord-Lieutenant of Ireland. In 1866, on the retirement of his party from power, he received the well-merited reward of an earldom; and, finally, from 1870 until the general elections of 1874, he was not the least trusted of Mr. Gladstone's Ministry as Secretary of State for the Colonies.

Although during his tenure of the Seals of the Colonial Office, Lord Kimberley had not the good fortune to complete any great constitutional works, he enjoyed the satisfaction of adding two provinces—British Columbia in 1871, and Prince Edward Island in 1873—to Canada, and of taking the first step towards the education of South Africa in the duties of autonomy by establishing a responsible Government at the Cape. Nor in an enumeration of Lord Kimberley's achievements as a Colonial administrator should it be forgotten that the Canadian question connected with the Treaty of Washington demanded incessant labour, and discretion of the highest order; while in a very different sphere the revision of the system of Indian Coolie emigration, and the settlement, with the aid of two important Commissions, of its minutest details, was a most important work. But as a whole, the period during which Lord Kimberley reigned in Downing Street was singularly uneventful. Nor was Lord

Kimberley the man to create events as some men can create them. If he is free from the Whig *laissez faire*, which was so conspicuous in Lord Melbourne, he has to the full the exceeding caution and the almost nervous dislike of undertaking any responsibility which can be possibly avoided, that are, above all things, Whig traditions. His fidelity to what may be described as the moral principle of his party, does not end here. With the Whig abhorrence of whatever savours of precipitation in action, Lord Kimberley combines the Whig coldness and reserve. Thus, at the Colonial Office he drew a hard-and-fast, and, to speak the truth, a rather needlessly ungenial line between the spheres of official duty and social pleasure. To his duty, indeed, he was devoted, but he did not consider that it was part of his duty to contribute something towards making England a pleasant place for the subjects of his Colonial Empire to visit. He was, in a word, the severely conscientious and circumspect official, and, unlike his successor, Lord Carnarvon, it never occurred to him to think whether he might not promote a kindly feeling between the Colonies and the mother country by condescending on occasions to receive the more distinguished of their representatives, when they happened to be in England, as host and friend. Yet human nature is not a consideration which even a Secretary of State and Cabinet Minister can afford to disregard.

The striking features of his career form of themselves an unmistakable index to the order of Lord Kimberley's abilities and character. His early and steady devotion to the work for which he had destined his life; his patient pursuit of right objects by the right way; a quiet disdain of parade, ostentation, or anything like sensational enterprise, and the total absence from his endeavours of all unworthy ambition, marked him out quickly as a statesman of a peculiarly solid and trustworthy type—one, indeed, who even at the immature age of thirty, when many men of future distinction have barely renounced the noisy pleasures of youth, could safely be intrusted amidst the intrigues of a foreign Court with the plenary disposition of English interests. Lord Kimberley is, as may be inferred from the honours he gained at college, a good scholar, and, what is a less certain consequence, a good writer also. With these qualities allied to his great capacity of patient application, and coupled with his large experience, he is now probably one of those most fully fitted members of the Liberal party to fill both ably and gracefully the office of Secretary of State. For foreign affairs especially his competence is indisputable. His opportunities certainly for gaining an insight into the mazes of European complications have been unrivalled. He was at the Foreign Office through all the days of anxious diplomacy following Magenta and Solferino, when with the audacious intrigues of French ambition and the conflict of Italian aspirations, the menacing alarm of Belgium and Prussia, and the weight of Austrian discomfiture, all the politics of Europe seemed involved in inextricable confusion. His service, too, at the Russian capital, from 1856 to 1858, and his official acquaintance with the Syrian troubles of 1860, have given him no common understanding of questions arising from the East. It is hence believed and hoped in many quarters that Lord Kimberley will live to be one of the most efficient Secretaries for Foreign Affairs that England has possessed.

As Lord-Lieutenant of Ireland, Lord Wodehouse (for he was not yet Lord Kimberley) held no idle or easy office, for he had to deal, in 1865, with the Fenian conspiracy. It is believed that the ambitious plot had been carefully laid of setting up in Ireland an Irish Republic by American aid, and it is undoubted that arms were imported, oaths taken, and secret drills held. Through the vigilance and promptitude of the Irish Government these designs were defeated, and the confidence placed in Lord Wodehouse was amply justified. A firm indifference to mere popularity and a settled aversion to the common methods by which popularity is gained, has always been one of Lord Kimberley's not least valuable characteristics, and as Viceroy of Ireland he benefited largely in popular esteem by the possession of this good quality. When he has assured himself that one way or one object is right, he is incapable of seeking his end except by the most direct modes of truth, and though he is not wanting in forbearance and tact, he will not say the pleasant thing where he is convinced that candour cries for the use of other words. Lord Kimberley's active intellect and natural disposition for work find employment hardly less, and perhaps of a hardly less satisfactory kind, in the unambitious field of county affairs. He is known in Norfolk as an excellent and hardworking chairman of Quarter Sessions, and in matters of municipal import, either for advice or active interposition, his experience and his talent for business make him a landowner as useful to his county as he is in the higher range of politics a statesman valuable to the nation. In Lord Kimberley's character the best and typical features of the English nobleman, gentleman, and statesman—honesty and fixity of purpose, a scrupulous recognition of the responsibilities of wealth and position, an orderly desire for honour without disturbing ambition or fanciful emotions, indifference to display, and a large capacity for work, with a sound intellect and a robust sensibility—these are forcibly and brightly portrayed.

XXVI.

MR. A. C. LYALL.

THE appointment of Mr. A. C. Lyall as Mr. Aitchison's successor in the office of Foreign Secretary to the Government of India, was admirably calculated to please those who took a just view of the requirements and opportunities of the post, and who were anxious to see something more than official ability of the conventional order enlisted in the administration of our Asiatic Empire. Mr. Lyall's career has been brilliant, and the experience which he has gathered in the course of it is immense. He has been brought into closer contact with more aspects of the many-sided Indian mind, has seen and lived amongst more varieties of native character, has been in more favourable positions for observing and analysing that marvellously complex entity which is vaguely spoken of as Indian feeling, than any of his contemporaries, and than many of his seniors. For as the eye sees nothing in the landscape which the mind does not bring to it, so to the Indian official who lacks the qualities of imagination, insight, and reflection, experience itself will be little better than an unedifying void. There are two great dangers to which our Indian administrators are exposed, and to one or other of which they frequently succumb. Either, like the representatives of a certain royal race, they learn nothing and they forget nothing, or unconsciously they adapt to a rigidly Procrustean bed of preconceived ideas—the principles of a school or the crotchets of a sect—the innumerable phenomena, inexhaustible in their interest, and priceless in their teaching, which are presented to them in the vast panorama of Indian life. Even a smaller man than Mr. Lyall might have been expected signally to profit by the practical results of two decades spent as he has spent them. Only a man of Mr. Lyall's remarkable powers could have transformed those results, by the chemistry of philosophic thought, and the exercise of intellectual power, into a culture and learning as admirable as they are rare. Mr. Lyall's career has not been uneventful, but there is no man of whom it would be more hopeless to form a just idea than from a mere recapitulation of its facts and episodes. The son of the clergyman of Harbledown, a suburb of Canterbury, and one of nine children, he was educated at Eton, and afterwards at Haileybury. Almost the last of the Haileybury race of Indian Civil Servants, he admits that the competition system supplies us with a distinctly superior average of Indian administrators.

We have, as Mr. Grant Duff pointed out in his "Political Survey," two sets of relations with Asiatic countries—the one Imperial, the other specially Indian. How the two interpenetrate each other, and consequently how great are the possibilities of the Indian Foreign Secretary, may be seen from a striking passage quoted by Mr. Grant Duff in an article on the foreign policy of Sir John Lawrence, which appeared in the *Edinburgh Review* just seven years ago, written by one "who had the best possible means of knowing what he was talking about." "Subject even to this limitation [the control of the English Cabinet] the Indian Foreign Office yet remains the focus of politics for half Asia—the storehouse of romance of all the East. Murmurs of Dutch aggression in far Sumatra, and whispers of piratical prahus lurking amid the unexplored isles of the Malayan Archipelago; rumours of French enterprise in the feverish rice swamps of Cochin-China, and quaint glimpses of Burmese life at the Court of the Golden-Footed Monarch of Mandalay—such are the varied contents of a mail packet from the Southern Seas. Out of the West come tidings of pilgrim caravans at Mecca, of pearl fishing in the Persian Gulf, or of burning slave-ships on the coast of Equatorial Africa; the outrages of the Christian Emperor in Abyssinia are not omitted, nor those of the Wahabee fanatic at Riad overlooked. North-eastward down the Himalayan passes of Bhootan and Nepaul the life that slowly stirs among the Lamas and monasteries of Thibet sends now and then a faint pulsation into Bengal; and lately the Valley of Cashmere afforded a passage to envoys from the uncouth Khans of Chinese Tartary. Finally, in the farthest north, beyond Afghanistan and the deserts of the wandering Turcomans, looms the giant form of steadily-advancing Russia." It is no exaggeration to say that Mr. A. C. Lyall is constitutionally adapted, in a very eminent degree—by temperament, genius, bent of study, and bias of mind—as well as qualified by unsurpassed and practical knowledge to discharge, as they have seldom been discharged, these onerous but nobly inspiring duties of the Indian Foreign Office. In proof of this it would indeed be only necessary to set forth in a dozen lines the summarised narrative of Mr. Lyall's official life, to follow him from Haileybury to Bareilly, where he arrived a week before the Mutniy; from Bareilly to the Bolundshar district and Philibeet; thence to Shahjehanpore, where he was distinguished for the interest which he took in the condition of the natives; to Agra, where he was for some while joint magistrate; to the Central Provinces, where his reputation first became firmly established on a broad and enduring basis. But it will be more interesting and more profitable to indicate the graphic evidence of his rare qualifications as they are contained in Mr. Lyall's writings.

Whether we regard Mr. Lyall as an author of prose or poetry, it is impossible not to be struck by the completeness with which he has assimilated the chief facts and cardinal conditions of Indian life. He has steeped his mind and bathed his imagination in the rich glow of an Indian sky, in the atmosphere that envelopes the temples and palaces which are the monuments of an antiquity mightier than that of Greece and Rome, in the religions and superstitions which divide Indian races, in prejudices which are gradually wearing themselves out, in aspirations which are still potent forces for good or evil. The web of his literary style is shot through with the changing tints of Indian life and thought. Superior to the vulgar trick of word-painting, which suffuses style with what is called "local colour," Mr. Lyall gives to those who have eyes to see and ears to hear, a marvellous reflection of the subtler features and the finer traits which the thoughtful student observes, and the earnest student would fain know. The essays which he has written in the *Fortnightly Review*—which do not so much merit republication as, in view of the immense value they would have as an educating agency in England, they demand it—are perfectly unique contributions to the history and literature of India. A popular writer Mr. Lyall is not, and if he can be said to have a defect as a writer, it is that his extraordinary power of condensing thought somewhat overstrains the attention of the reader. But it may be said without hesitation, that to have mastered the articles with which Mr. Lyall has periodically enriched the ablest of English reviews, is to have acquired far greater knowledge of India, a far more correct appreciation of the conditions of Indian life, than could be conveyed by a library of what is popularly called instructive literature. Mr. Lyall is a leading member of that band of authors who have succeeded in impressing the educated English public with the idea that India, and the variety of profound problems which India presents, deserve the deepest attention, and will repay the most careful investigation of the student of moral, political, and theological science. After reading and weighing well —the two processes are not to be accomplished without considerable labour—such papers as Mr. Lyall has published in the *Fortnightly Review* on "The Religious Situation in India," "Missionary Religions," and "The Origin of Divine Myths in India," there are many persons who will be tempted, not perhaps quite justly and logically, to exclaim, Why should Italy, Greece, Palestine, to such an extent monopolise the minds of our youth, when in England's Indian Empire we see the gradual operation of forces, the mighty evolution of principles, which contain many of the most momentous issues of Pagan or Hebraic antiquity, embodied in a shape more majestic and august? In the *Fortnightly* there was, about a year ago, a paper by Mr. Lyall on the influence of morality upon religious beliefs, which would have established the reputation of any writer on Indian subjects. There could be no better specimen of his style and calibre. The contrast between the moral attributes and duties of religion in ancient and in modern times—much of the epithet ancient being convertible with that which is contemporary in India—the political importance of theologic sanctions, the compensating check which political necessity exerts upon theologic superstition, the interaction of popular morality and religion in India at the present day—all these were described by Mr. Lyall with not more of circumstantial knowledge and freedom from prejudice than admirable moderation and philosophic fulness. Take the following, the concluding paragraph of the paper, as a specimen at once of the literary power as well as the speculative fairness of the writer:—

"Nevertheless, if these beliefs are prematurely submerged, we may have an awkward break in the continuity of theologic development, to which they appear unusually necessary; and it is not quite clear how this may affect morals. We may after all find morality in India, as elsewhere, looking dubiously at the ladder she has kicked down, and seriously alarmed at the decline of religious beliefs which has been the necessary consequence of her own rise. Or it may be that those are right who insist that Asia has always been too deep a quicksand for Europe to build upon it any lasting edifice of morals, politics, or religion; that the material conditions forbid any lasting improvement; that the English legions, like the Roman, will tramp across the Asiatic stage and disappear, and that the clouds of confusion and superstition will roll up again. Then, after all, the only abiding and immovable figure in the midst of the phantasmagoria will be that of the Hindu ascetic and sceptic, looking on at the incessant transformation of men into gods and gods into men, with thoughts that have been caught by an English poet, and expressed in lines that have a strange Asiatic note—

"'All ye as a wind shall go by, as a fire shall ye pass and be past;
Ye are gods, and behold, ye shall die—and the waves be upon you at last.
In the darkness of time, in the deeps of the years, in the changes of things
Ye shall sleep as a slain man sleeps, and the world shall forget you as kings.'"

There are other reasons which render this article valuable and typical. Mr. Lyall is not more a man of thought than he is of action. He has the temperament of the philosopher, but he has with it the true instinct of the practical administrator. His literary style bears the impress of this combination of gifts. He clothes the deep reflections of the ethical and metaphysical student in the precise and practical diction of the man of affairs.

To penetrate into India is to march into the heart of antiquity. If we can watch in the United States the working of that same democratic system under which we may some day live in England, we can in India note the picturesque illustration of feelings and prejudices, of social conditions and social divisions, which are of immemorial age, but which survive with all their freshness and much of their force to the present day. The warrior chiefs of the East, full of fire and full of vengeance, the contemplative, destructive, philosophic dreamers, are portrayed by Mr. Lyall in a series of poems, which are in simple truth magnificent. The soliloquy of a Hindoo ascetic watching the procession of the Prince of Wales at Delhi was originally published in an Indian paper. It is one of a series of poems which would form as valuable a manual for the student of India as Mr. Lyall's prose compositions. "Theology in Extremis," and "Meditations of a Hindoo Prince and Sceptic"—both of them printed in the *Cornhill Magazine*, the former in September, 1868, the latter exactly nine years afterwards—"The Old Pindaree" and the "Chief of the Rajpoot School," are beautiful as poems, but are not less remarkable for the capacity of which they give proof in the poet of identifying himself with the *nuances* of thought and character of strange and dimly comprehended nationalities. "Theology in Extremis" is the reflections of an Englishman taken prisoner by the Indian Mahomedans in the mutiny of 1857, who will not purchase life at the cost of apostasy from the faith of his fathers. It is not, as the poet shows, religious conviction, but English pride which prevents the doomed soul from repeating the short formula of Mahomedan faith offered him. The poem is a recital of his musings, and agonised questionings, Is there a God, and does He care for men? What is there behind the terrible curtain? This is the last stanza:—

> "Ay, but the word if I could have said it,
> I by no terror of hell perplext—
> How to be silent and get no credit
> From man in this world or reward in the next.
> None to bear witness and reckon the cost
> Of the name that is saved by the life that is lost.'

Of the "Hindu Prince and Sceptic," two stanzas will suffice to show the scope:—

> "And the myriad idols around me, and the legion of muttering priests,
> The revels and rites unholy, the dark unspeakable feasts!
> What have they wrung from the silence? Hath even a whisper come
> Of the secret, whence and whither? Alas! for the gods are dumb!
> Shall I list to the word of the English, who come from the uttermost sea?
> The secret hath it been told you, and what is your message to me?
> It is nought but the wide-world story how the earth and the heavens began,
> How the gods are glad and angry, and the Deity once was man."

Nor is Mr. Lyall less successful in a more epical and objective vein. Neither in spirit nor in graphic power can the speech which he places in the lips of the old Pindaree chief be surpassed. It breathes the atmosphere of battle. It clashes with the ring of steel. It illustrates in all their intensity the burning scorn, the unquenchable hatred of the aged warrior for the new rulers of India, "the hordes of hungry retainers, and well-fed slaves of the quill;" for starving ryots, sneaking Brahmins, and fat Hindus. At last he bursts forth—

"There goes my lord, the Feringhee, who speaks so civil and bland,
Till he raves like a soul in Jehannam if I don't quite understand.
He begins by calling me Sahib, and ends by calling me fool.
He has taken my old sword from me, and tells me to set up a school."

Then the old Pindaree bethinks him of the days when "the sword was king of the pen," and he was twenty-five :—

"Oh! I rode on a Deccanee charger, with a saddle-cloth gold laced,
And a Persian sword, and twelve-foot spear, and a pistol at my waist.

. . . .

My father was an Afghan, and came from Kandahar,
He rode with Nawab Amir Khan in the old Mahratta war."

Could any picture be more complete than that contained in the following stanza?—

"O, the chill of the pearly dawn! Then the crack of a sentinel gun
The gallop and glint of horsemen who wheeled in the level sun:
The shots in the clear still morning, and the white smoke's varying wreath,—
Is this the same land that I dwell in—the dull, dark air that I breathe?"

Again, hear the pent-up bitterness of spirit which finds relief in these characteristic lines—the last of the poem—

"Down in the street is a trader, my father gave him a bill,
I have paid that man twice over, and here I am paying him still;
He shows me a long stamped paper, and must have my land—must he!
If I were twenty years younger he'd get six feet by three.

"And if I were forty years younger, with my life before me to choose
I wouldn't be lectured by Kafirs, or bullied by fat Hindoos,
But I'd go to some far-off country, where Mussulmans still are men,
Or take to the jungle like cheeta, and die in the tiger's den."

To the same class of composition does the "Last Reflection of the Rajput Chief" belong—with its wonderful touches that call up a world of Indian landscape:—

> "The lofty wall which rounds
> The green oasis kept with care;"

the contrast between the blinding glare of the sand and the cool verdure of orange groves; the almost Æschylean figure of the "tribal demon's" image at the portal; the lines reminding one of the commencement of the chorus in the Agamemnon:—

> "Farewell the palace, to the pyre,
> We follow widows of the dead—"

the marvellous picture of the impending funeral; the echoes of battle which sound audibly; the reminiscences of a warlike youth; the established ascendancy of the English; the gradual dismantlement of forts and military strongholds, till nothing is left to the Rajpoot chief but the shade of his roof and a water-spring in a wilderness. Such are the stirring strains in which, as a poet, Mr. Lyall has introduced the English reader to the mysteries of India, and the great problems of Indian race. His poems are the worthy and more popular accompaniment of his prose writings. By both he has contributed to that good work which Sir H. Maine has in so conspicuous a manner advanced—the inspiration of the educated public in England with an interest in India—and no greater service for India or for England could at the present moment be performed than this. Mr. Lyall's writings are the best proof of his qualifications for the office which he now fills. As Home Secretary of the Indian Government he achieved a marked success, and there is every reason to believe that the success will be continued now that he holds the foreign portfolio.

XXVII.

LORD LYTTON.

In December, 1875, it was rumoured in England that Lord Northbrook had resigned his position as Indian Viceroy, and early in the following month it was known that Lord Lytton would be his successor. The announcement created a general sentiment of mingled surprise, curiosity, interest, and gratification. Lord Lytton had been twenty-six years in the Diplomatic service, and had gathered a large experience of Courts and capitals, as well as of the men inhabiting and the motives swaying then. But he had never permanently held any first-class Embassy, and to the English public at large he was best known as an accomplished *litterateur*, a poet of rare and real originality, the gifted son of a distinguished father. His acquaintances, his friendships were as cosmopolitan as they were various. He was equally on terms of intimacy with statesmen of the American Republic, with French authors, Italian diplomatists, painters and men of letters in England, German professors at Heidelberg, and German politicians who had been among his fellow-students at Bonn. He was at home in Courts and clubs, in salons and studios, and moved from one to the other with the perfect ease which is the fruit of perfect breeding. He had contributed as copiously to the literature of Blue Books as to that of Parnassus, and as his poems had attracted the attention of critics, so his reports on the political and financial condition of European States had commanded the approval of great men in Downing Street. There were other reasons which caused the appointment to be closely scanned. It was rumoured that England's inscrutable Prime Minister, Mr. Disraeli, had been specially struck by Robert Lytton when he was a Harrow boy, and had spoken to his father on the subject of his future at Knebworth. It was recollected that Lord Lytton the first had been among the most successful Colonial administrators of modern times, and it was speculatively asked whether Lord Lytton the second had imbibed any of those political lessons on the government of the dependencies of England which were contained abundantly in the two volumes of speeches and letters by the father, edited by the son. It was not forgotten that the great practical moral of Bulwer's last trilogy, "The Parisians," "Kenelm Chillingly," and "The Coming Race," was that the aristocracy, territorial or titled, of new or ancient lineage, which does not play a part in the political life of England is doomed, that the life of political action is nobler than that of poetic contemplation, and that, as Bulwer has told us in "Chillingly," the world is "a battlefield where the worse wounded are the deserters." Such was the philosophy of the father: what was the nature of the fruit, what the measure of fulfilment, which its precepts would find in the son? An immense deal of genuine pleasure was given by Lord Lytton's nomination to the highest office, which an English subject can hold, to all sorts of people—to diplomatists, to the cultured and intellectual classes, and especially to society in every European capital. The question asked on every hand was—now that Lord Lytton had been intrusted with the august and responsible office of her Majesty's representative in India—What will he do with it?

In Paris, where Lord and Lady Lytton were well known, where their social gifts and graces shone perhaps with a light more generally visible, and exercised an influence more vividly appreciated than in our own foggy climate, the appointment caused something like enthusiasm. In a very interesting letter which appeared in the *Times*, the Paris correspondent of that newspaper described the pang of regret, the keen sense of personal loss which Parisian society experienced when it was known that it was to lose "the Lyttons." It is not an exaggeration to say that the unique position filled by "the Lyttons" in the great world of the French capital had disposed of many a social prejudice against the English character. English diplomatists are too often without honour in their own country, and Lord Lytton's aptitude for political affairs and diplomatic achievements was less perfectly understood in England than on the Continent. English politicians knew that he had filled difficult positions, and had been sent on more than one critical mission; that having commenced his diplomatic career under his uncle, Lord Dalling, then Sir Henry Bulwer, he had enjoyed the advantage of the best training which a diplomatist could have; that when he had been specially dispatched to Belgrade, when afterwards he was placed in Copenhagen in the perplexed days of the Schleswig-Holstein Question, and when, later again, he visited the capital of the Hellenic Kingdom as the friend and counsellor of the young monarch, as well as in the share he had taken in the negotiations for a Commercial Treaty between Austria and England, and on the several occasions when he had acted as *chargé d'affaires* at Paris, he had shown not merely the skill of the official, but the sagacity of the statesman. Nor did they fail to bear in mind that Mr. Disraeli had proved singularly shrewd in his estimate of character, and that his selection of colleagues and officials had seldom been otherwise than successful. There was thus a general disposition to take Lord Lytton upon trust, and to believe all good things of him till such a belief should be rebuked by events. In some of the newspapers the appointment was criticised and even condemned, and a great deal was written with the purpose of showing that in virtue of certain physical and intellectual qualities, or the want of them, Lord Lytton was not the man who could ever be hoped successfully to govern India. In fact, the Indian princes and the Indian natives were spoken of as if they were phenomenal creatures whom it was impossible to approach without the possession of superhuman gifts and the exercise of magical arts. Very much the same sort of thing had been said when Mr. Disraeli's choice had fallen upon Lord Mayo.

So far as Indian opinion is concerned, it was not an easy thing to succeed so able and successful an Indian administrator as Lord Northbrook, and Lord Lytton had been in India a very little time before he found that there was a considerable body of prejudice which he had to overcome. The observations made by the Prince of Wales to the new Viceroy on the treatment of the native population produced a very deep impression, and Lord Lytton was not the man to feel strongly and to abstain altogether from giving practical effect to his feelings. It is not necessary here to recall the details of the Fuller case, and to reopen a closed controversy. The sequel is tolerably well known, and the effects of it have now, it may be hoped, disappeared. During the first year that he was in India Lord Lytton could scarcely do or say anything—deliver a speech, issue invitations to a dinner or cards for a great reception—without being accused in some quarters of a deep-seated, subtle, dark design to place a slight on the European population. Civil and military officials declared that he was either unable to comprehend the genius of Indian life and the conditions on which our Indian Empire is maintained, or else that he was deliberately working to undermine the fabric of our dominion. The explanation of these stories in the first instance is simple enough—the almost ludicrous sensitiveness, combined with the blind devotion to routine and tradition, which is the characteristic of a highly-organized officialism. It is much to have conquered the difficulties inseparable from a great and responsible position, to have succeeded in the business of administration when the obstacles which the administrator has had to surmount have been exceptionally heavy: it is even more to have overcome the persistent and unreasoning antipathy of a class, and to have trod the uphill path of an opposed career when the opposition has been that of a sentiment with which it is hopeless to argue. If Lord Lytton had been in any sense a weak man, if he had not, in fact, been a man of very exceptional tenacity of purpose and moral courage, he could not have gathered into his hands as firmly as he has done the tangled threads of Indian administration.

The great works which he has taken up are indeed, as yet, some way removed from completion, and there is sore trouble on the North-Western Frontier. But this is the sort of trouble which every Viceroy of India expects to encounter. The foreign and the frontier policy which Lord Lytton has pursued is that which he was sent out to adopt, and it cannot be criticized without criticizing at the same time the entire foreign policy of her Majesty's ministers. In his financial policy, assisted by the experience and the genius of Sir John Strachey, he has achieved a success beyond the reach of cavil or criticism. Judgment on his famine administration may be suspended till the Commission presided over by General Richard Strachey sends in its report. On the question of Indian taxation, Indian local government, and the employment of natives he is known to entertain opinions, and to be labouring for results, which the most Conservative of Indian politicians admit to be necessary, and the most thorough-going of reformers contemplate with enthusiasm. When Lord Lytton's financial policy is complete the whole system of the salt taxes wiil have been readjusted, and one of the most remarkable physical peculiarities of India—the colossal, thick-set, impassable hedge of prickly pear, which runs right across the Asiatic peninsula, and at the occasional gaps in which the salt tax is levied—will have disappeared, and the tax will be paid at the mouth of the mines. As regards the native question Lord Lytton, recognising the beneficent results of that *esprit de corps* which is only possible when men are organized into a distinct service, and not casually and erratically employed—finding their way by chance or by superior skill to certain positions—is understood to favour the idea of a high class native Civil Service. He would, in fact, redistribute the Civil Service into three parts —first, the Covenanted English Civil Service, the entrance to which would be in the future, as in the present, by open competition—competition, where it has once been established, being more or less of a necessary evil; the second, a high-class native Civil Service, with the express understanding that entrance to it is not to be by competition; thirdly, a service whose members would fill a great variety of offices of the lower kind, and would consist of English and natives indifferently. These are but a few of the works on which Lord Lytton is at present engaged; but they are enough to show how completely he realises the opportunities of his high office, and in how thorough a degree he has that combination of sympathy and sagacity which is of the essence of statesmanship. How lofty and complete is his sense of the Imperial dignity and moral responsibility of England's mission in India, was shown by the speech which he addressed to the native Princes at the greatest Durbar ever held, and the most magnificent pageant ever witnessed even in a land of pageants, that of May 1, 1876, when the Queen was formally proclaimed Empress of India. A characteristic quality of his statesmanship is the astonishing power which he has of acquiring a strong comprehensive hold of a new and elaborate subject, of at once perceiving its general purpose, and mastering its bearings. These are the attributes which mark his administration; but they are also not less apparent in the clear, powerfully-written Minutes which he sends to Downing Street, and which in their fulness attest not only the ready pen of the writer but the self-sacrificing zeal of the official.

XXVIII.

SIR HENRY SUMNER MAINE, K.C.S.I.

It is just thirty-six years ago that the Chancellor's English Medal in the University of Cambridge was awarded to "Maine of Pembroke," who in the year following was the successful candidate for the Craven Scholarship, and who had received the school training which qualified him for these academic successes at Christ's Hospital—the school of Porson, of Coleridge, and of Lamb. In 1844, Mr. Maine, still of Pembroke, stood first in the First Class of Classics, was Chancellor's Medallist, and a Senior Optime in Mathematics. He next gained a fellowship at Trinity Hall, and for a time was tutor of that college. He was called to the Bar at Lincoln's Inn, and also at the Middle Temple in 1850, and twelve years later, his Indian career began. He had been offered the post which he ultimately occupied—that of Legal Member of Council—a year or two previously, but the state of his health made him dread the effects of the climate. As a matter of fact, the change to warmer latitudes proved, in his case, decidedly beneficial. When Mr. Maine started for the East, he had been Reader of Jurisprudence and Civil Law to the Inns of Court, and

Regius Professor of Civil Law at Cambridge, and was known to electors as Revising Barrister for Middlesex. He was not merely known, but distinguished, as one of a band of writers, including Venables, Sandars, Lord Robert Cecil, Bowen, and many others, who, under the able guidance of Mr. Cook, had brought the *Saturday Review* to the high position it then held as a journal. Lastly, he was the author of a treatise on Ancient Law—a book pronounced by Mr. J. S. Mill to be profound, and yet as readable, in its delightfully lucid style, as many volumes which claim to be professedly popular,—the subject being the connection between the principles of ancient law and the lines of modern thought. If it may be said that the theme was one rendered more familiar to the German public, through the labours of Savigny and others, than to English readers, it was also one which had certainly never been treated in Germany itself with similar clearness and precision.

The year 1834 had witnessed the establishment of a Central Legislative Council in India in the place of the three previously existing at Forts William, St. George, and St. David—a measure urgently demanded by the chaotic condition, in this department, of the functions of the Government. The legislature thus inaugurated lasted twenty-seven years, though a considerable modification in its character took place in 1853. By an Act then passed, the Council was enlarged by the addition of members, called legislative members, of whom two were judges of the Supreme Court, and the others were appointed severally by the local Governments. It is enough to record the fact that the Act of 1853 was not thought to work well; the Council was said to have become a debating society, and the interests of the other Presidencies besides Bengal were not considered to be sufficiently kept in view. Sir Charles Wood therefore introduced the Councils Act of 1861, which re-established, for local objects, the Legislatures of Madras and Bombay, abolished the judge members, and introduced certain restrictions calculated to render the central Legislative Council less like the parody of a popular institution. These details are necessary to show the task that Mr. Maine had before him. It was a time of extraordinary activity. The Queen was proclaimed in 1858, and within three years the Civil Procedure Code, the Criminal Procedure Code, and almost immediately afterwards the Penal Code, all of which had been long in preparation, were enacted. In 1862 the High Courts of Bengal, Madras, and Bombay were established, that of the North-Western Provinces following in 1866. Small Cause Courts were set on foot, and the whole Police Department was reorganized. The machinery was thus prepared, the systematic arrangements were ready; but, with the exception of the Penal Code and certain acts affecting Revenue and Land Tenures, the substantive law was in a very uncertain and unsatisfactory condition. A law-giver was wanted, and in Mr. Maine a law-giver was found. To step from the study and the lecture-room into the arena of an Empire, and to have the opportunity of applying the wisdom suggested by antiquity, but moulded in the acutest minds of the age, to the daily lives and wants of millions, must mark a crisis or a triumph in the most brilliant and eventful of careers. There may have been such openings under the Roman supremacy, but they scarcely exist now in Europe, unless indeed it be in England.

That the years succeeding the appointment of Sir Henry Maine as Legal Member were not years of legislative idleness in India may be gathered from the fact that the Acts passed from the year 1862 to the year 1869, both inclusive, were two hundred and thirty-five. Of course they differed immensely in importance. There were such Acts as that relating to the emigration of native labourers to the Danish colony of St. Croix, and there was the Indian Succession Act of 1865. Perhaps the least tedious way of indicating what was done during the incumbency of Maine will be to take each year, and notice in the briefest manner the Acts which it produced. It need only be premised that in matters affecting revenue, and in subjects of merely local moment, the Legal Member was to a certain degree in the hands of others, and that in the details of civil procedure he was cordially supported in his labours by Sir Henry Harington, a civilian with a natural aptitude for drawing bills, who was a member of Council. In 1862 certain Acts were passed with reference to Stamps and Fees, but little else of importance; whilst in 1863 a Burmese Civil Procedure Act, and an Act enabling the Government to divest itself of religious endowments seem the most important. 1864 was a year of activity: Acts were passed to abolish Kazees, to amend the Law of Assurances, to enlarge the jurisdiction of Small Cause Courts, and, a delicate subject well treated, an Act regulating the marriages of Christians in India, having special reference to native Christians. 1865 was pregnant with important legislation: it witnessed the passing of the Act for the Maintenance of the Rural Police in the North-West Provinces, the Carriers' Act, the Indian Marriage Act, the Indian Succession Act, the Pleaders' Act, the Parsee Marriage and Divorce Act, the Punjaub Courts Act, &c. In 1866, the following Acts claim notice:—The Indian Companies Act, the Post Office Act, the Partnership Amendment Act, a new Registration Act, the Native Converts' Marriage Dissolution Act (settling a very nice and difficult question), the High Court Act (North-West Provinces), and two Acts affecting Trustees. 1867 witnessed the passing of Acts on Gaming, Customs, Stamps; on the duties of Administrators-General; while to 1868 belong the Oude Rent Act and Punjaub Tenancy Act; and 1869 was signalised by a new Customs Act, a new Stamp Act, an Act for the Amendment of the Criminal Procedure, and a Divorce Act; and this enumeration omits, of course, temporary Acts connected with the income-tax, salt duties, &c. On the whole, the result is most satisfactory; and if less praise is due to a Whipping Act, and none at all to the Punjaub Outrages Act—a retrograde measure, dictated by irritation, and not to be defended—and if the Criminal Procedure Amendment Act of 1869 was destined to be shortlived, still a large amount of sound and salutary work remains.

It may be easily imagined that the labours of which the merest outline has been here given, left little time to be devoted to other objects of interest in India. The Legal Member of Council, however, became Vice-Chancellor of the University of Calcutta, and in that capacity gave some excellent advice to the students, a body largely recruited from the section of Indian Society called Young Bengal. They were faithfully warned against the tendency to superficiality, which is a marked feature in the outcome of their miscellaneous studies, and, at the risk of unpopularity, were equally warned against the feeling deplorably common amongst them, that the condescension of accepting an almost iniquitously cheap education (considering who really pays for it) entitled them at once to the patronage of Government, and constituted a claim for provision and employment. Sir Henry Maine is an accomplished speaker, in the sense in which eloquence at the present day is accepted. Of the tawdry rhetoric now relegated to Scotch sermons and the lectures of itinerant moralists, he has no supply whatever. Tropes and metaphors find no favour with him. But his addresses may be compared to the best conversation—that is to say, the subject is treated as if the thoughts flowed in a natural succession, without artificial arrangement or studied juxtaposition; whilst the words employed are appropriate, forcible, and occasionally picturesque. If, as the matter increases in interest, the manner of expression becomes rather more ornate, and if these "purple patches" are previously prepared, they are worked in at any rate with neatness and effect.

Some curious notions have from time to time been put forward in print about Sir Henry Maine's qualifications and characteristics. A journal, the grotesque audacity of whose impossible proposals sometimes seems not unsuccessfully to simulate brilliancy, once suggested that the arrears on the Privy Council files should be cleared off by the appointment of Sir Henry Maine as special judge for two years, at a salary sufficiently princely to make it worth his while to accomplish the feat. Few men in England of his calibre would find such a task more intolerably tedious. Another newspaper, with ludicrous ignorance, has recently represented Sir Henry as selecting a favourable moment for joining Durand in seizing on the helm of affairs in India. Both of these ideas imply an utter misapprehension of Sir Henry Maine's distinctive qualities of mind. For the extent of his sound knowledge, few men perhaps have plodded less, or voluntarily incurred less labour. He has the art of finding at once what is worth retaining and rejecting the dross, and he has always kept steadily to his own subjects. That passion for sipping the arts and sciences, that hankering after the universal, which dilutes the usefulness of so many clever men, has never seduced him. He has placed his object steadily before him, and has adroitly made his reading, his acquaintance with specialists, and his general opportunities subserve to that end. To fag away at cases, or to jump at an opportunity of attempting to govern men, would be foreign to the views of one who has determined to become the first historical and comparative jurist of the day, and wisely employed his brilliant episode of law-making for personal culture in that direction. Since his return from India Sir Henry has held the offices of member of the Indian Home Council and Corpus Professor of Jurisprudence at Oxford. The two works he has published in connection with his chair, on "Village Communities" and the "Early History of Institutions," have greatly increased his reputation; whilst his Rede Lecture, at the other University, is a gem of pregnant thought, exhibiting, as indeed the other two books do, his Eastern experiences treated from the point of view of his life-long line of study. Sir Henry Maine's recent appointment to the Mastership of Trinity Hall, Cambridge, will lead to his resignation of the Corpus Professorship, but he will retain his place at the India Office. Advice at the Council Board is support to the Empire of a kind differing only in degree from active service in distant realms; and though the ultimate retirement to classic Cambridge will have been well earned, we hope, for the interests of India, it may not take place till a long-distant day.

XXIX.

SIR LOUIS MALLET, C.B.

THE position occupied by the Permanent Under-Secretary of State at the India Office is in some respects exceptional. On the one hand he is surrounded by a larger multitude of minor authorities than elsewhere falls to the lot of the highly-placed permanent officials; on the other, the law of change which operates in the case of all these throws his own fixity of tenure into stronger relief, and invests him, by force of comparison, with more of dignity and influence. There is the Council of Fifteen, at whose meetings he sits by in silence, without vote or voice; there is the Parliamentary Under-Secretary; there is the Secretary of State himself. But Secretary of State and Under-Secretary are dependent on a majority in the House of Commons; the Indian Councillor's term of office never exceeds, and by no means always extends to, ten years. The Permanent Under-Secretary survives generations and outlives dynasties. Placed in an atmosphere impregnated with mutability, he represents the one element that may relatively be called immutable, and he naturally acquires a knowledge, and with it a power, which may well console him, if he is of an ambitious, or, indeed, a conscientious turn of mind—believing that the knowledge which is born of experience is, above all things, necessary at the India Office—for any apparent sacrifice of dignity that the extinction of his existence as an active member of the Council may seem to involve. Authority naturally gravitates towards him. His advice is asked by his chief for the time being, by his Parliamentary colleagues, by the Indian Councillors. He is the channel by which all things and persons approach the supreme entity known as the State. He has the opportunity not only of continuous but of all-round work. The tendency is undoubtedly for members of the Indian Council gradually to assume the *rôle* of men whose chief duty it is to produce periodical papers on special subjects. There is naturally some difficulty in providing fifteen gentlemen simultaneously with a certain set or sets of documents, and, it may be, unwritten facts as well, and thus some at least of the number adopt a kind of official eclecticism, and occupy themselves with the particular work for which they have a leaning, and which chance throws in their way. Naturally, therefore, Sir Louis Mallet, whose appetite for comprehensive industry is almost insatiable, may have embraced, not without satisfaction, the offer of the position which he now holds at the India Office, made to him rather more than four years ago by the Duke of Argyll. His predecessor, Mr. Herman Merivale, died after it was known that Mr. Gladstone and his colleagues would resign. But the Duke of Argyll held the seals as Indian Secretary; he might have bequeathed the appointment to his successor, but technically his grace was responsible for it; he had six years' experience of the India Office—itself a sufficient reason why he should not hesitate to exercise his undoubted right in nominating a Permanent Under-Secretary.

The Duke of Argyll placed the post at Sir Louis Mallet's disposal, and Sir Louis Mallet resigned his place in the Council of the Secretary of State to accept the promotion. The position which he quitted was for several reasons one of a marked and, indeed, unique character. Up to the year 1872 Sir Louis was best known as a distinguished official at the Board of Trade, an eminent economist, and the conductor of some exceedingly difficult and successful politico-economical missions. But in 1870 the work in which he had engaged with so much energy seemed to have come to an end, and two years later the Duke of Argyll, the then Secretary of State, offered Sir Louis a place on his council. The new comer had no particular connection with India, no special knowledge of Indian affairs. But the appointment was not without a definite reason and fitness of its own. It had for some time been an imputation upon the Indian administration, at the hands of its purely commercial critics, that it did not pay sufficient attention to commercial affairs. Manchester sighed for the old days of the Company, declined to recognise the fact that India had passed from a trading speculation to an Imperial Government, and sought to perpetuate the traditions of the Board of Directors. Considerable pressure was brought upon the Duke of Argyll to nominate a representative of

English commerce and free trade when the next vacancy occurred. The difficulty was to find a suitable representative. When the Secretary of State came to consider the qualifications of which he was in quest, and to review eligible candidates in his mind, he not unnaturally arrived at the conclusion that Sir Louis Mallet was the man whom he wanted—a representative of the economical thought of England, and of its commercial as well as political life and usages, in whom, from the work which he had done, commercial men and economists might be expected to have confidence. Before, however, he abandoned his connection with the Board of Trade, there were some arrangements which he was anxious to carry out. The sphere of his duties had been rather the Continent and capitals of Europe than Whitehall, and the department which he filled had been to all intents and purposes a department of the Foreign Office. Sir Louis Mallet, therefore, suggested that his successor should take his place at the Foreign Office—the position which he had occupied at the Board of Trade being abolished. After some discussion and delay, this proposal was carried into effect, and Mr. Villiers Lister, who now reigns in the commercial department at the Foreign Office, may therefore be considered Sir Louis Mallet's successor outside the India Office. Even thus the Permanent Under-Secretary of State for India cannot be said to have completely severed his connection with his former office, and last year was placed at the head of a mission which went over to Paris on the subject of a commercial treaty with France.

The retrospect of Sir Louis Mallet's career is not without an interest and even a romance of its own. Born of an old French Protestant stock, he had for his grandfather one of the most distinguished French Publicists of the last century, Mallet Du Pan. With Mirabeau, Malouet, and others, he was the friend of moderation, in that period of French frenzy, when to be the friend of moderation was regarded as equivalent to being an enemy of the rights of man. As editor of the *Mercure de France*—a semi-official journalistic appointment—Mallet Du Pan incurred the wrath of the victorious mob, and had to flee for his life. After some months of wandering he found himself in England, an exile and penniless. His property had been confiscated, his library burned by Revolutionary incendiarists. Broken in health and spirits, he showed that he was not crushed. He at once set to work to found an international paper on the lines of the extinct *Mercure de France*, entitled, *Mercure Britannique*, published in London, and written in French. The new venture was a success, and in the first year its proprietor and editor made upwards of £1,000. He never lived to know a second year of its prosperity, the effect of his past anxieties and sufferings upon his nature was fatal, and in the first year of the present century Mallet Du Pan died. His works in more senses than one were destined to live after him. So profoundly impressed was Mr. Pitt, then Prime Minister of England, with the service which the French refugee had rendered in stemming the revolutionary tide, that he conferred a pension on his widow of £300 a year, and appointed his son to the Audit Office—an office, indeed, which Pitt may be said to have created for his benefit. He was a man of literary tastes and of a quiet disposition. Looking back upon the tremendous time of which his father had borne the brunt, he shrank from public life, and adopted as his motto, *Bene vixit qui bene latuit.* He never sought promotion beyond the Audit Office, and at the Audit Office, accordingly, his son, Louis Mallet, as a boy of sixteen, found himself. It was not an exciting apprenticeship, but it was an exceedingly useful one, and when, eight years later, young Mallet was transferred to the Board of Trade, becoming soon afterwards private secretary to Mr. Labouchere, the future and first, as well as last, Lord Taunton, he had acquired a complete knowledge of what may be called the mechanism of official life. Mr. Mallet, who was thus connected with the late Lord Taunton, was naturally educated in the exclusive atmosphere of Whiggism, and took his political faith from Whig prophets and interpreters. It was not strange therefore that when, in 1860, he found himself appointed the colleague of Cobden in the negotiations which ended in the conclusion of the Commercial Treaty with France, he should have felt some misgivings as to his company. Of Cobden he knew nothing, and had of course been taught to look at him through the not very favourable medium of Whig spectacles as one who was demagogue and socialist. Mr. Mallet, however, very speedily became convinced of the integrity of this dangerous personage, subdued by the charm of his self-sacrificing zeal, and fascinated by a sweetness of character which was irresistible, and to which Mr. Disraeli himself more than once testified. His mission to Paris, in 1860, was a determining event in Mr. Mallet's career. He had taken up his position; his principles had assumed shape and substance; the influence of Cobden had crystallised his convictions. During the decade that followed, Mr. Mallet had abundant opportunity of giving practical effect to these convictions. There were the conditions of the French Commercial Treaty to carry out; there was an Austrian Treaty of Commerce and Navigation to be executed. These were works which involved much European travelling, and when Sir Louis Mallet finally returned home, he had acquired an immense and varied diplomatic experience and political insight.

It may well have been no common disappointment to Sir Louis Mallet that his visit to India in 1875 was so abruptly cut short by illness. Still, though he can only say of our Indian Empire *vidi tantum*, it is something that he should have had the opportunity of catching a hurried glimpse of a part of it, and it may well be a satisfaction that before his return to England the rate of silver exchange had already become so depreciated, that whatever arrangements he might have concluded with the Viceroy could have only been provisional. The general views which Sir Louis Mallet holds on Indian affairs may be defined with tolerable clearness. He belongs, it may be said, generally to that school of Indian statesmen with which the names of the Stracheys are identified, and which consider, that if India is not to be governed according to English ideas, one of the chief reasons for England's Empire in India disappears. Believing that the great principles of economical science are universal, Sir Louis Mallet would insist on their application to India, and has no sympathy with those who advocate the expediency of "taking people as you find them." Neither has he any more sympathy with the propaganda of those doctrinaires, pure and simple, who propose to remove all causes of native discontent on *à priori* principles. He believes that in India, as everywhere else, there can be no good government without good finance, and that in this view the most urgent of the many urgent reforms required in India is the gradual substitution for the existing state of things of a sound fiscal and economic system. As Sir Louis Mallet has more than once pointed out, those reformers who, like Sir Arthur Cotton, declare that famines are preventable by colossal works of irrigation, and that it is the duty of the Government to undertake these, ignore the conditions under which all public works in India are performed—forget that no Government in the world would be equal to their performance, least of all the Government of India, where the officials change in the different localities every three years, where it can seldom or never happen that the official who executes the work is the same as he who has prepared the estimate, and where the permanent fixing of responsibility is next to impossible. This perpetual cry for Government works, Sir Louis Mallet might perhaps feel disposed to think is in a great degree the result of the fact that extension of public works means more lucrative occupation to the daily-growing class of Englishmen who seek their careers and make their fortunes as servants of the Crown in India. According to Sir Louis Mallet's ideas, the only real remedy for famine is to be found in enabling the people to improve their condition. Governed as they at present are, this is, of course, out of the question; but why not govern them so that it is out of the question no longer? Why not, instead of a system of land tenure which, varying greatly in different parts of India, is more or less defective in all, give them a system which should permit of the accumulation of capital on the soil? At the root of Indian famine lies the poverty of the Indian people. This poverty will not—according to Sir Louis Mallet's notions—be relieved till the occupiers of the soil are permitted to appropriate the margin of increment; till, in fact, they have more inducement than at present to bring the land up to the highest pitch of productive power. Meanwhile Sir Louis Mallet would assist the local authorities with loans, to aid native and local enterprise, but would do nothing for the people which in his opinion they can be made to do for themselves, and which it is outside the legitimate function of any Government to attempt for them.

XXX.

JOHN HENRY MORRIS, C.S.I.

It is thirty years since the present Chief Commissioner of the Central Provinces entered the service of the East India Company. Like his two great predecessors at Nagpore, he began his career in the Punjab—*arida nutrix leonum,* the training ground of so many in the foremost ranks of Anglo-Indian soldiers and civilians. In 1848 he was posted as Assistant to the Resident at Lahore. In 1851 he filled the office of Assistant Commissioner at Hoshiarpur. His subsequent appointments were to the Lahore Division, as Settlement Officer, to Mooltan in a like capacity, and to the Collectorate of Allahabad, whence, in 1863 or 1864, he was promoted to the Settlement Commissionership of the Central Provinces. After five years more he was appointed Judicial Commissioner, and in 1871 became the head of the local administration. In his account of the Central Provinces, the late Mr. Pritchard erroneously places him next in succession to Sir Richard Temple, Mr. Morris's immediate predecessor being Sir (then Mr.) George Campbell.

It will thus be seen that Mr. Morris's career, though very successful, has not been exceptionally rapid, nor can it be called brilliant, in anything like the sense in which the term applies to the services of the two distinguished men already named, and others who were almost his contemporaries. In fact, the main lines upon which the administration of the Central Provinces was to proceed had been laid down during the ten years preceding his assumption of the Chief Commissionership. Temple and Campbell drew the original outlines; it remained for their successors to fill in the details. The former were the architects; the latter are the builders. And the adventure and romance of the earlier time have given way to prosaic routine. Thus it is unlikely that any other Chief Commissioner will emulate Sir Richard Temple, who visited every quarter of his vast territory, explored its great rivers, and rode on horseback four thousand miles, or as far as from Cape Comorin to Peshawur and back, in the first year of his office. At least, that species of exertion is less necessary now than it was then. Still, there is now, and there will be for a long time, more scope for administrative work of a useful practical sort, in the Central than, perhaps, in any other of the Indian provinces. At Nagpore there is as yet small opportunity for the showy legislation of Bombay and Bengal; but throughout the vast territory of which it is the capital, there is an illimitable field for the engineer, the miner, and the agriculturist. The ruler of such a province is bound to be, before all things, a man with a turn for material improvement. Until this has made some headway, schemes like those which more advanced provinces have realised for art culture, and a Native Civil Service with or without donkey-races, may safely be postponed. In short, the career of a civilian in the position of Mr. Morris must be one of unostentatious, somewhat commonplace usefulness, rather than of such glory as the world ordinarily takes note of.

Whether Mr. Morris would have won distinction in a position of greater dignity and responsibility than that which he now occupies is probably a question which he himself may never have an opportunity of testing. But his fellow-civilians will admit his special aptitudes for the task of governing the Central Provinces. His seven years' experience in the separate departments of Justice and Land Settlement had already familiarised him with the details, as well as the general duties, of the administration-in-chief for which he was destined. For the long space of fourteen years Mr. Morris has afforded an excellent example of one who has identified himself, or who has been identified, with his province, and the probabilities are that Nagpore will continue to enjoy the benefit of his gifts, both of acquisition and of natural endowment, to the last. Mr. Morris will, perhaps, be content with recognition as one of the first in the second rank of Indian administrators—the men of sound, practical intelligence, capacity and liking for any amount of hard and often uninviting work; but, apparently at least, untroubled with the ambitions, the enthusiasms, and the grand ideals that usually go with genius. The educational and municipal projects that make more noise in other provinces find in him a steady and discreet supporter.

Of the two the latter has, it seems, made the greater progress during the present *régime*, and Mr. Morris states in his last Administrative Report that the non-official native members among those local bodies which are supposed to be, to a more or less extent, self-governing, are learning to feel a genuine and enlightened interest in their work. The Chief Commissioner very properly thinks that for a considerable time to come the pursuit of conservancy and sanitation will be rather more advantageous to his subjects than the study of Dr. Johnson. In the order of nature, which Mr. Morris is doing his best to respect, the flower—that is, the ornament—comes last; but in India there is an occasional tendency to attempt a reversal of the process. Hence unpleasant consequences, such as over-competition in the only learned profession which natives care for, that of law, and an overcrowding at the doors of the State service. It will not be Mr. Morris's fault if Young Nagpore, disappointed in his loftier aspirations, finds relief in what the Supreme Government calls seditious journalism.

There are two departments in which the Central Provinces have made greater progress under the rule of Mr. Morris than during the successive administrations of his predecessors—the Departments of Police and Public Works, including under this head the long-continued surveys of the mineral resources in which the province is believed to be so rich. Dacoity, or gang-robbery, is now well-nigh extinct. Another sign of improvement is the great increase in the number of lawsuits. It is no doubt the fashion to stigmatise litigation as the curse of India generally; but it is forgotten that the assertion of personal rights at law was well nigh impossible during the anarchic times of native dynasties. In this view the character of our fellow-subjects for litigiousness is only a mark of advancing civilisation, and the rapidly progressive rate at which original suits are filed in the one hundred and thirty lower courts of the Central Provinces shows the extent to which the reign of law has superseded that of brute force. In the Central Provinces, which perhaps comprise a greater diversity of races—from barbarous hill tribes to the most polished high-caste Brahmins—than any other Government in India, order has, within the last few years, been firmly established. In his railway enterprises even the English public are, in a measure, directly interested. The Eastern portion of Mr. Morris's dominions is perhaps the naturally richest grain country in India; and India, it appears, is destined to become one of the chief markets whence this country will draw its supplies of wheat. But between that Eastern portion—viz., Chattisgurh—and the rest of the world no railway, and hardly any road, communication exists as yet. The result is that the grain is over-stocked where it grows—selling for a fifth or sixth of the prices realised a hundred and twenty or fifty miles off, where adequate means of transport are available. The want of conveyance was sorely felt during the Bahar famine of 1874, and the recent famines in Madras and Bombay. Hence the persistency with which for many years Mr. Morris has been urging his railway extension projects upon the

Government. It is satisfactory to learn that one hundred and twenty miles of the line from Nagpore, eastwards, have been mapped, surveyed, and finally arranged for. When the line is complete the grain country will be brought into direct communication with the Western Coast.

Mr. Morris has always manifested a kindly personal interest in the feudatory chiefs, of whom there are fifteen in the Central Provinces. The most favourably known among them, viz., Udit Pertab Deo, accompanied the Chief Commissioner to the Imperial Durbar at Delhi; and it is to be hoped that he may have found in the title of a Rajah Bahadur and his elevation to a salute of nine guns, some consolation for the chronic rheumatism that afflicts his old age. It is almost needless to add that the results of a direct administration of feudatory estates have been as gratifying in the Central Provinces as they invariably have been elsewhere. The chiefships over which Mr. Morris assumed control three or four years ago already show surplus revenues in place of deficits, and it would be a fortunate thing for at least eight more of them if they were forthwith subjected to a like course of supervision. In brief, Mr. Morris is one of the best specimens extant in India of a round man in a round hole. In its geographical position, and its unsurpassed natural advantages for agricultural, mining, manufacturing, and commercial enterprise, the Nagpore territory possesses the guarantee of a great and prosperous future; and in devoting his energies to her material development, the Chief Commissioner may establish a reputation as durable as any which the majority of his contemporaries are likely to secure for themselves. It says much for a man of Mr. Morris's position and endowments that no one is jealous of him. Had he succeeded Sir John Strachey in the Lieutenant-Governorship of the North-West, his brother civilians, as well as the English population generally, would have unanimously recognised the appropriateness of the selection. But such an appointment would have entailed upon the Central Provinces a loss which they could very ill sustain, and which it would be extremely difficult to make good.

XXXI.

LORD NAPIER AND ETTRICK, K.T.

The question is often asked, what is the use of the subordinate Indian Governments? And generally the questioner, like jesting Pilate, does not wait for a reply. Yet a reply is not difficult. A very good case might be made out, and often indeed is made out, for the existing administrative machinery at Madras and Bombay. But if the question assumed another shape, and the inquiry were directed to the practical value of particular governors who have adorned the Madras and Bombay Presidencies, a response would be less easy. The truth is that a minor Indian governorship is pretty much what the holder likes to make it. For a competent man it is a field for most important and beneficent activity. An incompetent man may comport himself either as King Log or King Stork, according as his incompetence takes the form of lethargy or fussiness. In the one case his authority will fall into the hands of his colleagues in council and his secretaries; in the other, those officials will be engaged perpetually in preventing or remedying his blunders. In both cases the practical result will be, so far as he is concerned, to a great extent to efface him.

If one wished to point to a typical instance of a successful Indian governor, it would be necessary to go back a great many years for a better one than Lord Napier and Ettrick. Obtaining his government in the very prime of life, Lord Napier took with him to India large and varied experience gathered in well-nigh every great centre of diplomacy. The scion of a distinguished family, the Scotch Napiers of Merchistoun, one of whose progenitors fell at Flodden, whose motto is "Ready, aye, Ready," he can trace his lineage back to the reign of Edward III. The house is not only an ancient one; its representatives have rendered eminent service to their country and their Sovereigns for many generations past, and intellectual power has been its heirloom and tradition. It was a Napier of Merchistoun who invented logarithms, and it was the son of the great mathematician who was raised from the judicial bench to the Peerage. In more recent times the Napiers have been among the brightest ornaments of the British army and navy. Conspicuous beyond others of his family, or his era, in Indian history, is Sir Charles James Napier, G.C.B., the "bearded vision that swept over" and conquered Scinde, who was afterwards Commander-in-Chief in India, the sturdy antagonist of Dalhousie and Hogg. The two brothers of this distinguished man were General Sir George Thomas Napier, K.C.B., formerly Governor and Commander-in-Chief at the Cape, and General Sir William Francis Patrick Napier, K.C.B., the historian of the Peninsular War. Another branch of the family numbered among its representatives the late Admiral Sir Charles Napier, G.C.B., who commanded the British fleet in the Baltic during the last Russian war; while Sir Robert John Milliken Napier, Bart., represents the male branch of the family after the title had descended in the female line. Among its living representatives in the army at the present day may be mentioned William Craig Emilius Napier, Colonel of the 3rd Foot, and Governor of the Royal Military College at Sandhurst, the youngest and only surviving son of the late General Sir George Thomas Napier, K.C.B.

The memory of the achievements of his ancestors, and the consciousness of the family prestige, may well have acted as incentives to great exertions with Lord Napier and Ettrick. Entering the diplomatic service at the age of twenty-one, he was first attached to the English Embassy at Vienna, and the Austrian Court has not to this day forgotten the handsome and accomplished young nobleman, whose tranquil and polished manners and customs were an agreeable contrast to those of not a few of his colleagues. He was next appointed to the Teheran Mission, but did not actually join, and when he was four-and-twenty found himself at Constantinople, which under Sir Stratford de Redcliffe, who as the Great Eltchi then dominated the Sultan, was the best school of diplomacy in the world. Sir Stratford, though a mighty diplomatist, was not altogether a popular chief with his staff, and Lord Napier was one of the very few *attachés* who contrived to get on comfortably with him. Promotion was in store for the young Scotch nobleman. He was regarded favourably by the Palmerstons and Clarendons, and at a single bound leapt from the Secretary of the Embassy at Constantinople to that of Envoy Extraordinary at Washington. The position, however, did not suit him, and American society he found exceedingly uncongenial. He was next installed in the English Legation at the Hague, and then, four years after the conclusion of the Crimean War, he was transferred as ambassador to St. Petersburg, and in 1864 to Berlin. Thus, no English Statesman, it may safely be said, ever proceeded to India who could boast so thorough and extensive a training in European diplomacy. On the resignation of Sir William Denison, Lord Napier was selected to succeed him as Governor of Madras, which office he held for the usual six years, and afterwards, on the assassination of Lord Mayo, acted as Viceroy at Calcutta from February 24th till May 3rd, when he was relieved by Lord Northbrook, his place at Madras being taken by the late Lord Hobart.

Possessing an inquiring mind, and great power of work, wide intellectual culture and dignified manners, a gift of ready and courteous speech, and much natural tact, the several sections of the public service soon felt the presence of a chief whose *suaviter in modo* by no means excluded the *fortiter in re.* In the Revenue, the Public Works, and the Educational Departments of the Government Lord Napier was equally at home, nor would it be easy to overstate the advantage which resulted from his statesmanlike way of dealing with the questions which came before him. Again, he made a point of seeing things, as far as possible, with his own eyes, and not merely through the spectacles of official reports. No Indian governor since the time of Sir Thomas Munro has more assiduously visited the provinces under his rule, nor has any Indian governor of late years more completely won the suffrages of native public opinion. It is just this personal influence of a directing mind which is the prime safeguard of Indian administration. In no other way can the tendency to inveterate officialism, to redtapeism, and all circumlocution, inherent to the bureaucratic system, be so effectually checked.

It is much to be regretted that Lord Napier, since his return to England, has not published some abiding record of his Indian experiences. So close and practised an observer can hardly have failed to note much well worthy of being made publicly known, and to have formed views of his own on problems of Indian policy, with which it would be most interesting and important to have a further acquaintance than that supplied by an occasional letter to the *Times* on frontier policy. Competent critics who have had an opportunity of perusing some of his official papers, speak of them as showing gifts of a high order, both political and literary. That Lord Napier is an author as well as an art critic of no mean power is indeed well known to his friends, and is sufficiently proved to the general public from the book on "Modern Art," which he wrote when he was Secretary of Legation at Naples.

Since he left India, Lord Napier has been far from idle. One of his first appearances in public after his return was to preside over the Social Science Congress in 1872, and in the elaborate inaugural address which he delivered, he certainly displayed the courage of his opinions—opinions by no means palatable, it may be remembered, to many of his political friends. But the chief sphere of his activity has been the London School Board, and we believe it is pretty generally recognised that the great measure of success which has attended the operations of that very important body is due to no insignificant extent to the energy and assiduity with which Lord Napier worked while a member of it. He is well known, too, as a warm advocate of metropolitan municipal reform, and from time to time has spoken in the House of Lords upon various Indian and diplomatic questions—notably two years ago on the Imperial Titles Bill, which he warmly advocated—with the authority which attaches to his long and varied experiences. A few years ago it was asserted that he was again to be employed as an Ambassador, Constantinople being confidently mentioned as the sphere to be assigned to him; and upon a more recent occasion the rumour was revived. It turned out, however, to be incorrect, and Lord Napier and Ettrick still remains out of employ, enjoying a pension of £1,700 a year—certainly a very moderate award after nearly forty years spent in the public service. But it can hardly be supposed that further employment will not be offered to him. It may be that Lord Napier lacks something of the self-assertion which seems necessary for high political advancement. When, in 1876, it was suggested in several quarters that he would be the most fitting successor of Sir Henry Elliot at the Porte, Lord Napier withdrew altogether from the House of Lords, as if anxious not to remind the world by his presence in Parliament of the fact of his existence. His present mode of life is singularly tranquil and secluded, but there is not such a plethora of ability and experience available for our embassies or our governorships that Lord Napier can well be suffered to shelve himself in perpetuity.

XXXII.

LORD NAPIER OF MAGDALA, G.C.B., G.C.S.I.

The whirligig of time, which brings its revenges, redresses often the balance, when fortune has gone against a man in his early days. To those who have been denied ample opportunities in youth, and who might appear doomed, therefore, to mediocrity and obscurity in middle age, fame comes before the curtain falls with both hands full. Sir Charles Napier was an old man when he won his first battle; Sir Henry Havelock had been simply a regimental officer but a few years before he took honours as a victorious general. Thus also Robert Cornelis Napier, the younger son of an artillery major, born at Ceylon in the first decade of the present century, educated at the old East India Company's Military College at Addiscombe, seemed likely, when he entered the Bengal Engineers, to have nothing before him but a long vista of uneventful years, years busily and usefully spent, perhaps, but unillumined by the rays of that military glory which forms the true soldier's fondest and most constant dream. The duties which fell upon the young lieutenant were onerous and responsible, of course. An engineer officer has increasingly wide functions in the great field of Indian employment. He is called upon often to direct gigantic operations, to administer and govern provinces, to initiate and control vast public works. But his chances of active service, of a share in the great and stirring game of war, are often seriously restricted and curtailed. So it was that Napier, still only a captain, had served some twenty years before he saw a single shot fired. It had been a period of comparative tranquillity; the Indian Government had steered clear of complications which could be settled only with the sword, and it was not till the Sikh wars broke out that the avenue to military distinction was opened to men of Napier's stamp. But from henceforth, with one interval only of peaceful inactivity, Robert Napier was destined to take an important share in nearly all the military operations in which the Indian forces were to be engaged. He made his *début* in real war at the battles of Moodkhee and Ferozeshah, and was in the thick of both fights, was wounded, had horses killed under him, and was everywhere conspicuous for gallantry, intrepidity, and sound professional skill. He was in the advance upon Lahore at the close of the Sutlej campaign, was engineer in charge of the siege operations against the Kangre Fort; later, in the Punjaub he was for a time Engineer-in-chief before Mooltan, at the assault of which he was again severely wounded, but had recovered in time to be present at the battle of Goojerat and the subsequent pursuit of the Sikhs. These sanguinary struggles satisfactorily concluded, Napier, now a brevet lieutenant-colonel, lapsed once more into civil employment, acting now as pro-consul, surveying, reporting, minuting, and ruling great slices of the newly conquered districts. During this period he was seldom actively engaged in the business of a soldier, except when the turbulence of half-tamed frontier tribes needed chastisement and coercion; and Colonel Napier then kept his hand in at fighting by joining such expeditions as that against the Huzzunzie tribe in Hazara, or against those warlike Afreedees who remain insurgent and unquelled to this hour.

Then came the epoch of the Crimean war, a season full of pardonable jealousy for all those able and ambitious Indian soldiers who, by the very nature of the contest, were debarred from taking part in it, and who may be excused if they envied the opportunities afforded their comrades in the service of the Queen. Few but a small band of alarmists, or of men gifted with unusual prescience, would have been disposed to admit that within a couple of years of the fall of Sebastopol India would itself be in danger, that Indian officers would have their hands full of work, that military problems of extreme difficulty would arise, calling for prompt and energetic solution, that prizes and rewards would fall upon the successful to an extent equal to any the Crimean soldiers received. Colonel Napier's time came with the Indian Mutiny. He was actually in England on furlough when it broke out, but he was among the first to hasten back and lend a hand in the great task of preserving the land of his adoption to the British Crown. Of all those who returned then to India, burning with impatience, thirsting for revenge, resolutely determined to fight it out to the last gasp, there was none who, under a quiet, unassuming aspect, was stirred with greater enthusiasm, or nerved with a braver spirit, than this little Colonel of Engineers. Small in stature, of modest and retiring demeanour, who spoke always with incisive shrewdness, but never much, only those intimately acquainted with Colonel Napier's high qualities and intrinsic merit would have diagnosed from his external man the character of a dashing and successful military leader. But Outram knew him well, and directly he landed offered him the post of chief of the staff to the force which was on the point of starting to reinforce Havelock and assist in the relief of Lucknow. History has already done justice to the chivalry with which Sir James Outram declined, although senior officer, to supersede Havelock in the chief command, nobly urging that as Havelock had had all the toil he should also have the triumph of the actual relief; but Outram's abstention naturally kept his staff also in the background, and Napier was in no position of prominence until the Residency was actually entered, was again surrounded, and a second time besieged. Within the walls, however, there was great scope for his scientific knowledge as an Engineer officer, many demands upon his professional skill. He was engaged repeatedly upon independent operations, in sorties, such as that which led to the capture of Phillip's "Garden Battery," or in the rescue of the siege train guns which had been surrounded and cut off in the suburbs; and in all, by his skilful dispositions, his unerring judgment, and his ready adaptation of circumstances to the occasion, success was invariably, completely, and cheaply obtained. It was his misfortune to be once more severely wounded, but he was not long incapacitated from performing his duties, and he was soon in the forefront again, now as chief of the staff after the second relief, yet again as commanding engineer at the siege and capture of Lucknow. Thoroughly valued and appreciated now by all, Brigadier Napier was next intrusted with a purely military command, a privilege which prejudice has perhaps too studiously refused to men of his branch of the service. Napier's bearing and behaviour soon proved that an Engineer officer of the right stuff can handle troops easily and successfully if he only gets the chance. In the operations of the Central Indian Field Force, Napier commanded a division, and contributed in no small degree to the ultimate suppression of the revolt. That his special attainments and training should fit him pre-eminently to give substantial aid at the reduction of Gwalior, or in the recovery of the fort of Powrie when it fell into rebel hands, was natural enough. What there was less reason to expect from Napier were the dashing exploits of a *beau sabreur*, the headlong and impetuous energy of the brilliant leader of light horse. But in their way his feats in the pursuit and overthrow of Tantia Topee, and his chase of the rebel Feroze Shah may be classed with the best partisan enterprises; with the lightning raids of the American cavalry in the great Civil War, or even with the Russian General

Gourko's splendid performances in the last war in the East. With only one squadron of Hussars and a handful of infantry mounted on camels, he hunted Feroze Shah for five days almost without intermission, halting only after thirteen or fourteen hours in the saddle, and from sheer exhaustion, then on again and on lest the scent by delaying should grow cold. The affair against Tantia Topee was on a larger scale, the pursuit had lasted longer, the final victory was more decisive in its results. Here Napier commanded a small column of horse artillery and light cavalry, in all only six hundred strong, but manœuvred it with such masterly skill that he routed four thousand rebels, killed hundreds, captured elephants, baggage, tents, guns, and dissipated the whole force. Created for his services upon this occasion a K.C.B., Sir Robert Napier's greatness now "full surely was a-ripening." When in the following year it became imperative to send an expedition to bring the Chinese to account, Sir Robert Napier was selected as obviously the fittest man to be second in command to Sir Hope Grant. His position was nominally that of a subordinate divisional general, but it has now come to be generally understood that he was a leading spirit in the conduct of the war, and deep in the counsels of the General-in-chief. Fresh honours very properly fell to his share at the end of the campaign, honours which culminated later in his appointment as Commander-in-chief at Bombay, a distinction which had before been granted to a "Company's" officer. Fortune still smiled on him while thus employed, and brought him a new opportunity for winning military renown. The details and incidents of the Abyssinian Expedition are perhaps too fresh in men's minds to need more than a passing reference here. They are chiefly interesting as illustrative of the character of the general in chief command. The physical difficulties of the march to Magdala were at first sight well-nigh insuperable, while the liberality of the Government, which was prepared, as it seemed, to pay any price to insure success, placed at the disposal of the head of the enterprise appliances, plant, machinery, tube wells, steam-engines, stores, and supplies in such lavish profusion, that a soldier less scientific and with a less practised head, might well have been thrown off his balance, bewildered by the means at his disposal no less than by the obstacles in his path. If the actual fighting with Theodore's troops was infinitesimal, the pains taken to put the army before Magdala in fighting trim were colossal, and proved that Sir Robert Napier added to those qualities of good generalship he had already displayed much patience, great breadth of view, and sound administrative skill.

Although advancing in years, it would be a grave error to call Lord Napier one of the "has beens" as yet. Those who have seen him in his present post as Governor of our great Mediterranean fortress, must admit that he gives full proof of a hale and hearty old age. Active and energetic as of old, he clings still to Indian habits, is up every morning with the lark, spends daily many consecutive hours in the saddle, and will ride as straight to hounds as any reckless subaltern on the Rock. His clear intellect and well-stored mind still serve him ably in the discussion and settlement of grave military problems. There is as yet no abatement of that painstaking minuteness with which he treats every subject. That his value is fully appreciated by the ruling powers was shown last spring, when war seemed imminent. As soon as the Government had actually decided, under certain contingencies, to take the field, Lord Napier was recalled from Gibraltar for the express purpose of assuming command of the expeditionary force. He has remained in England for several months, acting as trusted adviser on all the serious points recently at issue, and although he has just returned to the Rock, to continue a government marked already by much administrative reform and common sense, it is understood that he remains there at single anchor, and at any moment of emergency within the next few years he will be again intrusted with the functions of supreme command.

XXXIII.

THE EARL OF NORTHBROOK.

SOMEWHERE about the middle of the last century a young German arrived in this country from Bremen with a resolute determination to make his way. He was led by fate to Exeter, and at Exeter he was smiled upon by fortune. He went into the wool trade, at that time a thriving department of industry and commerce in the West of England, was first clerk, then partner, and ended by finding himself head of a highly prosperous concern. Having succeeded as a merchant, he enjoyed the leisure of a country gentleman. He invested in a house and some land at Larkbear, a suburb of Exeter, and when he passed away left behind him two sons. The elder remained at Exeter, the younger resolved to perpetuate the adventurous spirit of his sire, and to try his luck in London. He was not unrewarded for his enterprise, of which, indeed, the monument remains to this day; for he laid the foundation of the great house of Baring, which in its new home in London was destined completely to eclipse the glories of its original dwelling-place at Exeter. Francis Baring achieved other than purely commercial successes. He was elected a member of the Court of Indian Directors. He went into Parliament. He became a personage in the House of Commons. Like his father he sighed for a Tusculum. The opportunity offered, and he bought the property of Stratton, in Hampshire, which happened to come into the market, and which in the fulness of time went to his son, the representative of the third generation of the English or Anglicised Barings. He also engaged in political life, and acquired, in one way or another, considerable experience of our Indian dominions. The head of the family in the fourth generation surpassed the distinction of his predecessors. He was successively a Lord of the Treasury, Secretary to the Treasury, Chancellor of the Exchequer in Lord Melbourne's Government—succeeding in that post Mr. Spring Rice—First Lord of the Admiralty, was created a baronet, and was promoted to the peerage. His wife was a daughter of Sir George Grey, and his son by the marriage was the future Viceroy of India. Never had any foreign settlers in England enjoyed so rapid a rise. In the course of less than a century, the descendants of a Teutonic soldier of fortune had advanced to the front rank in the life of their adopted country, and in little more than a century one of them had filled the highest post which an English subject can hold.

As a boy the destined Viceroy of her Majesty's Indian Empire, gave no pronounced promise of future greatness. He was a bright amusing lad, fond of field sports, fond of fun, fond of the open air, and perfectly contented to speak no language except his own. He was not idle at school; he was fairly industrious at Oxford. But his prevailing tendency was a disposition to take life easily. It became a question what to do with him, and an offer from a friend of the family, Mr. Labouchere, at that time (1846) President of the Board of Trade, to take him as his private secretary arrived opportunely. Mr. Baring set to work with a will, and acquired the reputation of a trustworthy and capable official, who knew well how to combine social pleasures with routine duties. Eminently circumspect in his demeanour, he had a keen capacity for enjoyment, and he did not seek to control it within any very austere bounds. For the next ten years he continued to lead much the same life, doing well all which came to his hands to do, but not displaying the signs of great intellectual calibre. After leaving Mr. Labouchere, he served as Private Secretary to Sir George Grey, at the Home Office, and Sir Charles Wood, at the India Board. Gradually the spectacle of ability and application that in the persons of his successive chiefs he saw before him made an impression on his mind, and Mr. Baring was seized with a desire to distinguish himself. He went into Parliament as member for Falmouth. He received the first and conventional instalment of political promotion in his appointment to a lay lordship of the Admiralty. He was transferred to the India Office, and at the India Office he appeared in a new light which astonished his friends. "I begin," said his father about this period to a visitor at Stratton, "I begin really to think we shall make something of Tom. I once thought he would never be anything more than a good whip. But now I see no reason why he should not develop into a Cabinet Minister." Mr. Baring left nothing undone which could merit this opinion. His entire existence was devoted to his office. Never had an Indian Under-Secretary with such an insatiable appetite for work been known. As a rule, the Parliamentary Under-Secretary does nothing more than represent, more or less imperfectly, Indian interests in the House of Commons. But Mr. Baring insisted on personally performing a multitude of purely official duties. He made himself a master of administrative details. He descended to such particulars as to give instructions to the clerks on the subject of the copying of letters and the arrangement of documents. His influence upon the internal and technical business of the India Office survives visibly to this day.

He was still an Under-Secretary of State—this time at the War Office—when the news of Lord Mayo's assassination arrived. He had gone to the War Office when Mr. Gladstone came into place and power, as Mr. Cardwell's subordinate, not indeed with satisfaction, but with resigned equanimity and a determination to make the best of it. He was a peer, and inasmuch as the number of peers who are possible in the Cabinet is strictly limited, he was heavily weighted in the race for high political promotion. But such good work as Lord Northbrook did at the War Office was quite sure to meet with recognition and reward. The times were exacting, and Lord Northbrook rose to their level. He had just won for himself by the speech in which he introduced the Abolition of Purchase Bill, and the manner in which he subsequently defended the measure, the highest praise of his colleagues, when the lamentable death of Lord Mayo occasioned a vacancy in the Viceroyship of India. The names of three peers came before the Cabinet as those of possible successors to Lord Mayo—Lord Dufferin, Lord Bury, and Lord Northbrook. If it seems surprising that the area of selection in the case of a post so envied and brilliant should be limited, it must be remembered that in the nature of things it is not easy to secure as Governor-General of India an English statesman who is also an English noble, and who would be admitted by universal consent to be in the first rank of English statesmen. A Cabinet Minister would hesitate to accept it. Family ties and domestic considerations may prevent others from undertaking the splendid responsibilities of the position. It was offered to Lord Northbrook, and with the offer he at once closed. India could scarcely have hoped to secure a better man. Of many of the qualities which he displayed in his Indian career it is impossible to speak too highly. His industry was unflagging. He set no limit to his personal exertions. He had no favourites, he was under the influence of no coteries. He went everywhere himself, saw everything for himself, and himself judged everything. There are disadvantages as well as advantages incidental to the administration of a Viceroy, who possesses this capacity for work, and who exercises it so indefatigably. As a rule, the opinion of the Governor of India on matters of high policy is merely the opinion of secretaries of departments. It was certainly a distinct gain to have a statesman at the head of affairs who delegated nothing to secretaries of departments, and who never failed to animate and dictate the official utterance. On the other hand, a Viceroy who devotes so much time and thought to details is necessarily prevented from giving adequate consideration to questions of supreme importance, and, it may be, from indicating or developing such a policy as the circumstances of the time require.

Lord Northbrook's administration of India was respectable rather than brilliant. Arriving in India shortly after there had been an immense expenditure on public works, an expenditure against which Sir Charles Wood, his chief mentor and guide in public life, emphatically protested, Lord Northbrook aimed, above all things, at giving the much-burdened people of India an interval of rest. He abolished the income-tax, and thus, when the time of pressure came, as come it did, he was precluded by the lines and spirit of his own policy from imposing fresh taxes. The famine of 1873 arrived, and although it passed off without any loss of life, it sounded the death-knell of Lord Northbrook's Indian career. Nothing can have been more admirable than the courage and devotion displayed by Lord Northbrook throughout the whole of this trial. For eighteen months, from the winter of 1873 to the spring of 1875, he stayed at Calcutta. But no self-sacrifice, however unsparing, or singleness of purpose, however heroic, could convert a deficit into a surplus. The financial consequences of the famine were the prelude of Lord Northbrook's retirement. When the Tariff reforms for 1875 were brought in, the Cotton duties had no place in the list. Lord Salisbury's disappointment at the omission was extreme. The Secretary of State had given his Lancashire clients a pledge that their grievance should be dealt with. Of this circumstances did not admit, and hence there arose a slight disturbance in the harmony of the relations between Lord Salisbury and Lord Northbrook. Had it not been for the fatal obstacle which the famine placed in the way of his plans, Lord Northbrook's financial policy would have been a success. As it was, he succeeded in reducing the military expenditure, and paving the way for several fiscal reforms. His foreign policy may be described as one of adherence to the principle of masterly inaction laid down by Lord Lawrence, and is certainly in direct antagonism to that of Lord Lytton. That Lord Northbrook is somewhat deficient in flexibility and originality may be admitted. That he is pre-eminently adapted for the administration of a policy whose principles are fixed cannot be denied. He is not the man to reorganize an Empire in a period of storm or stress; but of a good system in times of peace no better or more practical exponent could be found.

XXXIV.

LIEUT.-GEN. SIR HENRY NORMAN, K.C.B.

After an active career of thirty years' duration, signalised by many public services, alike in peace and in war, Sir Henry Norman has taken his place in the Council of the Secretary of State for India. His claims to the appointment were of a character that could not be ignored, while his singularly varied experience, his practical knowledge, his marvellous command of the details of Indian military administration, will bring an element that was much wanted to the deliberations of Lord Salisbury and his advisers. Sir Henry Norman has shown that he possesses not only the eye for rapid combinations, which is one of the distinctive attributes of the soldier, but a certain capacity for the gradual and laborious development of ideas which is by no means always found in the military mind. Endowed with a memory so minutely tenacious that in his younger days the contents of the *Army List* once mastered, reference to it for the future was superfluous, he has always possessed the power not only of accumulating facts, but of arranging in the order of their relative importance the results of his observation or study. Sir Henry Norman, therefore, goes to the India Office as one who has had almost unexampled opportunity of watching the practical aspect of the questions now especially prominent in Indian administration, and as one who carries about him ever ready for immediate use the rich storehouse of valuable facts acquired in the course of his eventful life. The more closely the Secretary of State and his councillors identify themselves with Indian opinion and experience, the more completely they look at administrative details through Anglo-Indian spectacles, the greater the guarantee for a working unanimity between Calcutta and the Indian Office. Independently, therefore, of his own eminent personal qualifications, the new member of Council is the representative of a class, the presence of whose representatives at Lord Salisbury's board is matter of congratulation in the interests of our Indian Empire.

The story of Sir Henry Norman's official life is the story of not a few of the most momentous passages in the annals of British India during the last three decades. Thirty-four years ago he was nominated to a cadetship in the Bengal military establishment, and on Christmas Day, 1847, he was promoted to the rank of lieutenant in the 31st Regiment of Bengal Native Infantry. Stirring scenes and great events awaited the young officer. The Maharanee had pitted herself against the British Government at Candahar, Cabul, Cashmere, and Rajpootana, and the long train of causes to which the second Sikh war must be attributed was already in motion. The atmosphere of the whole Punjaub was tainted with the spirit of mutiny.

The revolt of Sultan Mohammed Khan was followed by the defection of Shere Sing, and on the 10th of October, 1848, Lord Dalhousie having instructed Lord Gough to assemble an army at Ferozepore, set out for the scene of operations. "Unwarned by precedent," said Lord Dalhousie, at a banquet given to him at Barrackpore, before his departure, "uninfluenced by example, the Sikh nation has called for war, and on my word, Sir, they shall have it with a vengeance." It was no idle vaunt, and in the several engagements, commencing with the passage of the Chenab, which followed, young Norman, who was adjutant of his regiment, won his spurs. The conflict at Sadoolapore was rather a series of demonstrations and an artillery duel than a battle. Shere Sing retired in perfect order, and six weeks elapsed before the two armies met each other on the bloody and indecisive field of Chillianwallah. After this the Sikhs made a retrograde movement towards the Chenab by the Goojerat route, and, anxious to retrieve the results of the more than equivocal victory at Chillianwallah, Lord Gough gave the enemy battle at Goojerat. Here the duty of storming the key of the Sikh position fell to the brigade to which Lieutenant Norman's regiment belonged—a desperate service in which the losses of his corps amounted to more than 140 men killed and wounded. Decisive as was the triumph of the British troops at Goojerat, their labours were not yet over. The arduous toils of a long and splendid pursuit commenced. There were forced marches and desperate fatigues. But the 31st Bengal

Infantry bore up admirably; and Lieutenant Norman brought to the professional ambition of the soldier the spirits of youth and the endurance of a splendid constitution. At the Manikyala Monument, the traditional trophy of Alexander the Great, some of the Sikh army surrendered, and at Rawul Pindee the remainder, in all 16,000 men with 41 guns, laid down their arms, and their leaders, Sirdars Shere Sing and Chuttur Sing, gave up their swords. A few days later the Afghans were driven beyond the Khyber Pass. This more than avenged the losses of Chillianwallah. All the guns captured there by the enemy were recovered, the Punjaub was annexed, and Lord Dalhousie informed the Lahore Council of Regency that the Sikh dominion was at an end.

The campaign which thus terminated in an immense increase of our Indian dominion provided young Norman with something more than the opportunity of military display. Its experiences gave him an insight into the defects and excellencies of the troops of the Native States of India, which he has since turned to admirable account. He then learned to appreciate at their real worth the admirable qualities of the men and the innate incapacity of their chiefs. He saw soldiers whom, in the presence of competent commanders, no dangers or difficulties would daunt. But the commanders were not competent. They were fond of pleasure and luxury; they were distracted amongst themselves by jealousies which they had not the tact to conceal. Such professional sentiments are not, indeed, peculiar to Asiatic officers, but when they exist among European officers they are at least decently veiled, and, except in very rare instances, are not allowed to make themselves felt. But the fixed principle of promotion, whose recognition is so powerful in European armies, is unknown in armies officered by Asiatics, and hence the door is open to every sort of underhand influence and intrigue. Sir Henry Norman has had many opportunities of seeing Indian warfare in its various phases—opportunities forthcoming not only in his first campaign against the Sikhs, which came to a triumphant end under Sir Walter Gilbert, but during his subsequent residence at Peshawur. Here he remained for six years, and with the name of Peshawur the name of Sir Henry Norman will ever be intimately associated. It was from Peshawur that he proceeded as an officer in the force ordered to move against the Afreedees in the Kohat Pass, partly for the purpose of striking awe into the insurgent tribes, partly for the sake of exacting specific vengeance for the murder of some English sappers. The expedition brought fresh laurels to young Norman. He was not only formally thanked by the chief, Sir Charles Napier, but he was made—a distinction very rare in the case of so young an officer—Brigade Major, and on several subsequent expeditions against mountain tribes occupied the position of principal staff officer. In 1855 he served as Assistant Adjutant-General at the first camp of exercise ever formed in India, at Umballah, and a little later, rejoining his regiment, took the field against Sonthal; was for four months in command of a separate detachment, and was thanked by the Commander-in-chief in India for surprising and capturing a rebel chief. The third period in Sir Henry Norman's career commences with the outbreak of the Indian Mutiny, and includes such achievements and experiences as the capture of Delhi, the operations of Greathed's force, the relief and capture of Lucknow, in the course of which, as well as in the campaigns in Oude and Rohilkund, he gained signal distinction. For the part he took in the suppression of the Mutiny he received a medal and three clasps, was created a Companion of the Bath, and was awarded, when he became a Captain in 1860, the brevets of Major and Lieutenant-Colonel; he was twenty-five times thanked in general orders and dispatches for his services in the field. When the black mutiny was quelled, and the white mutiny broke out—the European troops at fifty stations striking, not so much from any innate sentiment of disloyalty as annoyance at the manner in which the transfer was made from the Company to the Crown—Sir Henry Norman occupied the difficult post of Adjutant-General. It is scarcely surprising that after all this, in 1860, he should have been compelled to return home on sick leave. But even during his compulsory furlough he did not permit himself to remain idle. He did good work as Assistant Military Secretary for Indian Affairs at the Horse Guards, and in 1863 was made one of Her Majesty's aides-de-camp. On his return to India he was appointed Deputy Adjutant-General, and was subsequently Military Secretary of the Indian Government under Lord Canning. In 1870 he was elected military member of the Viceroy's Council

—a position that he held till last year, and in this period he was twice President of the Council. Then Sir Henry Norman began to think of setting his face homewards. He did not, however, choose the direct route, and travelled to England by way of China, Japan, and America.

The value of Sir Henry Norman's nomination to the Indian Council is not exclusively to be estimated by his military experiences. He has had, it must be remembered, much to do with the creation of the present Staff Corps system, and there are certain points in connection with this which must inevitably, ere long, come before the consideration of the Secretary of State for India and his colleagues. Further, at a time when any sudden change in the ever mutable face of European politics may compel us to rely for reinforcements on our native Indian troops, Sir Henry Norman, who, duly appreciating the great aptitudes and abilities of a race of born soldiers, recognises in them an inexhaustible recruiting ground, will be able to give most valuable counsel. There are reasons over and above his professional attainments which will cause much satisfaction at Sir Henry Norman's promotion. The amiability of his character and his countless acts of charity have added a lustre of their own to his achievements as a soldier—qualities which confirm his claim to be considered one of those representative men by whose goodness as well as greatness our Indian Empire has been built up.

XXXV.

SIR BARNES PEACOCK.

The form of East lives in the marble of Chantrey; the brushes of Zoffany and George Chinnery have respectively preserved for the citizens of Calcutta the features of Impey and of Russell. These and other works of art are found on the staircase and in the apartments of the High Court, but there is no representation of Peacock. And yet, probably, in the long list of chiefs of the old Supreme Court, which, commencing with Sir Elijah Impey, terminated with himself, there is not one name more distinguished for legal acumen and for accurate and extensive learning than that of Sir Barnes Peacock. He can dispense with marble and with canvas, for he has left a lasting memorial of his abilities in his elaboration of the codes and in the large body of decisions which still command the reverence of Bench and Bar in India. It was with unfeigned astonishment that in 1852 the legal profession learnt that Mr. Peacock, Q.C., of the Home Circuit, was about to give up all his excellent prospects and proceed as Law Member of Council to India. Macaulay, taking up the same appointment nearly twenty years previously, had said, "I know well how dangerous it is for a public man wholly to withdraw himself from the public eye," and Jeffrey had designated the news of his proposed departure as "a solemn and melancholy announcement." The step might be considered as probably more suicidal to a rising barrister than even to a politician. Mr. Peacock had been called to the Bar at the Inner Temple in 1836, and had received his silk gown in 1850. It was understood that his acute mind had detected the legal flaw which opened the prison doors to O'Connell and his friends—the Traversers—and changed a penalty into a triumph through the streets of Dublin. He was a recognised leader of the Bar, and at the age of forty-two might reasonably be expecting the prizes of his profession to soon come within the reach of his grasp. His practice was most lucrative, and he had not therefore the excuse of Macaulay, to whom means were of paramount importance. However, Mr. Peacock went to India, and if, as was asserted at the time, the state of his health was the cause, he apparently found in a tropical climate complete immunity from threatened pulmonary disease.

The arrival of Mr. Peacock in the East was nearly contemporary with a great change in the character of his appointment, and in the constitution of the Legislative Council. The legal member was made also a member in the executive branch. Previously, he had had no power to sit and vote in the Executive Council, except when meetings were held for the purpose of making laws and regulations. The Legislative Council was increased; the Chief Justice of Bengal and one of the puisne judges of the Supreme Court selected by the Governor-General, were added to its members. The Governor of each Presidency and the Lieutenant-Governors were empowered to appoint a representative councillor. "Consequent upon these changes, discussion became oral instead of in writing; bills were referred to select committees instead of a single member; and legislative business was conducted in public instead of in secret." When Mr. Peacock's term as Member of Council was up, he was offered and accepted the chief justiceship; but as under the Act of 1853 the Chief Justice was a member of the Legislative Council, the connection of Mr. Peacock (at that time created Sir Barnes) with law-making lasted from 1852 to 1861, when the Indian Councils Act deprived him of his seat. Although the number of Acts passed during that series of years seems small when compared with the fertility of the Maine and Stephen periods, still some were of paramount importance, and had been long in preparation. The hand of Sir Barnes was visible in several, notably in the Civil Procedure Act; but it is chiefly in connection with the Penal Code that his name will be remembered. Lord Macaulay's fame as an essayist and historian has obscured with splendour his reputation as a theoretical lawyer, and so little interest was taken a short time ago in the Code, whose draft is entirely due to him, that Miss Martineau could with impunity pronounce it, in a public journal, a complete failure. But nothing could be further from the truth. Sir Fitzjames Stephen has said, "The Penal Code was a draft when Lord Macaulay left India in 1838. His successors made remarks on it for twenty-two years. . . . . It was enacted in 1860, and came into operation on the 1st of January, 1862. The credit of passing the Penal Code into law, and of giving to every part of it the improvements which practical skill and technical knowledge could bestow, is due to Sir Barnes Peacock, who held Lord Macaulay's place during the most anxious years through which the Indian Empire has passed. The draft and the revision are both eminently creditable to their authors, and the result of their successive efforts has been to reproduce in a concise and even beautiful form the spirit of the law of England." The Indian Councils Act of 1861 has been termed, with moderate pleasantry, an Act for the Abolition of Sir Barnes Peacock. The real truth is that he was gradually driven into an opposition to Government by his own sense of right, and by the impossibility, based in his nature, of deferring to authority concerning subjects on which he thought differently. But the position of controller of Government tendencies was scarcely suitable for the Chief Justice. Peacock took a great interest in the Legislative Council, and was nominated its vice-president in 1859. Few of the members could speak: they were full but not ready men, and had been accustomed only to writing minutes and reports—talking on their fingers, if the expression may pass. Mr. James Wilson was of course an exception, and he, as a House of Commons man, was a little tempted, in this teacup agora, to ravage where there seemed no chance of resistance, and roar where little likelihood existed of reply. But he could never produce any impression on Sir Barnes. A small, clean-cut man, with a pale, thoughtful face, would rise from the vice-presidential chair, which seemed worlds too big for him, and commence, after one of Wilson's tirades, with a dryness absolutely slaughtering, "I am afraid I can scarcely concur in any of the opinions just enunciated by the honourable member." Then the previous speech was dissected with the appalling calmness of Fergusson operating for the stone. When the opposition went so far as to think of negativing a grant of money awarded by Sir Charles Wood to the Mysore Princes, that functionary determined to exterminate the enemy. The most ardent admirer of free institutions could scarcely lament the blow. Not, indeed, that the grant was right, and not that the opposition was unreasonable; but still the anomaly of a Government thwarted by its own nominees was great, and afforded a spectacle of disunion amongst high authorities, which, in the particular circumstances of India, was worse than unedifying.

To Sir Barnes, on his release from legislation, fell the task of inaugurating the High Court, a tribunal formed from the amalgamation of the old Supreme Court with the Civil Service Court, commonly known as the Sudder. It was a task requiring tact and patience, and the success of the experiment is certainly in a measure to be attributed to his wise presidency. As a judge he passed many weighty decisions—one, on a revenue point of considerable importance, if it excited some opposition gained great notoriety. On the criminal side, he tried several cases which created much public interest; amongst them may be mentioned that of Shibkissen Banerjea—a Hindoo of wealth and position—and Dr. Crawford, charged with the forgery of a will. Sir Barnes was courteous to the Bar, but being by temperament strong-willed, and not easily reached through his emotions, he was sometimes accused in later years of asperity. He never left a point that was once raised without complete examination and settlement, and this habit appeared perhaps to some of the more eager spirits at times tedious. He retired in 1870, and on arriving in England was made a Privy Councillor, was appointed a member of the Judicial Committee of the Privy Council in July, 1872, and has since been made a judge of the Court of Appeal. There are extra-professional methods of obtaining notoriety and of gaining influence. Sir William Jones, when a puisne judge, astonished India, and subsequently Europe, by his linguistic attainments and his knowledge of the sciences. A beautiful tree, radiant in its season with crimson blossoms, the *Jonesia*, bears his name down to posterity in the records of botany. Russell Street, in Calcutta, is called after a Chief Justice, who was the pioneer in forming a quarter of the town in his time new. As Legal Members, besides the illustrious Macaulay, Cameron was distinguished by elegant learning, Drinkwater Bethune by an interest in the natives, of which a Female School still records the remembrance. Chief Justice Peel was a horticulturist of great knowledge and success; whilst Mr. Justice Phear acquired a reputation as a lecturer. But Sir Barnes Peacock confined himself to his duties; and it may perhaps be attributed to the absence of popular gifts that, as was mentioned at the outset, the only memorial of him exists in the work that he performed.

A hale age may be fairly attributed to active habits in a climate suited to his constitution; for Sir Barnes is well preserved for his years, and shows no symptoms of the man who at forty feared the profession he had chosen would prove too much for his strength. In India he was very fond of riding, knew and selected a handsome horse, and formed, with his jockey figure and neat seat, one of the best-known features of the Rotten Row of Calcutta, which is there called the Course. The neighbourhood of the Indian metropolis presents features which cause astonishment that the site was ever chosen for that of a great city. Over the dead level expanse, the sea marshes intersect the tracts of culturable land, so that swamps which destroy and fields which nurture are inextricably mixed together. The noble river flowing seaward, with an impulse received far earlier in its course, leaves tracts contiguous to its banks less encumbered with water, where the tropical vegetation is luxuriant and rich. Besides his handsome town residence, Sir Barnes occupied a country retreat to the southward, in a situation suitable for sport, and characterized by the strange, but not unpicturesque, features that have been mentioned. More than one son has found employment in the East, so that the family name is not likely at present to pass away even from those who do not trouble themselves with the history of the past. The benefit of wholesome legal enactments is one which is enjoyed by tens of thousands who have no cognisance of the benefactor.

But to those who have examined with care the annals of Indian administration for the last quarter of a century, the work of Peacock will be quite familiar; and there is little doubt that those best qualified to judge will declare that he had a great task to do—and did it well. It was a task curiously interrupted by one of the greatest social eruptions of modern times—the Mutiny. Seldom is a law-giver called upon to pause and consider whether the State itself can hold together; to turn from thoughts of future generations to thoughts of danger to life and limb in the present; to dream of established tranquillity when affairs looked blackest and least hopeful; and to preserve a judicial calmness when the cheeks of the best and bravest were blanched with the suddenness of an appalling catastrophe.

XXXVI.

SIR DIGHTON PROBYN, V.C., K.C.S.I., C.B.

THOSE whom duty or inclination, or both, take to Court ceremonials—unless they be blinded by the brilliancy of the scene or dazed by their near proximity to the august presence—will have noticed, upon the steps of the throne, and among the immediate surroundings of the Heir Apparent, a stalwart form in the scarlet tunic of a lieutenant-general, his manly breast covered with a blaze of decorations, that inscribed "For Valour" conspicuous among medals for Indian and Chinese campaigns. A closer inspection will discover a hale, strong man, still in the prime of life, his frame rejoicing in inches far above the average height, in symmetry perfect, in proportions magnificently moulded. His figure is well knit and active still, to a degree not usually the case at forty-six; his good right arm, with which he has in his time done doughty work, is still as nervous and muscular as of old. It is a striking head, handsome and well posed; the beard flows long and naturally; the eyes are bright and fearless, but, like his speech, having no tinge of that professional *hauteur* which frowns somewhat contemptuously upon the *pekin* or humble civilian of the workaday world. Yet this distinguished soldier is no less modest and unassuming in language and demeanour than he is unmistakably gallant in his carriage and bearing. It would be impossible to gather from his own lips the admission that he had deserved well of his country even in the slightest degree. He is as reticent in his talk concerning his own achievements, as he is gentle and unaffected in his ways. Nevertheless he has gained during his brilliant military career a world-wide and enduring prestige. His deeds of daring and personal prowess were once on every tongue. It is well known throughout India how splendidly he has behaved; how he has led repeatedly to victory squadrons of irregular horsemen, in race alien, but in spirit well disposed to ourselves; how, by his own conspicuous example, he has instilled into their souls the same ardent courage which animated his own; how he has taught them to despise danger and to forget there was such a word as fear, to charge straight home when the order was given, to sit calmly in their saddles and be shot down with unfaltering self-sacrifice if the occasion needed it, to fight on with unyielding tenacity against the most desperate odds, even when encountered hand-to-hand. Prodigal, even to recklessness, of his own life, an unrivalled horseman, excelling in the skilful use of sword, pistol, or lance, these with his own kindly encouraging words and the unremitting care with which he watched over the wants of his men, have endeared him to all, and have won from them a devotion which he could call upon to produce extraordinary results. Few sights in war have been better worth seeing than Dighton Probyn at the head of the horse which in time came to be called by his own name. The serried ranks of richly-attired troopers, with their gorgeous blue and white turbans, wound in graceful folds down over their ears and cocked rather on one side, their eyes gleaming fire, their sabres thirsting for blood, admirably mounted, and splendidly handled and led, would bear comparison with any cavalry in the world. The time may yet come when other regiments of this class will have their efficiency tested more severely perhaps than at any time heretofore, but they can scarcely fail in the trial while we have English officers like Probyn to show the way and such loyal hearts to follow his lead.

The dread Mutiny of 1857, which, with all its fell disasters, has yet the merit of having brought so many distinguished officers to the front, was the starting-point also of Dighton Probyn's brilliant military career. Born of an old family long connected with India, his father having been all his life in the service of the Company, and his mother a Macnaghten, a name familiar in India as a household word, he went out to the East as a young cadet in 1849. While serving in the 6th Bengal Light Infantry, he became adjutant of a regiment of Punjaub Irregular Cavalry engaged in frontier disturbances, and commenced thus his acquaintance with that warlike and chivalrous people, the Sikhs, whose best swordsmen and best horsemen, with all their best energies, were in after days to be placed unreservedly at his disposal. He was still but a subaltern when the chance of distinction came to him. Delhi was beleaguered, and every available man was hurried away, not without risk, from the Punjaub to reinforce the small army before the place. Probyn went down with a selected squadron of his own regiment and became part of the cavalry force under Sir Hope Grant, having as comrades and colleagues other officers little less famous than himself as leaders of irregular horse. Hodson, who came to a soldier's death at Lucknow, was one of them; another was "young" Nicholson, as he was affectionately called, who lost his arm at the assault and died soon afterwards, it was believed of grief at his brother's untimely end; a third was Watson, now commandant of the Central Indian Horse, who went as chief of the cavalry contingent to Malta; and the fourth was the subject of our sketch. Of all these three—Nicholson, Watson, and Probyn—Sir Hope Grant speaks in his journals in the most glowing and flattering terms, but he says especially of Probyn, although he takes him to task for want of caution, that "it would be difficult to imagine a more brilliant, dashing, daring irregular officer." Throughout the siege, and in the operations which followed, Probyn's feats gained him the admiration of the whole force. He was insatiable for the fight, foremost in every fray, ready to throw himself and the men he led against any opponents, no matter what their superiority in strength. He was for ever challenging the enemy to single combat; picking out a standard-bearer, attacking him, and spoiling him within sight, perhaps at striking distance of his fellows, charging often and routing the rebels with a small handful of troopers; or if the tables were turned and he seemed in danger of being outnumbered or overpowered, hacking and hewing his way out against seemingly overwhelming odds. He was man enough always for two or three at a time; even when himself wounded he has cut down and killed his assailant. The close of the siege of Delhi saw him in command of a squadron, and a captain. As such he was with Greathead's column at the battle of Agra, distinguishing himself highly in several sharp cavalry affairs; he was at the first relief of Lucknow, at the relief of Cawnpore, at the reoccupation of Futtehghur, and having rejoined the head-quarters, was present at the siege and final capture of Lucknow. But now, as the inevitable consequence of the severe toil through which he had passed, sickness overcame him, and he was compelled perforce to return to England, losing thus any active share in the successful movements which closed the campaign, if such it could be called. Just then came the outbreak of war with China, and Sir Hope Grant was nominated as Commander-in-chief of the Expeditionary Force. Probyn, although absent, was offered the command of the 1st Sikh Cavalry, as it was called, a newly raised regiment, and gladly accepted the post. Hurrying back with all haste, he was in time to sail with the expedition, and to command Probyn's Horse throughout the operations—a campaign not inglorious, in which his Sikh horsemen, when pitted against the hordes of Tartar cavalry, proved themselves immeasurably superior. Our allies the French, no mean judges, who for the first time saw our so-called Indian irregular cavalry, spoke of Probyn's and Fane's in terms of the highest praise. They were, indeed, two magnificent regiments, well mounted and well equipped, the temper and *physique* of the men undoubtedly first-rate throughout, and right good was the service they did.

After the return from China, with the single exception of the Umbeyla campaign, short but sanguinary as it was, Dighton Probyn sheathed his sword, and since then courtly duties have with him mainly superseded the stirring business of the camp. He held, for a time it is true, the post of Commandant of the Central Indian Horse, but on the arrival of the Duke of Edinburgh in the country in 1869, he was specially attached to the royal suite, and was again, and naturally, selected to accompany the Prince of Wales to India. Appointed subsequently, and in succession, Equerry and Controller of the Household, Sir Dighton might be presumed to have accepted the *rôle* of the courtier and to have forsworn the career of arms. But although he is in the Court, it may fairly be said of him that he is not of it, that his tastes and predilections are rather towards privacy and retirement than the excitement and constant movement which characterize life within the precincts of a palace. He has, however, secured for himself a high measure of respect and esteem, no less from his colleagues than from the gracious Prince he serves. He is known to have weight with his royal master, and to use such influence as he possesses with discretion, but without repudiating the responsibilities it involves. Whether he would be content to be thus tied with silken chains in gilded chambers should the trumpet sound the alarm for war, remains to be seen. The temptation to sally forth again into the field would probably prove irresistible; nor is it likely that the Prince himself would desire to hold him back, but rather to get the start of him in the race for fame. It is, on the other hand, somewhat unfortunate that Sir Dighton Probyn should have reached so soon the exalted rank of a lieutenant-general. He is perhaps more especially fitted to be the leader of a compact body of half a dozen squadrons or of a brigade than to direct the movements of a numerous and important force. But the old spirit is still undimmed, and to omit him from the list of those who should be called on to lend their aid in case of war would be a distinct misfortune to the national cause.

XXXVII.

MAJOR-GEN. FREDERICK S. ROBERTS, V.C., C.B.

It has been the custom with a numerous class of discontented and dissatisfied growlers to repeat with rather wearisome iteration that the palmy days of India are at an end; that it is no longer possible to shake from the pagoda tree a plentiful harvest of rupees; that young tyros in the military school cannot now hope to emulate the achievements of the great warriors and administrators who gave England her Empire in the East. The career which they enter is said to be barren of opportunities, the horizon is limited and circumscribed. There may be some foundation for the complaint, inasmuch as but few find it easy nowadays to bridge rapidly the great gulf which separates nameless obscurity from resplendent famo; but it is nevertheless true beyond all question that there is more than one distinguished young soldier in the service of the Empress of India who has been fortunate enough to carve out for himself a very substantial slice of distinction, although still only in the early prime of life. No case can be more aptly quoted to illustrate this position than that of the subject of the present memoir

—a staff officer of high reputation and an increasing prestige, who, from the high platform of assured professional success, can look back with satisfaction to the by no means remote epoch when he came out to India as an unknown and but recently emancipated Addiscombe cadet.

Frederick Roberts, with all the world before him in his first start in life, possessed a single, but far from valueless, advantage, in the fact that his father was also serving the Company, and had attained already to general officer's rank. As soon, therefore, as the strict conditions which governed staff appointments even then in India, could be fulfilled, and the subaltern had graduated in the vernacular of the country, he was advanced to the dignity of an A.D.C. The comparative ease of a post on the personal staff was, perhaps, not particularly congenial to an eager young spirit such as his; but it must have given him insight and experience at an early age into matters which continue for some time beyond the ken of those who remain altogether in the regimental groove. But the moment there was a prospect of active service he rushed at once into the field. The outbreak of the Indian Mutiny saw him appointed as Deputy Quartermaster-General to his own arm, the artillery, and as such he served all through the arduous siege of Delhi, being present at its capture. From this his first "baptism of fire," in which he was brought face to face with death in several unpleasantly close encounters, he continued to be actively engaged until the great Mutiny came to an end. He was in almost every skirmish, every action, every pursuit. Already realising thoroughly the scope and importance of the duties of the Quartermaster-General, with which, in truth, he has ever since been intimately connected, he did admirable service as a pioneer and scout. He was repeatedly in imminent danger; he passed through many hairbreadth escapes; yet he was for ever pushing forward in the forefront. His bravery was on a par with his impetuosity. He was mentioned no less than three-and-twenty times in dispatches, and always for daring deeds that deserved to be chronicled. It was recorded of him that he "constantly displayed the most marked gallantry." In stature by no means above the middle height, his small but well-knit wiry frame held the heart of a lion. They gave him the Victoria Cross because he recovered a standard from two rebels, pursuing them in hot haste as they made off, and slaying them with his own hand. On the same day he cut down a sowar with a single blow of his sword and killed him on the spot. And so it was to the very end of the campaign. He saw most of the fighting—Lucknow, Cawnpore, Gwalior—and was in the thick of it all, and at the end of it was only a subaltern still. Promotion could not be bestowed upon him—such are the peculiar conditions of our army, and notably of the artillery—until he was a captain, and that he became, and brevet major in the same year. His ascent of the military ladder was henceforth rapid enough, and equally fast came fresh openings, and more and more important changes and posts. But it was not until the Abyssinian expedition that he came very prominently to the front. Here, still employed in the department of the Quartermaster-General, the whole of the arrangements for the embarkation of the forces at Zoulla fell into his hands. His ready tact and courteous forbearance in dealing with the naval officers upon whom the execution of details principally fell, contributed mainly to the success of the whole operation; and Sir Robert Napier so fully recognised the obligations he was under to Major Roberts, that he chose him to proceed to England with the dispatches which announced the satisfactory conclusion of the campaign. This gained Major Roberts another step in rank. But it did more. Identified so closely with the success of the whole of the undertaking, he shared also in the triumph awarded to the victors, and was fêted and made much of on every side.

Since Abyssinia Colonel Roberts has never ceased to be employed whenever there was work of a difficult nature to be done. He went on most expeditions, and always justified the reliance placed in him. At length the post of Quartermaster-General of India fell vacant, and he was clearly the man to fill it. But the appointment carried with it the local rank of a major-general, and he was still only a lieutenant-colonel, and therefore ineligible. So anxious were the authorities to secure his services that they left the post vacant—he himself being appointed to act until he reached the grade of full colonel, and thus bridged over the gap in rank. That the confidence in his fitness was fully deserved has since been proved by the success which has waited upon his tenure of office. To him is mainly due the preparation of the now well-known "Route

Book of Bengal," a work of infinite value, which lays down in precise terms the various lines of march throughout the Presidency. Regiments, detachments, or private individuals, wishing to travel from point to point, need only consult the "Route Book," and following the details given in this section or that, are in a position to settle satisfactorily their itinerary.

Very recently, and in view of probable complications with Afghanistan, he was appointed commissioner upon the Scinde and Punjaub frontier. Here he has gathered up fresh experience, and busied himself in paving the way for those important operations which are now imminent. How highly he is valued by the supreme authorities may be gathered from the fact that he was summoned to Simla to confer with the Viceroy the moment it was known that the Ameer had refused to receive Sir Neville Chamberlain's mission. Within a couple of days he had returned to his command; and it is now announced that when hostilities actually commence he and his division will be in the van.

It may be safely predicted of him that he will do right well in any work that may be entrusted to him. He is essentially a soldier; not altogether and exclusively a scientific one, for his continuous Staff service has removed him for a long space from the artillery, to which he first belonged; and now, as a general officer, he may be said to have paid it a final adieu. He is a man of action; and yet his mind through years of training and experience is stored with precedent, and he can think for himself, or, if need be, argue persuasively with others. To the military mind he commends himself by a close adherence to military ideas; scrupulously neat and natty in appearance, an excellent horseman, quick in all his movements, prompt in his decisions, sharp and peremptory in voice, he is naturally suited to command men. With comrades of his own or subordinates of every rank he is popular in the extreme. "Bobs," as his old friends call him to his face, as many others who would not so far presume, do also behind his back, is known and liked by a very wide circle in India. A thorough gentleman in thought and deed, unselfish and unsparing of personal effort when there is work to be done, his ready sympathy and cordial recognition of the efforts of others make it a pleasure to serve with him or under his orders.

Of all the good soldiers which India has given us—and the number is not limited—there is none upon whom reliance can be more implicitly placed in the sharp crisis which is now at hand.

XXXVIII.

SIR HERCULES G. R. ROBINSON, G.C.M.G.

THERE are many methods by which success in the difficult art of Colonial administration may be achieved. A man of supreme power and ability, self-reliant and secure in his own judgment, will mark out a course for himself and pursue it undeviatingly. In the plenitude of his wisdom he claims to know best, hoping that in the long run his judgment will be accepted as right, and that justice finally, if tardily, will silence opposition and reverse hostile criticism. Men of weaker fibre, whether merely easy-going or led away by a fallacious astuteness, lay their account in acting up to the advice of the statesman who said, "When in doubt do nothing," and trust to masterly inactivity to secure the best results. To neither of these, however, is supreme success uniformly and certainly conceded. Autocratic imperiousness on the one hand often defeats its own object by arousing a spirit of opposition which, under milder measures, would have never appeared; while, on the other, the *laissez aller* principle which characterizes various shades of incompetence, leads its adherents not seldom into difficulties and failures of the most disastrous kind. The Colonial governors whose careers have been marked by the most conspicuous and satisfactory results have been those who have not been betrayed into either extreme; who have known when to act with promptitude and vigour, and when to abstain from interference; who, in a word, have been remarkable for their consummate tact in dealing with men and affairs. It is because he has possessed this quality in an eminent degree that Sir Hercules Robinson has gained a deservedly high reputation as an able and successful representative of the Crown.

Commencing official life early, and in posts of comparatively small responsibility, Sir Hercules Robinson has progressed steadily and uninterruptedly to charges the most onerous and important. After a year or two of regimental experience at an epoch when the military profession offered but narrow prospects even to the most capable and aspiring, he gladly exchanged his commission in the Royal Irish Fusiliers to take civil employment under the State. An Irishman of a good family in Westmeath, who had married early and well, a daughter of Lord Valentia's, he had not long to wait for an appointment. There was plenty of work for good and energetic young men to do at the time when dread famine devastated the Emerald Isle. As one of those who helped to organize and administer the gigantic scheme of State relief which found food and labour for starving thousands, Mr. Robinson gave such proofs of quick-wittedness, shrewdness, and capacity for affairs, that when the famine was over his preferment to other duties came as a matter of course. He was still barely thirty when he commenced his Colonial career, graduating, as many of his colleagues have done, in the forbidding climate and narrow sphere of usefulness of a West Indian Island, as its governor. But first at Montserrat, and afterwards at St. Kitts, he proved to those who ruled in Downing Street, and who then, as now, were not slow to avail themselves of the abilities of those who served them loyally and with sound discretion, that he was of the stuff of which good administrators are made. Never throwing difficulties in the way of Colonial Office action, a willing subordinate, he had clearly the knack of making himself acceptable to those whom he ruled. Everything went smoothly when Mr. Robinson was at the helm; there were no unpleasant hitches, no threatening storms, no breakers ahead betraying the neighbourhood of dangerous shoals. Of pleasing address, in his way a dandy, to the extent of appearing always scrupulously well dressed, and with trim bouquet proverbially blooming in his button-hole, he looks invariably what he is, a gentleman every inch, not only in external appearance, but in spirit and in conduct. Short-sighted observers who do not search below the surface, may have been so far misled or dazzled by his outward mien, as to question whether there are in him any of the sounder and more solid qualities which go to make a really great man. But it would be a grave error to deny him undoubted ability, and of a rare kind—the ability to rule and govern others quietly, and with no great parade or show, to really guide when it might seem that he was guided, to persuade when others more talkative might fancy their own arguments were carrying the day. That this faculty of governing is understood and appreciated at the Colonial Office is best proved by the fact that there has been no break in his pro-consular service for nearly a quarter of a century. When once admitted into the ranks as a trained and disciplined administrator, he won his way into the foremost ranks. From the West Indies he went to Hong Kong, in succession to Sir John Bowring, where he won golden opinions; thence again to Ceylon in time to act as host and genial entertainer of the Duke of Edinburgh; thence to New South Wales, where he still continues—his tenure of office, greatly to the delight of the colonists, having recently been extended another year. The reins of Government in an old-established Colony like New South Wales—one which having passed through many vicissitudes, has now entered upon a career of assured wealth and prosperity —may be easier to handle than those of a younger community, where elements are more unsettled and political passions run high. But there are, nevertheless, in the older Colonies so many difficult social duties to discharge, so much nice and accurate discrimination required to keep everything in equilibrium, that the Governor who in charge of one of them earns widespread popularity, has established his right to be considered a successful administrator in the fullest sense of the word. But Sir Hercules Robinson has also proved himself capable of grappling with the most difficult Colonial questions by the admirable manner in which he dealt with the matters in dispute between her Majesty's Government and the natives of Fiji. It may be that the annexation of Fiji has not proved an unmixed blessing, and that many difficult problems remain to be solved, but, at least, no fault can be found with the measures introduced by Sir Hercules Robinson for carrying on the Government immediately after the hoisting of the British flag.

Kind-hearted, full of *bonhomie* and friendliness to all who are brought in contact with him, Sir Hercules is one of the most highly-esteemed and popular men in the service of the Crown. He makes himself agreeable, smooths down difficulties, softens asperities, and keeps the whole system of which he is the centre in thorough working gear. He does this almost by intuition, but he succeeds also because he gives himself no airs. There is nothing of the great *bahawder* about him; he is easy of access, civil, and obliging to all who approach him. He welcomes his guests at Government House with a genial cordiality which makes them feel at home directly, and in these matters he is ably aided and seconded by Lady Robinson, who is one of the most charming hostesses in the world. It is not easy to find fault with such a man as this; but critics there are who take him to task for his love of the turf. Racing is in its way a passion for him. Nothing gives him more pleasure than to own racers and see horses run. To those, whether friends from whom he might reasonably ask to be saved, or detractors who would read him homilies and treat him to much unkindly criticism, he openly avows his predilections, and declares that he cannot see where is the harm. He trains and runs horses—true; but he never bets, not a sixpence, and he always runs to win. If he is to blame for liking to see a trial of speed between the animals he so dearly loves, there are many in the same boat with him. Horse-racing may degenerate in this country into an unsatisfactory substitute for the gaming-table, and by degrees alienate from it the more reputable elements of society, but in the abstract it is essentially British in character, and if properly carried out it tends into a good direction. It is its abuse only that is hurtful, and if all owners and patrons were as "straight" as Sir Hercules Robinson, the "turf" in England would stand higher than it does now. But his love of sport is catholic in character. Races he perhaps prefers, but he is also a great *shikarri*, a keen sportsman, who, when at Ceylon, as elsewhere, proved what he could do with a gun. To none of these tastes will his countrymen be disposed to take exception. The official who can on occasion make a telling speech, indite a clear and concise dispatch, work for long hours in the disposal of business or the discussion of public affairs, has many of the leading qualifications of administrative efficiency, but he will gain rather than lose credit with those who surround him, whether Celt or Saxon, if he knows the good points of a horse, can shoot straight, and ride well to hounds.

XXXIX.

THE MARQUIS OF SALISBURY, K.G.

Less than twenty years have passed since Lord Robert Cecil used to be one of the most regular of journalists who made the afternoon pilgrimage of Fleet Street and the Strand. The young man with the severe cast of countenance, the clearly-chiselled features, and the slightly stooping figure, was well known to his contemporary publicists, though he had few words to exchange with them. At this time the young nobleman, who was living by his pen, had, and could have, no idea that the full honours of an ancient peerage would shortly descend to him. He was the second son of an exceedingly austere father; he had recently married, had a seat in Parliament, but no expectations save from his fine intellect and strong will, and received an allowance from his father wholly inadequate to the social needs of his position. He had passed through Eton and Oxford, had distinguished himself at the former by his distaste for the sports and pastimes of the place, by his devotion to the crucible and the laboratory, by the success with which he dabbled in photography and botany, as well as studied French, German, and modern languages generally. At Oxford he had condescended to win an "idle fellowship" at All Souls'. His tutor at Eton was the Rev. W. G. Cookesley, a name carrying with it pleasant memories and genial associations wherever old Etonians are to be found, and perhaps the most striking recollection which Lord Robert Cecil's schoolfellows entertain of him in those remote days is that he was signally destitute of the smartness and trimness which is, for the most part, a characteristic of Eton boys. When he quitted Oxford, before he settled down in London, he travelled pretty nearly round the world. The pilgrimage of this planet was a new thing then, and novelties had an attraction for the pilgrim. He was unaccompanied; he took a delight in roughing it in America, Australia, and elsewhere, and displayed an aptitude for overcoming difficulties and conquering obstacles by dint of sheer hard work and resolution, which may be thought to have foreshadowed the address and determination with which some years later he mastered the complicated details of the Indian Budget after three days' study, or rescued a railway company from the abysses of mismanagement and the impending fate of ruin.

Before he was five-and-twenty Lord Robert Cecil was returned for the borough of Stamford, previously represented in Parliament by a politician also destined to become subsequently Secretary of State for India—Sir Stafford Northcote. But at this time Lord Robert's energies were directed into the channel of journalism rather than of Parliamentary politics. His connection with literature was decidedly an impediment to his political success, and was regarded by his family and his friends as a lamentable aberration from the proper course. Both of his friends and his family he saw exceedingly little, and became a good deal of a Bohemian and an Ishmaelite. His speeches in the House of Commons at this time are marked by bitterness and acridity, qualities for whose exercise he also found an opportunity in the *Saturday Review*, then under the charge of Mr. Douglas Cook, one of the best newspaper editors of modern times, who gave his aristocratic contributor much valuable advice, that has since borne rich fruit. It may be mentioned that it was while writing for the *Saturday Review* that Lord Salisbury's attention was first actively turned to Indian affairs. He at once commenced to study them, with results which were apparent not merely in the columns of the daily and weekly Press, but in the speeches made by him in Parliament on the subject of the Indian Mutiny and the Indian Bill. Meanwhile, the heir to the Marquisate of Salisbury had shown himself to be a considerable personage, and had established his reputation as a political force in the House of Commons, with which it was plain both his own party and his opponents would have to reckon. It was the favour which was born of fear, but it had much the same effect as the favour which is born of love. His repeated attacks, in the *Quarterly Review*, on the Derby-Disraeli combination of 1856, prevented the return of the Conservatives to office, and let in Lord Palmerston and the Whigs. The great feature in all these attacks, and indeed in the general political conduct of their author at this period, was an enthusiastic hatred of Mr. Disraeli, and persons began to ask whether an avenger had not arisen from the bones of Peel, and the future Tory Premier was not destined to feel during the remainder of his career a thorn in his side. Lord Robert Cecil's social position and prospects had changed too. He had, by his brother's sudden death, become an elder son. Thus, as a prospective marquis, and a most formidably pungent critic, he became more than ever a person to be appeased.

Political office in England is quite as generally given for the purpose of muzzling dangerous and irrepressible *frondeurs* as by way of rewarding the zealous services of staunch friends. When, in 1867, Lord Derby was called upon to form an Administration, he was compelled, by the exigencies of his position, to offer Lord Cranborne the Secretaryship of State for India. The office was elevated and responsible enough for the severe and imperious ambition of the ultra-Tory member for Stamford. A natural affinity has been discovered to exist between the genius of Burke and the theme which he handled in his impeachment of Warren Hastings; and the barbaric splendour of the country which the English pro-consul had ruled, may well have been irresistibly fascinating to the copious and gorgeous eloquence of the orator. Something of the same kind of relation there may be said to be between the temperament of Lord Salisbury and the office to which he was promoted, something of the same adaptation of the post to the man. The Secretary of State for India gloried in the burden of the work which was laid upon him, and which, to a great extent, he had laid on, and even created for, himself. Eleven years ago the clear, terse, brilliant statements —witness his famous Budget speech, delivered after three days' preparation—of Lord Cranborne in the House of Commons were a refreshing contrast to the long, loose, rambling, inaudible utterances of his predecessor, Lord Halifax. But Lord Cranborne was not to hold the helm of the India Office for long. The democratic concessions of the Derby-Disraeli Reform Bill vexed incurably his Tory spirit. He resigned his place in the Cabinet, and the pent-up torrent of his indignation with Mr. Disraeli found vent in a bitter opposition to the bill, and in a series of fiery attacks on its chief author. No consideration, Lord Cranborne vowed, would ever make him go again into the same lobby as the Semitic statesman—only Lord Cranborne used much more emphatic language—whom he stigmatised in the House of Commons as a "political adventurer," the professor of a policy of legerdemain, the "destroyer of that mutual confidence which is the very soul of our party Government." Mr. Disraeli received these attacks with cynical composure, smiled sardonically, and remarked, "The young man's head is on fire." Lord Cranborne had not yet abandoned—for the matter of that he has not abandoned it to this day —his connection with literature, and the next number of the *Quarterly Review* contained a memorable article against the Derby-Disraeli policy in the old slashing vein, entitled the "Conservative Surrender."

But, great as is Lord Salisbury's hatred of Mr. Disraeli, his love of power is even greater. Mr. Gladstone's Administration went out; Mr. Disraeli formed a Cabinet, and Lord Cranborne, who had in the meantime taken his place in the House of Lords as a full-blown Marquis, consented to serve in that Cabinet as Indian Secretary. This office he held for just four years, and it is by his administration of it during this period that his character as an Indian statesman must be judged. Of the salient principles of his administration it is not necessary to say much. His policy may be described as one long and very practical illustration and endorsement of the views of the late John Stuart Mill, that India should be governed from Downing Street rather than in Calcutta. Whatever its merits or demerits, the decision at which Lord Salisbury arrived, and which he enforced, was that her Majesty's Viceroy and his Council should enact no great measures save after consultation with the Secretary of State. A Tory above all things, Lord Salisbury became as keen a Free Trader as he once was Protectionist, and by his condemnation of the protective import duty imposed on British manufactured cotton goods won the hearts of the traders of Manchester. At the India Office, Lord Salisbury did not only work very hard—he extended his industry to details needlessly minute. He insisted upon seeing and forming an opinion on all papers. The consequence was that he really had not the time necessary to devote to the meditation of great questions. He has carried the same habits with him to the Foreign Office, and it may be said that the motive which prompts these habits is more laudable than their results are uniformly admirable. There is danger in using a razor where a common knife would do as well, and creative statesmanship necessarily leaves much more than Lord Salisbury is always inclined to do, to clerkly industry.

His reign at the India Office was distinguished amongst other things by the appointment of Lord Lytton to the Vice-Royalty, and Sir John Strachey to the financial ministry, and also for a complete shifting of the ground of our foreign policy. Up to the close of the Duke of Argyll's administration we had the policy of Lord Lawrence—that of masterly inactivity. Directly Lord Salisbury came in he reversed all this, and set to work to change our relation with the Ameer of Cabul —with what results we now know. But he left the result as a legacy to Lord Cranbrook, and he is now rather known as the writer of the famous circular, and as one of the parties to the Salisbury-Schouvaloff memorandum, than as the author of a new Indian policy.

As Chancellor of the University of Oxford, Lord Salisbury has passed a bill, one of whose cardinal objects is the abolition of such sinecures as the All Souls' Fellowship which he once held himself, and he seems to have been strangely amenable to academic influence in the new regulations as to the age of competition wallahs, the reduction of the limits of which is mainly due to the recommendations of Sir Henry Maine, now Master of Trinity Hall, Cambridge, and Mr. Jowett, Master of Balliol. One innovation in a matter of detail, it may be mentioned, has been made by Lord Salisbury both at the India Office and the Foreign Office—the new writing-machine; the adoption of which, however, is, we believe, confined to his lordship's room. As a Parliamentary speaker Lord Salisbury has much improved. He has acquired mellowness without losing force. In the House of Lords he has an audience more congenial and critical than in the present House of Commons, and, contrary perhaps to his expectations, finds that there is no reason to regret his translation to the Chamber of the hereditary legislature. In society Lord Salisbury is pleasant and popular, with plenty of talk on plenty of subjects, eschewing political topics as far as possible, and infinitely preferring experimental chemistry. It is believed by some persons that Lord Salisbury is destined to succeed Lord Beaconsfield, as leader of the Conservative party. It is feared by others that under the leadership of Lord Salisbury, the wonderful organization will not remain a triumphant party very long. Lord Salisbury is a great minister, and in his way a statesman, but before a man can lead he must conciliate, and this is exactly what Lord Salisbury cannot or will not do.

XL.

THE NEW SECRETARY OF STATE FOR INDIA.

Just twenty-two years ago a barrister, who was even then verging on middle age, was pacing in moody solitude and reverie his chambers in the Temple, when he was roused from his musings by the announcement that the chief electioneering agent of the Conservative party, whose prospects were not at that time particularly bright, had called, and was anxious to see him immediately. The barrister in question, who was none other than the eminent Conservative politician who has just succeeded Lord Salisbury as Secretary of State for India, was constitutionally impatient under disappointment. On that particular day he had received, and was then suffering from, the blow of a very severe disappointment. An application for "silk" had been made on his behalf to the Lord Chancellor; it had been refused, and the victim of the refusal, Mr. Gathorne Hardy, was anathematizing his evil star, and not perhaps invoking benedictions on the head of the keeper of the Queen's conscience. Nine years previously his *amour propre* had been mortified by a discomfiture as unexpected as it was bitter, and from the effects of which he had even then scarcely recovered. He had presented himself as candidate in the Tory interest for his native borough of Bradford, and had been rejected. He did not, indeed, appear before the constituency as the member of an ancient Yorkshire family, which had a traditional claim to the allegiance of the town. The defeated aspirant to its representation came of a modern stock of respectable yeomen, who had been settled for a generation or two in the neighbourhood, and who had prospered exceedingly. Mr. Gathorne Hardy's father, "honest John Hardy," had finally achieved the distinction of being returned by his townsmen to Parliament, and his third son had thought that the position was to be hereditary. When he discovered his mistake, and while he was yet smarting under a sense of failure, he did the best thing he could, and discovered an anodyne in hard work. He had been called to the Bar some years previously, he had gone circuit, and displayed great promise as an advocate. To the profession of advocacy he therefore turned his attention, and such progress had he made in it that in 1856 he considered himself entitled to promotion to the rank of her Majesty's Counsel learned in the law. The negative with which the modest request had now been met by the Chancellor caused Mr. Hardy once more to reconsider his position. He had almost decided upon flinging up the law, abandoning all thoughts of politics, and retiring into the country to live on his estate, when the irrepressible Mr. Spofforth, who was then the manager of Conservative election contests, made his way into the room, informed Mr. Hardy that there was a sudden vacancy at Leominster, added with judicious flattery that the ball was at his feet, told him there were not five minutes to lose, and declared that it would be necessary for them to start within a couple of hours for the scene of the impending political battle. It was quick work, and Mr. Hardy was at first a little staggered at the proposal, but reflecting possibly that there was a tide which taken at the ebb leads on to fortune, and thinking that the moment for thus taking it had arrived, closed with the offer, and accompanied Mr. Spofforth that same evening to Leominster. In less than a fortnight he had been returned as member for the borough.

This was Mr. Gathorne Hardy's first start in political life. He was then forty-two, and, considering the great Parliamentary destiny which awaited him, it came rather late. He is now sixty-four—the youngest-looking man of his age in England, of upright figure, elastic walk, and with nerves as strong as in a man of forty-five—and in the interval of these twenty-two years he has filled several highly responsible positions, and crowned his successes by his promotion to the Indian Secretaryship and a seat in the House of Peers. Mr. Hardy's political history is that of the rise, progress, and culminating triumph of the Conservative reaction, and the Prime Minister has had no more valuable colleague than the senior member for Oxford University in the wonderful work which he has accomplished. If it is Mr. Disraeli who has vivified modern Conservatism with genius, it is Mr. Hardy who has infused into it earnestness. No more passionate appeals on behalf of existing institutions, good or bad, abuses or blessings in Church and State; no more bitter attacks on the friends of toleration and the enemies of privilege, have been made than by Mr. Gathorne Hardy. With a quick imagination, a power of repartee and reply naturally great, and which, cultivated by continual practice, has made him one of the most effective Parliamentary debaters of the period; with the gift of eloquence, always clear and fluent, and fairly forcible as well, Mr. Hardy has been something more than a plausible special pleader retained by Conservatism in defence of the principles of exclusiveness, and in support of restrictions upon civil and religious liberty which have long since become anachronisms. At the same time that he has given powerful and even solemn expressions to the most reactionary and impracticable doctrines of the Conservative creed, he has given them lucidity, coherence, and order, and with consummate skill has succeeded in reducing them to something which may be said to simulate the appearance of an intellectual system. He has shown, too, a felicity as rare as it is agreeable in these dull times. In the course of the debate on the Public Worship Bill four years ago, nothing could be better than his comparison of the cat, which, strolling up the floor of the House, bounded over the heads of the occupants of the Ministerial bench, not a little to their consternation, with the owl that, with similar suddenness, interrupted the sittings of the Synod or Dort. It will, of course, be understood that Mr.

Hardy is now promoted to the combined honours of the Indian Secretaryship on the ground not of any vaguely credited acquaintance with Indian affairs, but of his commanding abilities and his eminent services to his party. He has at different periods filled four separate offices in the Government, two of them carrying seats in the Cabinet. He had not been in the House of Commons two years when he was made Under-Secretary at the Home Office in Lord Derby's short-lived Administration of '58-'59. He was president of the Poor-Law Board, '66-'67; was promoted to the Home Secretaryship in the latter year, and remained in office till '68. It was at the Home Office that he won his first laurels as an administrator. No better selection could have been made by Lord Derby, and although Mr. Hardy was undoubtedly fortunate in coming after a Walpole, and before a Bruce—so that he had no formidable comparisons to fear—he showed a degree of administrative capacity which was in itself striking. His political importance he had, of course, immensely increased when in 1865 he successfully contested Oxford University against Mr. Gladstone. As regards the particular subjects on which he has spoken with conspicuous effect in the House of Commons, his fidelity to the principle of a religious Establishment was exhibited in his resistance to Mr. Gladstone's attacks upon the Irish Church in 1868; and he delivered a very notable argument against the principle that the relative amount of damage inflicted by the actions of a vessel which had escaped from a neutral port was chargeable to the nation which had been remiss in supervision, in the discussion which took place in the House of Commons five years ago on the "Three Rules" evolved from the Geneva arbitration. It is interesting to know that though Mr. Hardy was a member of the House of Commons when the China Question was discussed, and the Bill for the transfer of India from the Company to the Queen became law, he was silent on the former and had very little to say on the latter.

The part which Mr. Hardy was called upon to play when appointed Secretary of State for War was one of extreme difficulty. It is an undoubted fact that the accession of the Conservatives to power had filled some of the highest military authorities with vague hopes. To them Lord Cardwell's drastic treatment, his thorough-going reforms, and root-and-branch legislation had been most unpalatable. As far as was consistent with that proper subordination which soldiers in office, to their credit, never forget, they had resisted the measures which abolished purchase, which introduced the principle of short service, of localisation and of selection for regimental commands. They had been overborne, and they still looked back longingly at the institutions inexorably swept away. Therefore it was that more than one illustrious personage hailed Mr. Hardy's advent at Pall Mall with unmixed satisfaction. No Conservatives are more conservative than old soldiers in high places, and by all such Mr. Hardy was warmly welcomed as one who from his bias and opinions could not but be favourable to their cause. But they counted somewhat without their host. The new War Minister soon made it plain that he was opposed to all retrogression, that he accepted the situation as he found it, that he would administer the legacy left him by his predecessor without altering one tittle of its terms. Of his statesmanlike determination, and of the loyalty with which Mr. Gathorne Hardy has adhered to it, it is impossible to speak in too high praise. Had the originator of the various measures been himself, left to carry them out to their end they could not have been executed more unhesitatingly or in a more complete manner. Mr. Hardy's attitude may possibly have given some umbrage to those who had hoped other things, but he soon contrived to tone down possible asperities and pave the way to the harmonious working of the department. It was felt by all who came in contact with him that they were certain of courteous reception, of forbearance towards their own peculiar views, of prompt and generally accurate comprehension of even the most difficult points; yet more, it was soon seen also that, although Mr. Hardy was, when properly satisfied, prepared to give way, that he had, nevertheless, a back of his own. Firmness, combined with judicious concession, is one of the strongest weapons of the Administration, and Mr. Hardy throughout his tenure of office has never failed to enunciate his own opinions with decision and clear reasons, subsequently to carry them consistently into effect. His removal at a critical juncture like the present might at first seem to amount to a public loss, but he will be succeeded by a Minister whom he has in a measure himself trained. Colonel Stanley is in all the secrets of the War Office, and he may be relied upon to continue in the path which his predecessor has marked out for him.

In virtue of his position at the War Office, Mr. Hardy has, of course, been already brought more or less into contact with India, and remembering the traditional jealousy which exists between India and the War Office, the apprehension may suggest itself to some minds that devotion to the post which he now quits may tempt the new Secretary of State to increase by the further transfer of business from Pall Mall the expenditure already chargeable to our Indian Empire. That, at least, was the misgiving which was present to the minds of a few Anglo-Indian patriots in 1872, when Lord Northbrook gave up the Under-Secretaryship at the War Office, to succeed Lord Mayo as Viceroy. It is unnecessary to say how completely these misgivings were falsified by events. As it was then so will it be now, and as in the case of Lord Northbrook it was found a distinct advantage to the Indian Exchequer to have a Viceroy who had an experience in the inner working of the War Office, and who was on his guard against anything which could be construed as an attempt to relieve Pall Mall at the expense of India, so will it be in the case of Mr. Hardy. The loyalty of an English Minister is to the office which for the time being he holds, and the new Indian Secretary will transfer to the India Office and its affairs all the affection he may ever have felt for the War Office and the Horse Guards.

XLI.

SIR JAMES FITZJAMES STEPHEN.

UNFORTUNATELY, or fortunately, it is not given to many who have carefully thought out a subject in the study to find, during their lifetime, an opportunity of carrying theory into practice on an Imperial scale. Mr. Hare will, probably, pass out of the memory of men before his reform of the representative system is carried into effect. The foundations of the City of Health will still perhaps have to be laid when Dr. Richardson can no longer interest himself in its institution; and it is possible that the new moral world may continue to be encumbered with the *débris* of faith, property, and wedlock, when fate shall require the attendance of Mr. Bradlaugh. But the subject of this notice has been fortunate enough to devote a considerable portion of earlier manhood to the careful consideration of the laws of evidence, of contract, and kindred topics; to simplification of procedure, and condensation of statutes, and to have found a splendid occasion, in middle life, of carrying out his ideas in the ample arena of the Indian Empire.

The elements of law and literature seem to be woven into the tissue of the Stephen family; and one or other, or indeed both, to be present in most of its members. The grandfather, James Stephen, M.P., was a Master in Chancery; the father, the Right Hon. Sir James Stephen, was alike distinguished for his knowledge of political law and his high historical attainments. The father's brother, Sir George Stephen (still living at an advanced age), was a solicitor and miscellaneous writer of much excellence. His humorous "Adventures of a Gentleman in Search of a Horse" amused the lovers of light literature forty years ago. Sir Alfred Stephen, cousin to Sir James and Sir George, the present Governor of New South Wales, was a distinguished colonial judge. In the present generation, James Fitzjames Stephen worthily represents the family proclivity towards law, and his brother Leslie, as worthily, the hereditary taste for letters. Amongst the many interesting essays of the late Sir James Stephen, one entitled "The Clapham Sect" claims especial notice, as affording a lively sketch of a body of men who were bound together by a similarity of religious views, and by a common determination to use every effort towards the abolition of the slave trade. The group included Thornton, Wilberforce, Zachary Macaulay, the Chancery Master Stephen, and others; and it is not without a bearing on the attitude of the two Stephens of our day, in reference to certain grave subjects, to remember that the religious views held in common were those of a somewhat narrow Evangelicism.

Because those views were not the result of a patient inquiry after truth on the one hand, nor of a reliance on the traditions of authority on the other, but of a belief in a kind of spiritual intuition accompanying the reading of the Scriptures, the religion thus generated was a thing not to be discussed, but to be accepted, and compatible only with culture when kept wholly separate from it. And when we remember that the mother of Fitzjames and Leslie Stephen was a Venn, a name most rightly held in high estimation by the followers of the Low Church sect; and, furthermore, that the connection of Fitzjames Stephen with the party was strengthened by his alliance with the Cunningham family, whose head was the well-known pastor of Harrow, an eminent light of the school, supposed to be handed down to us in the coarse portrait of the "Vicar of Wrexhill," by Mrs. Trollope, we shall understand a certain feeling which both brothers have exhibited—the feeling, we mean, of having been "suckled in a creed outworn," of having lived to "find out" religion, a feeling which persons who had arrived at religion by thought, or who had even passed through it, instead of being brought up in it, would probably never have experienced, and certainly never have expressed.

The present Sir James F. Stephen, whom, for distinction's sake, we will call Fitzjames Stephen, was born in 1829, was educated at Eton, went to King's College, Cambridge, and afterwards to Trinity, was called to the Bar at the Inner Temple in 1854, took silk in 1868, and from 1859 to 1869 held the Recordership of Newark-on-Trent. Before his journey to the East, which gives him the claim to appear in this gallery—he was distinguished by his law works, his newspaper writing, and his great familiarity with that particular branch of legal learning which has been called into play by the prosecution of Ritualists, who have endeavoured to shelter themselves under enactments, or permitted practices, of the time of Elizabeth. The most important of his legal writings was the "General View of the Criminal Law in England"—a work which is marked with extraordinary originality and completeness. As a writer for the Press, he was long connected with the *Saturday Review*, and the fruits of his less ephemeral labours in that journal have appeared as "Essays by a Barrister." It was, we presume, in the hope of securing a foeman worthy of his steel, that Mr. Charles Reade endeavoured, more than once, to fasten reviews of his works on Mr. Stephen personally. Such attempts are, however, to be deprecated, as tending to fetter criticism, and to add new pages to the "Quarrels of Authors." Stephen seceded from the *Saturday* to the *London Review*, which for a short time sought to emulate in brilliance, and, at a respectful distance, to compete with the circulation of the elder journal. Untoward circumstances, however, led the fated vessel amongst the rocks of Exeter Hall, where it is understood she went to pieces, and all hands perished. After that, Fitzjames Stephen, who of course had left the *London* before its ill-starred voyage only to founder in Calvinistic waters, was credited with many of the best contributions to the *Pall Mall Gazette*, in which journal those to whom the vigour and clearness of his style were particularly acceptable, looked eagerly for traces of his pen.

In 1869 Mr. Stephen succeeded Sir Henry Maine as Legal Member of the Governor-General's Council in Calcutta, and in the control of the proceedings of the Legislative Council. An account of this council and of its gradual development has been given in the notices of Peacock and Maine which appear in these pages, and the fertility of the period of Maine's seven years' incumbency has been particularly commented upon. Yet, notwithstanding the fact that Stephen was only three years in India, and during that time had a severe illness, his tenure of office stands out with peculiar brilliancy. For without going into the details of particular measures, but simply gathering up a handful of his achievements, the Evidence Act, the Contracts Act, the thoroughly scientific readjustment of the Criminal Procedure Code, and the great progress made in the clearance out of obsolete or superfluous Acts, and the codification of existing laws into as small a space as they could conveniently occupy, constitute by themselves a monument to his reputation which will not pass away. When the labour involved in drawing up exhaustive Acts on Evidence and Contract is considered, it will be seen that no man, unless previously thoroughly acquainted with the subjects, could possibly have completed the task in the time. In other enactments he was doubtless greatly assisted by the skill of Mr. Whitley Stokes, the secretary to the Council, and the industry of Mr. Cockerell, one of the members, but the work we have particularly specified bears the Hall-mark of the legal member himself. The ready and powerful pen of Stephen enabled him to assist in the general conduct of affairs, more perhaps than any person who had previously held his office. It was generally reported that the minute in the time of Lord Napier and Ettrick's brief incumbency, on the unfortunate and misdirected zeal which led a wholly subordinate officer in the Punjaub to assume the functions of a Government which was within easy reference—was written by Stephen. The facts were put with singular lucidity, and with a firmness which the temporary infatuation of the Indian public rendered necessary. His speeches, too, were full of interesting matter, and if any one might consider that the special pleader showed occasionally—as in his endeavour to prove that the permanent settlement in Bengal and elsewhere did not exempt the land from further burthens—the ability of the pleading could not be denied. He held his appointment during the vigorous period of Lord Mayo's administration; a period, however, by no means exempt from financial and other difficulties. Nor can it be denied that the government of Lord Mayo scarcely met with that loyal co-operation in all quarters which it had a right to expect. However unpopular an income-tax may be, it can never be the duty of those who have to organize its collection to fan the flame of opposition to it, and to assist in denouncing, instead of attempting to mitigate, its oppressive character. More than once Stephen had to aid in strengthening the Government against foes who were those of its own household; and on one occasion, when devising a scheme of relief for a section of the Hindoos, whose marriages were interfered with by existing rituals—a piece of special legislation, of course, because nothing but special legislation would reach the evil—he was met by an attempt to raise the cry of the "Hindoo Church in danger," in the Legislative Council itself.

His career was drawing to its close, when the terrible tragedy at the Andaman Islands brought in a time of much anxiety and responsibility, which he shared with his friend, Sir John Strachey, who by the demise of Lord Mayo found himself provisionally at the head of the Government. A graceful mention of this period is to be found in his treatise on "Liberty, Equality, and Fraternity," which had been forming itself in Stephen's mind during his stay in India, was partly written on the voyage home, and was published shortly after his return. This work, which is full of vigour, clear in style, and shows much ingenuity of illustration, was not likely, of course, to be met with anything like universal acceptance. In so far as it blew away much sentimental vapour overhanging watchwords, which can certainly only be received under considerable limitations, it was doubtless calculated to do good. At the same time it approached other subjects in a spirit calculated to give pain to many good men, and one which was inconsistent with the admission of the extreme uncertainty attaching to them. The loud masculine tone pervading the pages of the treatise scarcely befits the writer, who, whilst acknowledging the mysteries with which we are surrounded, not only does not believe himself to know of any solution, but does not consider solution possible.

We can understand the fierce logic of Joseph de Maistre, because we know that he starts with the confidence that his foot is on the rock of eternal truth. But with one who could pen the beautiful passage in the last page of the volume, where life is depicted as a snowstorm overtaking us in a mountain pass, we should have thought the excessive gloom and terror of the situation would have induced a sadness whose natural effect would have been—not necessarily to weaken—but certainly, to soften. The slight tendency to be dogmatic, where dogma is held to be untenable, seems incongruous. And this tendency undoubtedly prevents the reasoning from being uniformly close; and, indeed, whilst fully admitting the power of the style, we must think some of the argument occasionally sadly at fault. Space only admits of one verification of this remark, in noting the fact that the statement, "If there is a God, but no future state, God is nothing to us," is more than once introduced as a self-evident proposition. It is nothing of the kind; it is a pure assumption, and any one attempting to convert it into a tenable proposition would have to break a spear with Spinoza.

Since his return Mr. Stephen has held the Professorship of Common Law in the Inns of Court, and was last year decorated with the Knighthood of the Star of India. He has acted, too, as judge by commission; and in this capacity it fell to his lot to charge the grand jury in respect to that remarkable case which obtained such notoriety as the "Penge Mystery." Sir James Stephen is now in the prime of life, and his powerful frame seems to indicate a degree of vitality which, we sincerely trust, will enable him to carry out his work in the still higher position which undoubtedly awaits him. Many will have been happy to believe that in his damaging letters on Mr. Bright's crude, hasty, and therefore ineffective, attack on the Government of India—not that the Government of India should not be attacked, of course it should, whenever it acts amiss—Fitzjames Stephen has shown the warm heart to which his powerful head has sometimes done wrong.

XLII.

GENERAL RICHARD STRACHEY, C.S.I.

It is less than eight years short of half a century ago that Richard Strachey received his commission in the Bengal Engineers. Though his highest reputation was not to be achieved by the sword, he had a decade's varied, active, and distinguished service. He was engaged in the Sutlej campaign of 1845-6, was on the staff of Sir Harry Smith, took part in the battles of Aliwal and Sobraon, being mentioned in the dispatches and decorated with a medal and clasps for his services. His younger brother, Sir John Strachey, filled every position which is open to an Indian civilian, not excepting the Governor-Generalship, the duties of which he held in the interval that elapsed between the death of Lord Mayo and the arrival of Lord Northbrook. General Strachey's experiences were scarcely less multiform—notwithstanding the fact that, except when he has been acting as his brother's representative, he has filled no office of the highest responsibility—if the total of his achievements as a civilian is added to his work as a soldier. Richard Strachey first showed what was his calibre, and what was the true bent of his genius, when he was employed on the Ganges

Canal. He had a large share in the construction of the chief works at Hirdwar, and he displayed not merely industry, energy, and assiduity in the discharge of his labours, but a rare power of initiative, and great scientific aptitudes as well. As in the earlier, so in the later stages of his career, his name and efforts have been closely and consistently identified with all that is enlightened and bold in the path of Indian progress. A complete record of his official life would be a tolerably copious chronicle of the development of the resources of India during the last quarter of a century. No Indian administrator, perhaps, has ever left the traces of his influence marked in such clear and, on the whole, beneficent characters; and, if a monument of his toils is sought, the student of Indian history has but to look around. The next step in his civil career, after the completion of the Ganges Canal, was made in the capacity of Secretary to the Public Works Department, whose policy he directed, and for the broad results of which he must be held responsible. He planned and carried out the narrow-gauge railway system, in the teeth of opposition and criticism. He constructed embankments and he built barracks. He was appointed Inspector-General of Irrigation Works, and it was while holding this office that he collected the experience which so eminently qualified him for the Presidency of the Commission to Inquire into Indian Famines. He was a second time Secretary to the Public Works Department, having during the interval which had expired since his first tenure of that position been employed in England at the India

Office in connection with the State railways of our Asiatic Empire. Four years ago he was nominated by Lord Salisbury a member of the Indian Council at Westminster. He exhibited in London the qualities which had already made his reputation in Calcutta. He took an active and a prominent part in the debates, and whatever the subject in dispute, he always had definite views and firm convictions, as well as the courage which such convictions and views inspire. When it was decided that a Commission should investigate the causes of the famine which had spread desolation through two Indian provinces, it seemed natural that General Strachey should watch over its proceedings, and the appointment which summoned him a twelvemonth ago to Calcutta was received with general satisfaction. Then came his brother Sir John Strachey's visit to England, and the General was called upon to fill the gap thus temporarily created in the Ministry of Finance. General Strachey's statesmanship, it will be perceived, is of what may be called the universal order, and it is comparatively matter of indifference to him whether he be required to organize a scheme of public works, or to draw up a budget, and to attempt the task of converting a deficit into a surplus.

But what is perhaps the most interesting, and certainly not the least important, aspect of his career, has still to be mentioned. General Strachey is not only eminent as financier and administrator: he has won the highest distinction in the wider fields of science. We hear much in these days of academic reform about the endowment of original research. Original research has never been conducted upon such a scale, or with such splendid results, as when Mr. Thomason, the wisest and most enlightened and far-seeing Lieutenant-Governor whom the North-Western Provinces ever had, secured for Richard Strachey the dignified but onerous task of undertaking a scientific survey of the Himalayas. Mr. Thomason was already acquainted with the devotion of his *protégé* to geology, botany, and mineralogy, and could form an accurate idea of the results that might be expected if a regular exploration of the physical characteristics of that mighty range of mountains was to be made. He succeeded in inducing the Governor-General and the directors to order such an investigation. Richard Strachey could have had no more hopeful, no more congenial opportunity, and one of the results was a contribution of a value undreamed of to the natural history of Hindostan. It is deeply to be regretted that only the official record of these researches has been given to the world. General Strachey has indeed for some time had in preparation a work which, if it is ever published, will be a full narrative of the labours of himself and his colleagues. But his official duties have been heavy and continuous, and the lettered leisure that is necessary for the completion of such an enterprise—an enterprise, however, that would form the due monument of his career—is still wanting. Thus, in the domain of natural history and the observation of those facts and phenomena which make science possible, General Strachey has performed a work as conspicuous and as original as in the Indian railway system, or in the department of

Indian Finance. Of the former he must be considered as virtually the inventor. It was his advice which led to Lord Mayo's determination to abandon the making of railways through guaranteed companies—a costly and even a ruinous policy, which has cost the Indian Exchequer many millions. Similarly it was General Strachey who was mainly instrumental in developing and shaping the great scheme for the decentralisation of Indian finance, whose execution was one of the chief triumphs of Lord Mayo's Viceroyship. Wilson, Laing, and other authorities had pointed out for many years past that the great evil of our Indian system was over-centralisation. Sir Bartle Frere wrote a pamphlet in which the same moral was powerfully enforced. All questions, however small and however local their nature, came up to the Central Government. The provincial governments were without financial responsibility, and, therefore, without one of the greatest incentives possible to economy and good administration. It is to General Strachey that the honour belongs of having first devised a plan that could give effective expression to the principle for which many generations of Indian financial reformers had contended. It may well seem remarkable that a man who has exercised so wide and deep an influence upon Indian policy has never occupied permanently a post of corresponding importance. He has been, and indeed at this moment is, Finance Minister of India. But he is so as his brother's substitute. The fact that General Strachey has thus been comparatively stationed in the background has perhaps served to increase the popular estimate of his influence. A certain sense of mystery has attached to the power and prestige of a man who has wielded immense strength without himself being the centre of that fierce light which beats upon the holders of high office.

XLIII.

SIR JOHN STRACHEY, K.C.S.I.

"The Stracheys" have already gained a name and a prestige in the history of our Indian empire, which confers upon them a kind of dynastic eminence. In some respects they may be said to resemble certain members of the gifted house of Napier. Brilliant intellectual powers, an extraordinary capacity of prolonged and intense exertion, a marvellous aptitude for great varieties of work, refinement of taste, habits of culture, a delicate and minute appreciation of excellence in literature and art, are common to both. A further noticeable quality which each has in common is an attachment to certain views which appear likely to become a tradition in the race, and a disposition to resent any opposition to them as something in the nature of a slight placed upon the family honour. Cases are not unknown in which, if the conduct of any one member of the *gens* is criticized, the whole clan musters in his defence. This is the kind of thing which has been noticed in the case of the Napiers, and something like it perhaps will have suggested itself *apropos* of the Stracheys. It is the same too with the Freres, and it was the same in a much more marked degree with the Mills. When it was wittily said that the moral of John Stuart Mill's autobiography might be summed up in the single sentence, "There is no God, but it is a family secret," it was but giving epigrammatic and pointed expression to a not uncommon family peculiarity. On the other hand, it would be a mistake to suppose that because one Strachey entertains an opinion, another Strachey declares it to be the embodiment of absolute truth. If the Stracheys grow restive under idle contradiction of the ideas which they may jointly happen to hold, Sir John and General Richard Strachey differ from each other on more than one important question of policy.

Still, the points of agreement between the two brothers are sufficiently marked. Roughly dividing Indian politicians and administrators into two schools, it may be said that the Stracheys are each of them to be found within the limits of the same section. There are, in the first place, those who believe in the all-sufficient wisdom of keeping things as they are; who maintain that men all the world over are the creatures of circumstance and custom, and that if a bad law or a bad system is the one under which the population has lived, it is relatively superior to a good one. Secondly, there are those who consider that for the improvement of mankind change in the customs of States, and interference with the traditions of rule, where traditions and customs are bad, is indispensable; and that when the rulers of a country whose resources at every turn want a more perfect development have been themselves educated in a higher civilisation, it is their duty to give the subject races the opportunity of profiting by superior advantages. It is under the latter of these heads that the Stracheys come, though Sir John Strachey, at least, is not prepared to go anything like the same length as are others of those whom it includes. While admitting that the responsibility of England in India is proportionate to its power, and that if India is not to be ruled according to English ideas then the English can have no right to be in India, Sir John Strachey would scarcely be disposed to admit that the end of Anglo-Indian Government is the amelioration of the social unit—the individual man. He looks at things *en gros*, and would probably maintain that in Indian administration only broad results were possible, and that cognisance could not be taken of single instances. Yet certainly no Indian statesman has worked more continuously or more successfully for the good of the vanquished race than Sir John Strachey. All the legislation with which he is most closely identified is of a character eminently philanthropic, and the first occasion on which he attracted attention was the accomplishment of a work of popular beneficence. He was the first Sanitary Commissioner ever appointed in India, and it was the report on cholera and sanitation which, in this capacity, he drew up, that caused him prominently to make his mark. Sir John Strachey's consciousness of the valuable hygienic service which, as a layman, he then rendered to the peoples of India, betrays itself, it may be, in what has always been, and still is, his contention, that if you want an effective sanitary commissioner you ought not to appoint a doctor—though this view was merely quoted by Sir John Strachey on no less eminent authority than that of Miss Nightingale. There is probably no other instance but that of Sir John Strachey of an Indian civilian who has successively held every office which an Indian civilian can fill. Appointed at an earlier age than most of his contemporaries, first collector and then magistrate, he passed through the different grades of judicial commissions, Chief Commissioner, Member of Council, till, during the interval that elapsed between Lord Mayo's death and Lord Northbrook's nomination, he discharged the functions of Viceroy. It would not be more impossible to overrate the value of this universality of experience than the fact that Sir John Strachey was not at the commencement of his career attached to a Government secretariate. Great as the distinction may be, no piece of promotion is more to be deprecated than that which places the young Indian civilian upon the staff before he has learned the active duties of his calling, or has acquired an experience with the *nuances* of the country. He who is prematurely appointed to the secretariate may rise to eminence, but will seldom attain to practical knowledge. His reputation, firmly established before that period, was increased by his close identification with the leading measure of Lord Mayo's administration, the decentralisation of finance, although Sir John himself is accustomed to say that the honour of this achievement belongs to his father, General Richard Strachey. Several great authorities had for years protested that the great evil of India was over-centralisation; but Sir John—or, as Sir John would say, General Richard Strachey—was the first to find out that the necessary practical remedial measures could be taken. The essential part of the new system is by no means, as is sometimes said, to diminish the control by the central authority of departmental expenditure. It is rather, in the first place, to increase the financial responsibilities of the provincial governments; and, in the second place, to give fresh inducements to good administration and economy. Before this reform was instituted the entire power of the purse lay with the Government of India. No local government had any income which it could call its own. But as in the case of individuals so in that of communities, no surer premium can be offered to extravagance than grants of money *pro rê natâ*, without any definite sum by way of allowance being fixed. There was, in fact, a rough scramble in which every local government endeavoured to get its fingers as deep as possible into the recesses of the ministerial purse. Under the new *régime* a kind of contract has been entered into between the central government and the local governments, the terms of which are an encouragement to the latter to develop and improve to the utmost their sources of revenue. In the old days excise fees were a branch of the Imperial exchequer, and the local authorities, without previous interest in its state, could not be expected to display much solicitude as to its collection. By the decentralisation of finance the local government receives for itself all that it can collect above a given figure, and the incentive to the exercise of economy and good administration is immense, for whatever profit may be forthcoming, that goes without deduction to the credit of the local government. Before Lord Mayo's time Sir John was one of the leading members of what is undoubtedly the most brilliant administration that India has seen of late years—that of Lord Lawrence, which included amongst others men like Fitzjames Stephen, Mansfield, and Maine. On Lord Mayo's death Sir John Strachey, as senior member of Council, held till Lord Northbrook's appointment the reins of the Indian Government in his hands. Doubts were raised in the Chief Court as to whether there had not been some informality in the proceedings of the trial of Lord Mayo's assassin; the Court further holding that if the proceedings were thus vitiated the trial could not take place again. Sir John Strachey and Sir James Stephen, who was then a member of the Council, discussed the matter. The former was then sitting as Governor-General, and it was discovered that as Governor-General he had power to pass an ordinance, with effect for six months. The question thus was whether the man should be hanged by Act or by ordinance. The ultimate decision of the High Court rendered the latter alternative unnecessary, but had it been necessary it would certainly have been carried out. Sir John Strachey has been as successful with famine administration as finance. He it was who first perceived that the famine relief movement was gradually degenerating into a great pauperising agency. He therefore exacted an honest day's work as the price of the benefits of the famine relief works, with the result that there was at once an enormous reduction in the number of applicants.

Throughout the whole of Sir John Strachey's career loyalty has been pre-eminently his guiding principle. It was conspicuous in the public service which he rendered under Lord Lawrence, Lord Mayo, and Lord Northbrook: it has asserted itself no less emphatically under the *régime* of Lord Lytton. At considerable pecuniary sacrifice he gave up the well-endowed office of Governor of the North-West Provinces to join Lord Lytton's Council as Finance Minister in 1876, and since he has been there the amount of work which he has got through is almost incredible. Sir John Strachey is indeed bound to the Viceroy by something more than the ties of official loyalty. Between Lord Lytton and his Finance Minister there exists a strong personal friendship, and something of that similarity of temperament and habits which often, but by no means invariably, is the guarantee of an intimate personal sympathy. Like Lord Lytton, Sir John Strachey has no taste for the physical sports and athletic exercises which fill so large a space in most Anglo-Indian lives; like Lord Lytton again, while gifted, as has been seen, with an enormous capacity for getting through work, Sir John Strachey prefers to do his work at his own hours, in his own way, and to vary work with intellectual relaxation in the manner and on the occasions which suit him. In width and variety of culture, in universality of taste and reading, in devotion to art and literature, Sir John Strachey exhibits a resemblance to Lord Lytton, and he still dreams of ending his days in Italy surrounded by the masterpieces of centuries. His career as an Indian administrator is probably now drawing to its close, but nothing short of physical necessity will induce him to resign until Lord Lytton's term of administration has expired. Not merely is there steadily operative with him the sentiment of personal devotion which caused him to labour with such protracted intensity at his desk before the Viceroy visited Madras last year, in order that he might be completely equipped with facts, that a serious illness supervened, but there remains much in his financial policy to complete. It may confidently be hoped that nothing will prevent Sir John Strachey's fulfilment of his purpose.

XLIV.

SIR RICHARD TEMPLE, BART., K.C.S.I.

There is not a little in the career of the present Governor of Bombay which should act as an encouragement and example for those who, lacking perhaps the genius of heaven-born Imperial administrators, are by no means devoid of their ambition. Sir Richard Temple is in the front rank of Indian statesmen; he has many—perhaps the most essential—qualifications which entitle him to that place; his fortunes have always been those which rare deserts only can command. But when a man has done all that Sir R. Temple has done, and done it, comparatively speaking, so swiftly, and with so little effort of painful exertion, it is natural to look for the secret of his success in something which we all recognise as the *cachet* of rare greatness. It is not to disparage the Governor of Bombay to say that this gift, or this combination of gifts, will not easily be found in his instance. A critical examination of his career will disclose the possession of few qualities which most young men of parts and promise may not boast that they have already, or may not at least hope to acquire. It is not that Sir Richard Temple fails to rise infinitely above mediocrity;

but when the conditions of his promotion are analytically investigated, little or nothing is to be found which men who are not much more than mediocre do not often possess. Exceptional success is usually to be explained only by the combined presence of exceptional causes. Either we trace the operation of happy accident in birth, the permanent influence of social advantages of rare value, the perpetual assertion of a remarkable personality, uncommon force of mind, or a rare faculty of intellectual originality and initiative. Whatever may be, or whatever we may imagine to be, the cause, we instinctively and immediately connect it with the effect, and the tyro who, at a distance, gazes admiringly on the achieved result, feels that such greatness is beyond his capacity, and should therefore be beyond his hope. But the aspirant for public honours will scarcely accuse himself of any egregious lack of modesty if, after having followed in his mind the successive stages of Sir Richard Temple's career, he comes to the conclusion that there is no reason why much of such a career should not be his own.

On the whole, natural and pardonable as this feeling may be, the competition wallah of respectable or even first-rate capacities who should venture from the spectacle of Sir Richard Temple's progress to prognosticate a course signalised by similar triumphs for himself, would make a mistake. It may be that the Governor of Bombay is not made of the stuff which we may expect to find in great generals who shape the plan of victorious campaigns, or of great lawgivers who reduce turbulent societies to order, establishing firmly and for ever among men the enduring foundations of a civil polity. Sir Richard Temple does not belong to the same class as Clive and Hastings; perhaps posterity will say that he has not left the impress of his mind so clearly upon the statutes of India as Fitzjames Stephen, or on the finance of India as John Strachey. But, in the building up of an Empire so complete and so vast as that of England, there are a time and place for the exercise of every variety of talent and gift, nor does it follow that the same quality of mind which is necessary at one stage of the construction of the fabric, is to be desired at those which follow. If Sir Richard Temple has seldom exhibited any trace of the aptitude of a master for reviewing or reconstituting the principles on which an Empire is administered, he has never failed accurately to note the condition of its administration, correctly to estimate the tendencies of the times, and the currents of popular feeling. In a word, if he has not shown himself a man calculated to mould the age according to his will, to fashion it anew after the model which seemed to him best, he has displayed consistently a surprising degree of activity and intelligence in judging of its capacities, and in judging also of the instrumentality by which the designs of its presiding spirits could best be carried into effect. This was exactly what those who knew him best even as a Rugby boy ventured to predict for Richard Temple. He was not a brilliant scholar, but he was a very plodding one, and it was only the other day that his private tutor, who was one of the masters in the school (since dead), remarked, when Temple's name was accidentally mentioned, how much he had been impressed by the thoroughness of his work as a boy. It was the same at Haileybury, where it was observed more than once that if there lived the youth to whom George Canning's description of Joseph Hume, that he was an extraordinary specimen of an ordinary man, could be applied, Richard Temple was he. When he got to India it was very soon perceived and very generally recognised, that over and above his remarkable energy, industry, application, and tact, the future Governor of Bombay had some noticeable gifts. His reports and dispatches were written in graphic and glowing English, and with consummate skill he succeeded in suppressing anything like the trace of elaboration or artifice. He never degenerated into commonplace; he systematically curbed any propensity to highflown oratory, and the result was that his official statements were useful not as mere bald, colourless narratives, but also as the suggestion of arguments. After he had made his mark in the Allahabad District in settlement work, and had carried his capacity for this especial task to the Punjaub, he attracted the quick eye of John Lawrence, and it was as his secretary that Temple first became known as an able writer, and we may add without unfairness, a reliable partisan. He was absent in England during the mutiny, but he returned in the winter of 1857—58 to become Commissioner of Lahore, and on a memorable occasion received the then Governor of India, Lord Canning, with something more than conventional distinction. But it was his administration of Nagpore which first caused contemporary critics to prophesy a future of exceptional brilliance for Richard Temple. Here, indeed, he left the mark of his ability and influence legibly inscribed in enduring characters. He found disorder and he left it order, he reduced neglect and irregularity into discipline and studied vigilance.

When his term of office in Nagpore had expired he became in succession Resident at Hyderabad, and Minister of Finance. While still holding this latter office be again went to England, and on his return found that his financial policy had received some severe criticism from Sir John Strachey. To these criticisms it would not, indeed, have been difficult to adduce a conclusive or satisfactory reply. But Sir Richard Temple, instead of entering into a controversy, decided to be judged rather by results. It is true that there was at the time a serious deficit; but then a deficit is the normal condition of Indian finance. It is also true that he reintroduced the income-tax, but arguments in favour of that impost were no more wanting then than arguments in favour of its existence are wanting now. Of Sir Richard Temple's famine administration all that need be said is that a comparison between the principles on which he acted in 1874 and in 1877, will show how considerably in that interval his views had changed. The fact that Sir Richard Temple is the first provincial Governor of India who has received a baronetcy since the days of Sir Frederick Currie, to whom the honour was awarded as a *souvenir* of the annexation of the Punjaub, shows conclusively the esteem in which his public services are held. His career has been coincident with many of the most prosperous episodes in Indian history, and if it cannot be said that he has created these episodes, he has at least in a very signal degree contributed to them. Pleasant and genial, both in society and in his bearing towards his official inferiors, he has an extraordinary power of creating among all those with whom he is brought into contact a real enthusiasm for work. He is thus a born departmental chief, with immense activity and unfailing buoyancy of spirits. The son of a distinguished amateur artist, he is no mean artist himself, and, educated to the saddle from his youth, he is an admirable rider. His hereditary seat, the Nash at Kempsey, marks a home of the same family from whom we have the Essays of Swift's illustrious patron, and which has supplied an heir to the strawberry-leaves of Buckingham and Chandos. If Sir Richard Temple does not belong to the stamp of men who, if we had not possessed already the Empire of India, would have made it for us, he has done good service towards securing and consolidating our possessions; and if he has not had occasion to create a policy, he has been the useful and successful instrument of that which others have devised.

XLV.

SIR JULIUS VOGEL, K.C.M.G.

For more than one reason, the Agent-General for New Zealand is to be regarded as a pre-eminently representative man. His career has been typical in its industry, its energy, its moral and intellectual qualities, its indefatigable perseverance, and its distinguished success, of the careers associated in a special degree with the national character. We expect the Englishman who seeks his fortune in a far country to do well and prosper. We expect that he should persistently refuse to admit the word failure to his vocabulary. The expectation is but too often not realised. That fact, however, makes no difference to the national idea, and this idea has at least been fulfilled in the case of Sir Julius Vogel. Secondly, he represents in his views and aspirations the Colonist quite as much as in his temper and achievements he does the Englishman. He has brought back with him to Great Britain not only the old dogged determination of the race to carry out in this country whatever he may take in hand, and to contribute to its execution all that lies within his power, but he has brought with him also a very definite conviction of the duties which Great Britain owes to her Colonial dependencies, of the advantages which she derives from them, of the responsibilities imposed by these advantages on her, and of the particular manner in which they can be most effectively discharged. As loyal a subject of the English Crown as it behoves a true-born Briton to be, he would like to see the bonds that unite Great Britain to her Colonies drawn more closely. He urges many powerful arguments in favour of making this connection yet more binding. But there is nothing whatever apologetic in his appeal. It would be a consummation, he tells us, greatly to be wished for, if prompt and decisive action is taken on the lines that he indicates. But the gain will by no means accrue exclusively to the Colonies. It will, in a word, be the cementing of a partnership quite as profitable to the senior as to the junior member of the Imperial firm. The champion of confederation who writes in this practical and dignified way, has an infinitely better chance of securing an audience and compelling consent than one who uses the language of a merely sentimental politician, or who adopts the maudlin metaphors common with patriotic rhetoricians of the fifth-rate order, who protest against the monstrosity of the mother country deserting her loving and longing children.

Sir Julius Vogel has had just a quarter of a century of active Colonial life. He went to Victoria in 1852. Nine years later he removed to New Zealand. His first appearance in public life in that colony was in the capacity of journalist, and a journalist of marked courage and enterprise. Five weekly papers existed at the time of his arrival in Dunedin. The pressure of advertisements upon their columns made Mr. Vogel think that there was an opportunity for enlarging the scope of the Press. He determined to start a daily paper. His friends dissuaded him, and recommended a tri-weekly issue. Mr. Vogel persevered with his experiment, and to him New Zealand is indebted for its first daily newspaper. From journalism he went into politics, was successively a member of the Provincial Council of Otago, a member of the General Assembly, a member of the Provincial Executive, and Colonial Treasurer of the Government. This last position Mr. Vogel assumed in 1869. It was a period of anxiety and trial for the colony. A deadly reaction after the stimulus afforded by the opening up of the gold-fields had fallen upon the country. Many substantial persons seriously meditated leaving the colony. The Imperial Government removed all the English troops, in spite of the remonstrance of those who considered that the time had not arrived for taking so significant a step. The colonists were at the very time actively engaged in repressing some native disturbances, and they were brought face to face with the fact that, in the present and all future difficulties, they had only themselves on whom to rely. The population of New Zealand was strictly limited. Mr. Vogel and his ministerial colleagues saw at once the necessity of extending it. They argued that the present population were already over-weighted with the debt left to them on account of past troubles with the natives, that the colonists were not in a position to bear the responsibilities of further troubles, that the North Island possessed but a mere fringe of settlement, and that the productiveness of the Middle Island languished on account of the want of means of communication between its various districts. Hence the Immigration and Public Works policy of Mr. Fox's Government, in which Mr. Vogel served. The mere title of this policy conveys but an inadequate idea of its extent and boldness. Its key-note was to render the recurrence of the Maori insurrection impossible by the construction of roads through the North Island and the temporary establishment of a force of armed constabulary, as well as to stimulate the productive energies of the country by the introduction and settlement of immigrants, the supply of water to the gold-fields, the purchase of Maori lands in the North Island as a public estate, and the construction of a grand system of trunk lines of railways extending through both islands.

It was an ambitious and comprehensive scheme, that excited not a little of adverse criticism at the time. The new immigrants, Mr. Vogel and his friends were told, would pour into Victoria, and New Zealand would be as barren of men as before. The results of the policy justified its wisdom, and both the public works and the railways have proved, financially as well as politically, remunerative. Immigration was conducted on a large scale, Parliamentary roads through disturbed districts were completed, and railways, which provincial governments had longed for, but had been unable to construct, were at once contracted for. It could not, indeed, have been executed without assistance from the mother country, and in 1870 Mr. Vogel came to England to negotiate a loan. Four years later he again visited the mother country—this time as Prime Minister—when he negotiated another large loan, and also made arrangements for connecting New Zealand with Australia by cable communication. It was then that he also carried to a successful issue the negotiations with the Bank of England which afterwards resulted in an Imperial Act authorising the inscription of Colonial stocks, under which, by opening up a new investment for trust funds, the means have been afforded of materially increasing the value and utility of Colonial securities.

Meanwhile, at the risk of losing many of his staunchest friends and supporters, he became the instrument of effecting a complete revolution in the system of governing the country—a revolution so comprehensive that few instances could be found of such an organic change being consummated without disturbance or bloodshed. Beginning his political career as an ardent advocate of the provincial system of government, the conviction gradually forced itself on him that the Central Government was better able to carry out the colonising work, which was the *raison d'être* of provincial governments, and that these ought to cease to exist. With characteristic determination, and at the temporary cost of much popularity, he undertook the task. The whole provincial system is now abolished, and there are few who still deny that the change has been attended with advantage. In 1875 Mr. Vogel was made a Knight Commander of the Order of St. Michael and St. George. Some idea of the ability and inexhaustible capacity of the man for work may be seen in the fact that at one and the same time he held the portfolios of Premier, Treasurer, Minister for Immigration, Postmaster-General, and Commissioner of Telegraphs, to the satisfaction even of his bitterest opponents. Colonial Ministries are, for the most part, exceedingly short-lived. Probably Sir Julius Vogel is one of the very few, if not the only Colonial Minister who, in the course of a decade and a half, has passed a full seven years in the enjoyment of place and power, and then voluntarily resigned the position on account of his health not permitting him to bear the continued strain on his exertions.

It was not to be expected that a man who had thrown himself with such ardour, devotion, and success into the politics of his colony, and who in a comparatively short time had won so commanding a position in the scale of Colonial statesmanship, would be content to rest on his oars when he again returned to the mother country to discharge the duties of the Agency-General. While he was yet a member of the Government, Sir Julius Vogel had, in a letter to the *Standard* in the month of May, 1871, sketched in outline a plan for the great scheme of the "Confederation of the Empire." He did, indeed, do something more than adumbrate the empty form of an ambitious dream. Sir Julius Vogel has shown himself throughout his varied and remarkable career above all things practical.

If he is sketchy he is also strictly constructive. If he declares that the materials for the rearing of an edifice are there, he does not fail to lay down tolerably precise instructions as to the manner in which the work should be undertaken. He has not only the courage of his convictions, he has the knowledge and the ingenuity to show that they may be converted into realities. Thus, his letter to the *Standard* was something more than the spirited expression of an imposing series of vague aspirations. It set before the public a design, and it contained definite hints as to the mode in which that design might be executed.

Since then he has materially elaborated those hints. He has held his own in the advocacy of the scheme against so subtle a reasoner as Mr. Lowe, and so logical as well as so experienced a critic as Lord Blachford. He has convinced many who were coldly sceptical; he has won the active support of not a few who, friendly to his suggestion as a theory, despaired of its realisation as a fact. In an article in the *Nineteenth Century*, July, 1877, Sir J. Vogel had no difficulty in demonstrating the unsatisfactory nature of the relations between the mother country and the Colonies. He then went on to show that if the disintegrating movement which is in progress is to be arrested, something definite must be done. A union between the different parts of the Empire during pleasure meant, he argued, separation sooner or later. The only preventive of separation is, he insisted, confederation, which, he explained, "Would be fraught with advantage both to the parent country and the Colonies in the shape of increased trade, increased value of property, the augmented happiness of the people, and the saving of much misery and disaster." His attempt to show that "its accomplishment does not present great difficulties" was met with an answer from Lord Blachford, which at some points must be admitted to have been logically complete. But nations are not governed by logic only, and the weak point in Lord Blachford's exceedingly able reply was that he failed to lay due stress on the conditions of sentiment and pride which are the chief factors in such a question. Thus Lord Blachford contended that the absence of perfect community of interest between its different members stamped the confederation scheme as impracticable; he refused to recognise that a community of language, traditions, habits, education, may be as powerful in its way as a community of material interests. "All questions of war," said Sir J. Vogel, with a correct insight into Anglo-Saxon feeling all the world over, "must be questions in which the people in Great Britain have common interests with their fellow-subjects in other parts of the world. If the quarrel is one because of an insult to British subjects or wrong to British property, the provocation is equally felt by every subject of the Sovereign of Great Britain."

But the most striking points in Sir Julius Vogel's case for confederation have to be mentioned. First, take what may be called the commercial argument. The Colonies, he says, so long as they remain an integral part of Great Britain will perpetuate for her the trade which she is losing with foreign countries. But it is said we can afford to lose that trade. It will only involve a loss of £140,000,000, and what is that when compared with the aggregate income of the country? "The fallacy of the argument," returns Sir J. Vogel, "lies in the fact that it presupposes more or less a community of ownership. If the thirty-two millions of people who inhabit this country drew each a proportionate share of the total income, the loss arising from the loss of foreign trade might, by a like equal division, be little felt. But there is no such equality. You cannot equally divide the consequences. You have first a number who primarily suffer, and to whom the loss means ruin. You have then around the principal group a widening circle of suffering, which becomes less severe as it enlarges in extent, till in the far background you have those who are only remotely affected. If this be well considered, it will be seen that the loss of a portion of the extensive trade of the country may mean a calamity which cannot be measured in its effects by dividing its extent into the total means of the nation." Further, English trade with foreign countries is diminishing through the agency of specific causes—high rents, the evil reputation earned by doubtful practices, misconceptions arising from the artificial system by which manufacturers and consumers are separated. Without her shipping, and without the capital which she herself supplies by loans for the purchase of her own goods, she would have but little foreign trade, and without her Colonies she would neither be able to own, nor justified in owning, such a merchant shipping as she possesses, and on which her foreign trade depends. But English capital and English industry must have some outlet or they will perish. If English money is invested in foreign countries, it goes to lands where her own laws give her no redress. Sir J. Vogel cites the silver legislation which is now proceeding in the United States as a warning on this head. The check upon foreign loans has led to an enormous increase in Colonial investments. Is not then the conclusion irresistible—first, that the Colonies are commercially useful to England; secondly, that the essence of this utility lies in the fact of their being legally a part of England? Finally, there is the absolutely unanswerable argument which Sir Julius Vogel gives in these words:—

"As fields for the labouring classes the Colonies possess irresistible fascination. They who do not go rejoice at least in the knowledge that they can do so, and there are few amongst them who have not friends there. The rest of the community other than the leisured few have interests more or less extensive beyond the seas. So much of that interest as is given to foreign countries it is certainly not desirable to increase, and if the Colonies are to become foreign countries the same objections would apply to the increase of British interests in them. If Great Britain can retain her dependencies for another fifty years, she must become powerful in the extreme. By that time her consolidated strength as compared with that of the rest of the civilised world would be nearly irresistible. As a mere matter of insurance, it would be better to maintain the connection, even at a heavy cost, than to have those dependencies added to the number of foreign nations. Between England with world-wide interests and England shut up within herself it is hard to see how there can be any hesitation. Divested of her exterior dominions she would become the theatre of fierce war between the labouring, the moneyed, and the landed classes. Flooded with foreign goods to repay interest on past loans, sufficient occupation would be denied to the people; the moneyed classes would dread investments abroad, would see no room for investments at home, and would fight against the taxation they alone could pay. A fierce onslaught would be made on the land, and year by year the aggregate wealth of the nation would decrease."

In all probability there is much good and great work for Sir Julius Vogel yet to do in the mother country. He has already made himself the champion of a noble and beneficent idea. He has done much towards showing that it is more than an idea. His views, supported as they are by facts and figures of the utmost significance, are receiving careful consideration in the highest quarters. It may be believed that before long Sir Julius Vogel will have a further opportunity of showing his skill and exercising his practical genius in the highest and greatest scheme of constructive statesmanship which has ever been proposed to the rulers of a mighty Empire.

XLVI.

FREDERICK ALOYSIUS WELD, ESQ., C.M.G.

THE struggle for existence which drives all conditions of men far afield in search of employment, lucrative and sufficient, is naturally a distinct advantage to the countries they elect to adopt as their own. Thus the strong-thewed labourer who gives a colony the best energies of his manly prime; the skilled artisan who lends his aid to the development of Colonial industries; the small but eager capitalist who carries to a new land the commercial aptitudes which might be choked or killed outright by competition at home, have greatly contributed to make our Colonies what they are. But still more have these Colonies benefited by the influx of immigrants of a higher stamp, by the occasional arrival of cadets of great houses whom the changes in our social constitution do not nowadays permit to find a satisfactory career at home. Where competitive examinations stand in the way of easy admission to the public service, where soldiers and sailors must climb slowly and sadly the professional ladder without a faint hope of help from influential friends, when the Bar denies its favours until the hair is grey or altogether gone, and pocket boroughs no longer exist to give the heaven-born statesman his first start in political life, an enterprising spirit does wisely if, instead of deploring the changed conditions of affairs, he yields to the promptings of his own plucky heart to fly and carve out his fortunes in other climes. Such arguments as these prevailed with one young man some five-and-thirty years ago, who by birth and position might reasonably have looked for advancement at home. When barely out of his teens, Mr. Frederick Weld resolved to seek in the new antipodean world some avenue to wealth and distinction less crowded than any in the old. He came of an ancient stock; he was one of the Welds of Lulworth, a well-known Catholic family long seated in Dorsetshire, where they had bought castles and lands from the Howards, and had been famous always for their staunch adherence to the faith they professed even in the darkest days of religious intolerance, marrying and intermarrying with Arundels and Stourtons, Cliffords and Peters, and giving sons and daughters to the service of their Church. Of the latter not a few in succeeding generations took the veil, and among the former was one of the Squires of Lulworth, who himself made the vows, and rose to great eminence as a Cardinal and one of the Papal Conclave at Rome.

Frederick Weld was educated at Stonyhurst, a college standing on land which had once belonged to his family, and went almost direct from thence to New Zealand in 1843. For ten years following his life was uneventful. It was the life of the struggling but indefatigable colonist, who worked hard with his hands, and nevertheless could use his head and the mother wit which was his own in storing up and assimilating the real experience which has since stood him in such good stead. In these early days, too, he began to display the eager and inquiring spirit as an explorer which has characterized him ever since. He was the first to traverse great portions of uninhabited lands in the interior of the Southern (or Middle) Island of New Zealand, and that his travels were soberly and seriously undertaken was fully shown by the able scientific papers upon them which he subsequently contributed to the journals of the Geological Society. He visited the Sandwich Islands, and wrote shrewdly concerning the volcanic eruptions there. He might have attempted more in this direction, but the arena of political life opened for him with the establishment of Constitutional Government, and almost from the first he took part in the management of Colonial affairs. As one of a small band of politicians, shrewd and intelligent men, who recognised at once the needs of the colony, he worked hard to start fairly the new coach of representative government. A thousand difficulties beset their path. The old Crown officials, not yet pensioned, thwarted them covertly at every step; the Home Government could not quite readily agree to give up the reins of control; more especially the native question threatened ere long to rise into the most serious proportions. No colony has had more difficulties to cope with in its dealings with aborigines than New Zealand with its Maoris—a race at once of diplomatists and warriors, who, whether in the council chamber or in the field, have shown themselves no mean antagonists for our best men. Mr. Weld long identified himself with the native question. He was for some years Minister for Native Affairs, and throughout his best efforts were directed not to exterminate, but to preserve and civilise the whole of the tribes. This mastery of the subject brought him naturally very prominently to the front, when an unwise policy, too persistently pursued, had culminated in a bloodthirsty and what promised to be a nearly interminable war. The courage with which Mr. Weld accepted the offer of the Governor to form a ministry at the moment when the danger was greatest, cannot well be overpraised. The war had lingered on too long already. A split threatened with the Southern Island, which was compelled to contribute to the expenses, but yet not actively concerned in the war waged in the Northern. A policy of interference was paramount at Government House and in Downing Street. There was much of real statesmanlike genius in the bold and determined way Mr. Weld grappled with the situation. He saw clearly that divided authority and divided responsibilities were at the root of all the mischief, and he claimed his proper place and his full functions as Prime Minister in a representative government. He was ready to stand or fall by his acts, to continue in power or to resign forthwith, according as he succeeded or failed. But while in power he must be supreme. The fearlessness with which he vindicated the principles of Colonial self-reliance was unbounded. The colony, he maintained, was prepared to govern itself at all hazards and at all costs. That this might entail the withdrawal of the Imperial troops even in the midst of a serious war did not turn him aside from his views. If needs be the troops must go; the colony would do its best to terminate the war with its own levies, in which it must be confessed he had considerable faith. That the policy of Mr. Weld was sound and satisfactory was fully proved by its cordial endorsement and acceptance at home. In the House of Commons ministers and a large majority, after a lengthy debate, made this plain, and there is little reason to doubt that, had Mr. Weld continued in office, the pacification of the Northern Island and the general settlement of the Maoris would have been much more promptly secured. But he was in a measure a martyr to his own principles. Although the Crown approved, a strong party in the Colonial Parliament opposed his measures, defeated him more than once, and in deference to the majority he resigned.

Returning now to England in indifferent health, he spent two or three years at home, to proceed in 1869 to Western Australia as Governor, being one of the first, and nearly the only, Colonial politician who had been thus advanced to Vice-regal honours. A statesman so thoroughly imbued with the value of representative institutions would naturally be disposed to extend their practice wherever opportunity offered. This he saw in Western Australia. It was then, and still is partially, a Crown Colony, ruled from Downing Street, instead of governing itself. It was, in truth, hardly ripe for political autonomy; a large percentage of its population had but just entered into the condition of semi-freedom which is conceded to ex-convicts on tickets-of-leave. These were scarcely entitled to enjoy the franchise, and the concession was therefore more estimable theoretically than practically possible. But such a measure of representative government as could safely be given Mr. Weld secured to Western Australia, and the concession, whether premature or not, was only one among many proofs of his untiring anxiety to promote the moral and material prosperity of the Colony committed to his charge. He was equally eager to develop its commerce and its resources. He sought to open up its mineral wealth, to find an outlet for its vast supplies of magnificent timber, to provide it with harbours and additional roads. Above all, he gave free play to his old passion for exploration, and combining business with pleasure, made repeated peregrinations of the provinces, travelling generally on horseback, and spending sometimes weeks and weeks together in the saddle. Some idea of his personal endurance may be gathered from the fact that on one occasion he rode nearly a hundred miles with a broken rib.

All that he laboured to bring about in Western Australia he is now strenuously seeking to secure for Tasmania, his present home. This colony, since it escaped the old convict taint, can scarcely be said to have advanced with the times. It was said, a year or two back, to be worse than stagnant—to be really retrograde. It was asserted that the grass grew in the streets of the principal towns, that trade languished and drooped, that the public buildings were falling into decay. If this was even partially true, it is equally certain that Mr. Weld is striving hard to do away with the reproach. Tasmania is richly endowed with those natural gifts which should make a country wealthy and great. It owns vast forests of the most valuable timber, an abundance of mineral, coal, whale-fisheries, a highly productive soil. The wool it grows and the wheat it raises will compare with those in any of the markets of the world. That it should progress favourably under the governorship of so able and eager an administrator as Mr. Weld is natural enough, and although the commercial condition of the colony is still somewhat unsatisfactory, it is now making rapid strides ahead. It may not reach its ancient prosperity during Mr. Weld's tenure of office, but it can at least thank him for being put in the right road. There as elsewhere he has gained golden opinions, not only for his administrative but for his social qualities. Of singularly genial manners, he is kind and considerate to all who approach him, and he is so deservedly famed wherever he has been for hospitality as cordial as it is ungrudging, that he leaves only the pleasantest memories behind. If his health and vigour remain unimpaired—and he is still in the prime of life—there is every reason to hope that he will in due course rise to the highest pro-consular honours.

XLVII.

SIR GARNET WOLSELEY, K.C.B., K.C.M.G.

Bacon has said that a wise man will make more opportunities than he finds; yet he who is supremely successful in life owes it rather to his having done his best in whatever comes to his hand. Those who are prompt to avail themselves of every opening that offers, who never refuse or reject a chance, who when they have once put their hands to the plough never turn aside, but persevere steadfastly, are certain to prosper in the end. No man has less reason to quarrel with fortune than Garnet Joseph Wolseley; no man within certain limits has done more to deserve her smiles. From the earliest outset of a singularly eventful career he has shown himself willing to undertake any task, whatever the duties and responsibilities it might entail. Bringing great natural powers, a quick intelligence, much energy and enterprise, to bear upon the smallest charges, he has come by degrees to be intrusted with the highest, and can thus far boast that often as he has been tried in the balance he has never yet been found wanting. Nevertheless luck seemed sorely against him at first. Condemned to a profession which might be honourable enough, but which could never afford much outlet for talents above the common, young Wolseley was eating his heart in a land surveyor's office in Dublin when the Queen's commission came for which he had so earnestly yearned. Descended from an ancient stock, the Wolseleys of Mount Wolseley in the county Carlow, and himself a soldier's son, the lad might well be forgiven if he cherished ambitious dreams. His first chance presented itself without a moment's delay. The regiment to which he was gazetted, the 80th, just then formed a part of the expedition to British Burmah, and he joined it in time to be present and to distinguish himself at the storming of Pegu—yet more, while still only an ensign and in his teens, he was severely wounded, and honourably mentioned in dispatches for his bravery in the raid against Myatoon, the well-known robber-chief. Having thus received his baptism of fire, Wolseley was soon called to play a more serious part in the great game of war. He was now a lieutenant in the 90th Light Infantry, a distinguished regiment, the cradle of many gallant soldiers, and with it he landed in the Crimea in 1854. In that dreadful winter all men were sorely tried, and none more so than the Engineer officers, upon whom fell the conduct of the extensive siege operations in progress. Their numbers, never large, had been yet further reduced by wounds and incessant toil, till it was deemed necessary to call in assistance from outside by enlisting the services of a certain number of promising recruits from regiments of the Line. Wolseley was one of these. His youthful training and the irksome routine which had once been so distasteful stood him now in excellent stead. Had he never served his apprenticeship to the business, albeit in a humble walk, he would not have been in a position to perform the *rôle* of an assistant-engineer in the trenches before Sebastopol. As such he did right good service continuously, save when incapacitated by wounds, throughout the siege and until the fall of the place. In the assault upon the Quarries, their capture and subsequent defence, in the disastrous attack upon the Redan on the 18th June, hotly engaged in every sortie, heading the advance with wool-bags, or freely adventuring his life with the volunteers, who pushed forward the flying sap, Wolseley richly deserved the brevet, the medals, and the rewards which fell to his share at the close of the war.

It might have been the fate of another to have vegetated now in country quarters, but it was Wolseley's to be in the thick of the fight wherever there was fighting to be done. Scarcely was the Crimea over than the horrors of the Indian Mutiny burst upon the country, and Wolseley, still with the 90th, was hurried off to the struggle. They were among the earliest reinforcements. The 90th went therefore with Outram to the relief of Lucknow; they served under his orders in the defence of the Alumbagh, and the subsequent siege of Lucknow. Major Wolseley was a prominent figure throughout. His indomitable pluck, his conspicuous zeal as a regimental officer, added to the prestige he had already gained, marked him out as pre-eminently suited for more responsible employment upon the general staff, and as a deputy-assistant quartermaster-general to the division of Hope Grant he took a conspicuous part in all the operations of that force. Scarcely was India tranquillised when fresh opportunities came to Wolseley, now a lieutenant-colonel. Sir Hope Grant, the chief to whom he had already given his allegiance, and to whom he felt bound by the strongest obligations to the last, was nominated to command the expedition against China in 1860, and Wolseley went with him as a matter of course. Still in the department of the quartermaster-general, but in a higher grade, Colonel Wolseley proved himself to be possessed of the most valuable qualities of the staff officer. Eminently useful in organization, of untiring energy, active and forward in reconnaissance, with the almost intuitive perceptions of the true soldier when the opposing forces met in the shock of fight, Wolseley, after the Taku forts had been captured and Pekin fell, had so far made his mark that it was quite understood he would never again go upon the shelf. Naturally, when the Trent affair threatened to develop unpleasant complications with the United States, and Lord Palmerston, with commendable promptitude, threw a large force of troops into Canada, Wolseley was selected to go too. The storm-cloud blew over, the bulk of the forces were withdrawn, but Wolseley remained as Quartermaster-General in Montreal, devoting himself for the first time during his service to the humdrum duties of a garrison town ; yet even here he displayed so much industry, judgment, and good sense, that at the termination of his tenure of office he obtained the unusual recognition of reappointment for a second period of service, and thus stayed in Canada, happily for himself, to be on the spot when a new opportunity fairly dropped into his mouth. The rebellion of the squatters in the Red River territory, who had established a Government of their own at Fort Garry, could not be suffered to pass unchecked, and a respectable force was organized, in spite of the remoteness of the scene, and dispatched to reassert the Queen's authority, under Wolseley's command. There were not wanting military critics at the time who depreciated this expedition as a mere military picnic or promenade; but although it escaped from first to last the sterner realities of sanguinary warfare, the affair was beset with such serious administrative difficulties, that to triumph over them as Wolseley did, with the means at his disposal, was a sufficient proof of his capacity and a substantial reason for advancing him to more important trusts.

Returning to England with the star of a Knight Commander of St. Michael and St. George, Sir Garnet Wolseley had now placed his foot securely upon the ladder, and if the topmost rungs were still some way above him, it rested, humanly speaking, only with himself to say how much higher he would climb. He was secured at once for the Horse Guards staff, and, entering upon the duties of assistant adjutant-general at head-quarters, was quietly moving on in a groove of useful but mechanical mediocrity when he was called upon to give his aid in quelling one of the most threatening "small wars" with which England has ever been vexed. That nothing but prompt and adequate measures, wisely and judiciously applied by a firm hand, could satisfactorily terminate the Ashantee troubles, was now quite obvious, and the Government, having decided to act with vigour, prudently resolved also to give the general they had chosen *carte blanche*. Now at once were developed in Sir Garnet Wolseley those faculties of leadership of which he had given fair promise already. An admirable judge of character, he has the rare gift also of securing the personal devotion and attachment of all who serve with him. Directly he was nominated, the best officers in the army rallied round him to a man. There were, of course, his old friends and comrades who had gone with him in the canoes to the Red River, John McNeil, Redvers Buller, poor Huyshe, Butler, of the "Great Lone Land." To these were added many rising names, known best perhaps in their own military circles, but which were certain some day to be more widely celebrated. Colonel Greaves, at first prevented, joined him at last, as chief of the staff; Home, most energetic and pushing of scientific soldiers, was to be his Commanding Engineer. He secured the pens of Henry Brackenbury and Maurice to collaborate his dispatches; Evelyn Wood, Baker Russell, T. D. Baker, ill-fated Alfred Charteris, and the boyish Lord Gifford, were among those who started with him for the Coast. Others followed with all reasonable speed—adjutants of Guards, Staff College students; a professor, as Colonel Colley was then, gladly resigned his chair to come in at the death. Wolseley had, in truth, the pick of the best brains of the profession, and if the victorious march to Coomassie was primarily due to his own patience, foresight, and tenacity of purpose, he was himself deeply sensible, and has never since forgotten, all he owed to the able lieutenants at his side. Born to all seeming under a lucky star, Sir Garnet's good fortune never deserted him from first to last in this trying, but happily completely successful, campaign. There were times, doubtless, when a spirit less stout and resolute might well have quailed: when illness decimated his ranks and robbed him of valuable and trusted subordinates, when swarms of savages infested and endangered his line of communications and supplies, when his men were being struck down by deadly Ashantee slugs as he stood in their midst. But those who were with him through it all—through the long, dreary struggle with a lethal climate while the preparations were slowly and laboriously perfected for the decisive advance, through the toilsome march, its obstacles, its bloody skirmishes and disastrous fights—declare that Wolseley was always intrepid and undismayed. His head was cool under the hottest fire: he received the direst and most compromising news with a smiling face. When the risk was greatest, and the consequences that must follow failure and reverse terrible and disastrous in the extreme, Garnet Wolseley never hesitated or halted, but calmly, and with admirable self-reliance, was resolutely determined to go on and win.

It needs no abnormal prescience to predict for a man of this stamp a brilliant future in the days to come. He is a Lieutenant-general before he is forty-five, and it is rarely that an English officer arrives at this exalted rank when still in the full heyday of youth and vigour. Sir Garnet Wolseley is, in truth, at this moment the very incarnation of "go." His figure is spare, well knit and active; his bright, eager face, although his hair is fast turning to silver, is still quite young and keen. He can get through more work than most men; can hold his own with a bevy of merry, light-footed girls at lawn tennis, or sit for hours in grave debate at the India Council, or yet again rapidly dispose of piles of official papers at his desk. He wields a fluent and incisive pen; besides minor works, he has published the invaluable *Soldier's Pocket-Book*, which has taken rank already as a military manual and classic; his papers on "Military Questions," in the *Nineteenth Century*, have gained something more than a mere *succès d'estime.* He is a soldier *par excellence;* high military commands and great military renown are his most cherished aspirations and dreams, but he has given evidence of great administrative talents in the line of civil government, both on the Gold Coast and at Natal. His selection to fill the post of first Governor or High Commissioner of our latest acquisition, the island of Cyprus, is now about to afford him fresh opportunities for displaying the stuff of which he is made. The task set before him is one of no ordinary difficulty, especially to a man of active mind. Instead of organizing and pushing to a successful finish some small campaign, instead of dealing with large questions of colonial policy, he has to sit down and patiently take up the threads of a Government he finds to his hand—the legacy of the unscrupulous Pacha and unspeakable Turk. It will be his duty to adapt and alter what he finds till it suits English ideas and supplies a model for neighbouring provinces; he will have to attract local emigration, to till the fertile but fallow lands of Cyprus, to encourage the employment of English capital and increase the revenue till it can at least recoup this country for its outlay upon the island. All this must he accomplish in a seemingly unattractive spot, amid squalid towns and a pestilential atmosphere. If at the end of his term of office he has purged Cyprus of its worst evils, and set it moving steadily along the high road to prosperity, he will have accomplished a great work. But the test is crucial, and far more severe than any to which he has hitherto been put in his uniformly successful career.

THE END.